Banking and Finance
on the Internet

Banking and Finance on the Internet

MARY J. CRONIN, EDITOR

 VAN NOSTRAND REINHOLD
I(T)P® A Division of International Thomson Publishing Inc.

New York • Albany • Bonn • Boston • Detroit • London • Madrid • Melbourne
Mexico City • Paris • San Francisco • Singapore • Tokyo • Toronto

Van Nostrand Reinhold is an International Thompson Publishing Company. ITP logo is a trademark under license.

The ideas presented in this book are generic and strategic. Their specific application to a particular company must be the responsibility of the management of that company, based on management's understanding of their company's procedures, culture, resources, and competitive situation.

Printed in the United States of America

Visit us on the Web! http://www.vnr.com

For more information contact:

Van Nostrand Reinhold
115 Fifth Avenue
New York, NY 10003

Chapman & Hall GmbH
Pappalallee 3
69469 Weinhurn
Germany

Chapman & Hall
2-6 Boundary Row
London SEI 81-IN
United Kingdom

International Thomson Publishing Asia
60 Albert Street #15-01
Albert Complex
Singapore 189969

Thomas Nelson Australia
102 Dodds Street
South Melbourne 3205
Victoria, Australia

International Thomson Publishing Japan
Hirakawa-cho Kyowa Building, 3F
2-2-1 Hirakawa-cho, Chiyoda-ku
Tokyo 102 Japan

Nelson Canada
1120 Birchmount Road
Scarborough, Ontario
M1K 5G4, Canada

International Thomson Editores
Seneca, 53
Colonia Polanco
11560 Mexico D.F. Mexico

1 2 3 4 5 6 7 8 9 10 QEBFF 02 01 00 99 98 97

Library of Congress Cataloging-in-Publication Data

Banking and finance on the Internet / Mary J. Cronin. editor.
    p. cm.
    Includes bibliographical references and index.
    ISBN 0-442-02488-1 (cloth)
    1. Banks and banking—Computer network resources.   2. Banks and
banking—Data processing.   3. Investments—Computer network
resources.   4. Investments—Data processing.   5. Internet (Computer
network)   6. World Wide Web (Information retrieval system)
I. Cronin. Mary J.
HG1708.7.B36   1997
025.06'332—dc21
                                                                97-20309
                                                                    CIP

Contents

             on the Web   231
             Mary J. Cronin, Boston College

CHAPTER 9   **Breaking New Ground: WallStreet Electronica**   251
             *Carlos Otalvaro, Noah Otalvaro, and Francisco
             Otalvaro, WallStreet Electronica*

CHAPTER 10   **International Banking and the Internet**   271
             Andreas Crede, University of Sussex

APPENDIX A   **Banking and Financial Services Resources
             on the Web: Directory of Directories**   307

APPENDIX B   **Financial Services Technology Consortium
             Membership**   319

             Contributors   323
             Index   327

Introduction

MARY J. CRONIN
BOSTON COLLEGE

The debate about moving secure investment and banking transactions to the Web is over—the Internet has emerged as a key competitive arena for the future of financial services. Now the race for revenues, market share, and on-line advantage has begun in earnest. The stakes are high in terms of profits to be won or lost and critical opportunities for future growth and business development. The outcome of the electronic commerce strategies set in motion during 1997 will help to determine the fate of institutions as diverse as multinational investment houses, huge data processing conglomerates, mutual fund giants, and local community banks. The scope, cost, and security of the investment, financial management, on-line purchasing, and banking options that will be available to consumers for years to come are being shaped by today's financial services alliances and networked solutions.

It is no surprise, then, that banks and brokers are flocking to the Web. According to a Datapro study, only 7 percent of U.S. banks were offering any type of electronic commerce on the Internet in 1995, whereas more than 32 percent had established plans to support transactions on the Web by the end of 1997. Even community banks, not historically in the forefront of technology adoption, have joined the rush to cyberspace. Almost 50 percent plan to open a Web site by the end of 1997, and of these 27 percent will offer secure banking transactions. A study by the American Bankers Association estimates that home banking will increase by 600 percent between 1995 and 1998. The Tower Group predicts that by the year 2000 U.S. banks will spend more than $700 million annually on their Internet presence. On-line investment opportunities, broker services, and secure trading on the Web have grown even more quickly. Forrester Research reports a 100 percent increase in investor transactions on the Web in 1996 and projects more than 10 million Web trades annually by the year 2000.

Although these growth statistics are impressive, they indicate only part of the impact electronic commerce on the Web will ultimately have on U.S. and international financial services. Many questions about the viability of existing business models and the relationship of electronic commerce to traditional industry channels remain unanswered. On the surface, all the players in the industry seem to be moving in the same direction—toward a home page on the World Wide Web and a predictable set of electronic commerce applications. Dig deeper and the definition of Internet opportunities and threats quickly diverges according to the size and core business of the institution.

In fact, moving financial services to the Internet creates a totally new competitive landscape. Instead of operating within clear-cut service boundaries, well-established financial organizations suddenly find themselves competing for customer loyalty and liquidity. What's more, the competition may come from a technology provider, a tiny start-up, or a telecommunications titan as easily as from within the industry. The advent of Web-based commerce has added new layers of complexity and unpredictability to the worlds of commercial and retail banking, mutual funds and brokers, back-end processors and front-end financial software providers.

When the risks are real and the uncertainty of outcomes is still high, there is no value in simplistic formulas for success or one-size-fits-all solutions. It would be premature to predict which companies will emerge as winners in on-line financial services or even to sum up the impact of the Web on the industry as a whole until significantly more data are available. Rather, this book presents the latest technical developments and electronic commerce strategies from the perspective of a variety of financial services institutions, from the large, well-established corporations to consortia and standards setters to smaller companies doing business primarily on the Web. In the process, it examines financial services and electronic commerce issues as they impact a number of key participants, including

▷ banks
▷ brokers and mutual funds

▷ software and technology solutions providers
▷ consortia
▷ card issuers and backers of digital trust
▷ transaction and financial processing services

Each of these groups has developed a set of strategies and products to incorporate the Internet and the Web into future business development. Yet even when they are designing services based on a common standard for electronic commerce, there are significant differences in vision and practice, stemming from the present competitive position, and the flexibility to make major course adjustments. Often their public announcements point toward overlapping agendas and alliances, but their institutional interests lead to competitive conclusions. By collecting contributions from authors with different institutional backgrounds and financial services experience, this book presents a balanced picture of where today's financial services experts and practitioners agree and where their strategic directions compete or conflict.

New partnerships and electronic commerce product announcements have become a daily routine for the financial services industry. It's obvious that the momentum to move to Web-based business models is increasing and that the traditional distinctions among service providers are blurring. But what are the critical turning points for the industry as a whole? With rapid changes at work within the industry, sorting out the significant developments and long-term trends can be a challenge. In chapter 1, "Defining Net Impact: The Realignment of Banking and Finance on the Web," the editor discusses how secure electronic commerce is driving change in financial services and analyzes the potential for the Internet to become a universal channel for trusted settlements and exchange of value. As the Web begins to replicate core banking functions, a variety of nonbank institutions are ready to move into the transaction settlement business and to assume on-line trust broker roles. Technical advances in managing networked security and digital trust are intersecting with increased consumer activity and expectations on the Web. Attracting a significant percentage of customers to Web commerce will require enhanced convenience; value-added, integrated information; and simple, fast user interfaces. In addition to concerns about security and uncertainty about how to select the appropriate service, home Internet users are still limited by dial-in connectivity speeds and hardware requirements for delivery of multimedia information and services. Finally, chapter 1 discusses the central role of digital trust and identity in extending the applications of electronic commerce to the whole spectrum of financial services and analyzes the implications of nonbanking institutions assuming the role of digital trust broker.

Chapter 2, "Frontiers of On-Line Financial Services," coauthored by Ravi Kalakota and Frances Frei of the University of Rochester, focuses on the strategic, technical, and business issues driving banks to reexamine their approach to delivering services. Drawing on their extensive research in banking operations and infrastructure, the authors analyze how nonbanking competitors are moving into traditional bank territory, and they discuss how bank managers are responding to this threat. They point out that it is essential for banking strategists to understand the difference between delivering customer services on the Web and earlier, largely unsuccessful investments in proprietary home banking systems.

Kalakota and Frei conclude that many banks are doubly disadvantaged in this new arena of on-line competition, because (1) they still rely on inflexible back-end processing systems that limit their ability to provide real-time, integrated financial information to customers; and (2) they still do not have a strategic plan that will guide the transition to full deployment of on-line financial services. The chapter ends by posing some of the core questions that bank managers must address to move their institutions successfully into the electronic commerce environment of the future, including managing financial supply chains, developing innovative on-line products, competitively pricing services, and attracting more customers to do business on line.

One bank that has of necessity come to terms with these questions is featured in chapter 3, "Banking on the Web: Security First Network Bank and the Development of Virtual Financial Institutions," by Kim Humphreys. As the first bank to open for business directly on the Web, Security First Network Bank (SFNB) aimed to demonstrate the viability of on-line banking via the Internet. This virtual bank's success in providing advanced security and service options attracted thousands of technologically sophisticated customers in its first year. But the real challenge for the future is growth and diversification as the country's largest banks begin to flex their muscles on the Web. SFNB has posted steeper and steeper losses over the past year, a trend that the current steady, slow rate of customer and account growth is not likely to reverse. Executives are focused on the much more lucrative market for the Security First banking software and secure infrastructure solutions and have established a target of selling the S1 system to at least 55 banks during 1997. But with losses of $108 million in the first quarter of the year and only 24 banking customers signed on, the results are still far from assured.

The SFNB case illustrates the potential and the perils of virtual business models for smaller institutions in an industry heavily populated with deep pockets and increasingly cutthroat competition. Financial products and services on the Web must be bolstered by strategic alliances and back-end growth strategies to ensure the long-term viability of any new venture.

This long-range strategic outlook on electronic commerce is a significant factor in the Liberty Financial projects described in chapter 4, "From Web Strategy to Implementation at Liberty Financial Companies" by Iang Jeon and William P. Rice. After testing a new virtual marketing and distribution model with its innovative WebSaver Annuity product, Liberty Financial's executives have set out to capture the lead in implementing commerce on the Web. One core component, a flexible, modular IT infrastructure, is already in place and forms the foundation for secure, personalized on-line services and products.

Through its diversified holding companies such as Stein Roe Mutual Funds and Keyport Insurance, Liberty aims to bring innovative, customized service to the next wave of customers who are just connecting to the Internet. Even though their initial product offerings are already available on the Web, Liberty strategists continue to emphasize long-term leadership and growth opportunities over short-term revenues and profits. From their vantage point, fine-tuning the technology to support customization and integrated financial information and offering advanced security features such as digital certificates for customers and brokers will soon be a competitive necessity for all financial service organizations. Sustainable advantage will come from building stronger customer relationships and more value-added services into the Web delivery channel. And the companies that learn how to do that most effectively will win the loyalty of present and new customers when the Web becomes the primary channel for financial services and transactions.

Billion dollar bets have already been placed that the world's smallest, most portable computer platform—the chip embedded in smart cards—will become the engine moving a critical mass of business and consumer transactions to the Internet. A recent Dataquest report predicted that the market for smart cards will burgeon from 544 million units in 1995 to 3.4 billion units by 2001. Killen & Associates forecast that the annual volume of smart card/e-cash transactions will exceed 10 billion by 2001 and that technology providers, not banks, are the most likely beneficiaries. However banks respond, this level of growth will certainly fuel the competition for consumer loyalty and digital dollars by channeling more funds into electronic commerce applications not tied to traditional banking and financial services systems.

In chapter 5, "Smart Cards in Web-Based E-Commerce," Scott Guthery describes the transformation of smart cards from primitive calculators for debit/credit transactions to the hottest technology for on-line financial transactions and security solutions. The technical breakthrough of fitting Java programming applications onto card chips, allowing a single card to be used with multiple vendors and for different types of transactions, is only the beginning of the story. The new generation of Java cards will include built-in security and digital identification to protect consumers and customize transactions from any network access point. In the process, they will become vital links between banking, consumer credit card transactions, Web commerce, and electronic cash. Visa International, the world's largest consumer payment system, with 561 million cardholders and more than 20,700 member financial institutions, has already announced plans to standardize its global card payment business on the multiapplication Java chip card described in chapter 5.

Standards and who sets them are critical questions for the next phase of electronic banking and financial services, and the acceptance of standards often hinges not on superior technology but on jockeying for competitive advantage. In chapter 6, Dan Schutzer, Vice President at Citicorp and President of the Financial Services Technology Consortium (FSTC), describes how the Internet has shifted the standard-setting process toward open platforms and outlines the projects undertaken by FSTC to ensure that banking services will meet future consumer demands for integrated, convenient, and easily accessible financial products and transactions.

He points out that despite the ferment around electronic commerce and smart cards, banks today still have intrinsic advantages in market penetration. Almost every U.S. household has some relationship with a bank, and checks are second only to cash as the preferred method of payment. In order to capitalize on these advantages, banks need to move toward more cost-effective and flexible on-line services. Schutzer describes in some detail how standards for electronic checks and Internet bank payments systems will help to ensure that banking institutions retain their central role in future financial exchange models.

The emergence of standard solutions for electronic commerce poses strategic challenges as well as opportunities for the well-established corporations that have built a business around efficient and cost-effective back-end processing of data and financial transactions. As Chuck White, President of Electronic Commerce Payment Services at First Data Corporation, explains in chapter 7, processing services firms have also been forced to reconsider their revenue sources, organizational structures, and customer/competitor relationships by the move of banking and investment services and front-end customer interfaces to the Internet.

First Data Corporation's 23 separate business divisions, having successfully penetrated a variety of separate markets such as comprehensive credit and debit card services, merchant authorization, processing and settlement for banks, check acceptance and risk management, accounts receivable recovery, mutual fund transaction agent services, consumer fund transfers, and check clearing must now develop strategies to add value through service integration. Lacking the name recognition of front-end software providers such as Intuit and Microsoft and vertical integration potential of global payment processors like Visa and American Express, First Data is developing an Internet strategy based on alliances and innovative, integrated services that will add value to its existing customer base while opening the door to new business development on the Web.

Moving mutual fund information and trading services to the Web, as described in chapter 8 by Mary Cronin, in collaboration with Julie Kever, Vice President for Interactive Product Development at Charles Schwab & Company, was a natural offshoot of Schwab's aggressive use of technology to reduce costs and maintain its reputation for innovative services. The development of a mutual fund Web presence required a significant collaborative effort from different groups within the corporation, as well as extensive usability testing with customer groups. The strategic impact of this site is not measured primarily by its popularity with customers, although this is certainly an important goal; the Web also plays a key role in Schwab's future plans to expand its product and service offerings to include financial planning, retirement fund management, and insurance options. The potential of the Internet to reduce customer-support and transaction costs and simultaneously provide consolidated, value-added financial services to a growing share of the U.S. population makes Web commerce a competitive necessity for Schwab and other well-established investment companies. The Web also provides a new channel for Schwab to reach the international investment community, as Internet connectivity continues to increase at a rapid pace around the world.

If the established international financial institutions don't move quickly enough, they may find that virtual competitors have made significant market inroads. As chapter 9, "Breaking New Ground: Wall-Street Electronica," documents, the rise of investment services and electronic brokerages on the Web represents an unprecedented opportunity for small, agile, and technically sophisticated companies. Carlos, Noah, and Francisco Otalvaro make a case that the independent, Web-connected investors will demand services that are best provided by a new combination of personalized, intelligent on-line services.

Banks outside the United States have been slower to accept the viability of the Internet for secure commerce and reluctant to contemplate the redesign of legacy systems to deliver account information and transaction support via the Web. Nevertheless, the pace of change is accelerating according to Andreas Crede in chapter 10, "International Banking and the Internet." Among the barriers Crede identifies are the high cost of Internet connectivity for banks and consumers in most countries, the continuing investment that banks are making in expensive, proprietary networks and software solutions, and lingering concerns about privacy and security on the Internet. The aggressive stance of U.S. financial institutions and the growing movement to participate in multinational strategic partnerships is weakening these barriers, as many of the world's leading banks reevaluate their electronic commerce strategies.

The issues and insights presented in each of these chapters deserve attention in their own right as direct documentation of a critical moment in the meshing of financial services and electronic commerce. Taken together, they provide a multifaceted perspective that is well matched with the complex and sometimes contradictory developments of an industry in transition. No matter how savvy the expert or seasoned the strategist, any one point of view is unlikely to capture the full import of the changes taking place in banking and finance today, or even to consistently identify the developments that will have enduring impact. The debate about moving secure investment and banking transactions to the Web is indeed over, but analysis of the dimensions and the direction of this revolution is far from complete.

The ideal analysis would blend the experience of practitioners and executives from leading corporations with in-depth research and expertise in the key technical areas. Such a framework would help to decipher the patterns that presage a major industry-wide shift to new models of commerce, competition, and growth. This book brings together that combination of expertise and diversity to provide a many-sided view of the ways in which the Internet is changing and challenging different facets of financial services. Like the industry itself, it represents a divergence of opinions and business models, as well as significant agreement about some core issues and developments. And like the Web, it represents a work in progress.

1

Defining Net Impact

*The Realignment of Banking
and Finance on the Web*

MARY J. CRONIN
BOSTON COLLEGE

Introduction

Bill Bates has a lot of banking and financial management work to accomplish before midnight, and it is already 10:30 P.M. This is definitely the week to decide about another round of mortgage refinancing and loan consolidation. His sister wants to talk about a long-term-care insurance plan or assisted-living option for Dad before he heads back to Florida for the winter. The evening's e-mail brings a mixed message from Bill Jr. at college—he may be able to get a tuition rebate if he dedicates next semester to volunteer work in South America. But what will that mean for his college loan and work-study packages? And will it be okay if he graduates a year late? He really needs to decide by tomorrow.

Those are just the new items on the evening's list. Bill has already promised to visit his daughter's eighth-grade class to speak about his work in the entertainment industry, and he wants to back up the anecdotes with some current data on industry structure, revenues, and profits. It is also time to prepare the monthly performance report for his investment club, pay the household bills, and make some

Keogh plan estimates for his wife, based on her new income from freelance designer work.

So with all this work ahead of him tonight, why is Bill smiling? Because he is about to open up his personal finance management site on the Web and tackle all of the tasks on his list in one productive session. Recurring items such as bill payment and monthly investment performance reports are already built in to his on-line profile, so all he has to do is click on these headings, review and approve any changes in numbers, and set the automatic bill payment and report generation processes in motion.

A visit to the mortgage planner section of his site retrieves his existing loan and rate information and calculates the difference in monthly payments, as well as the new processing costs and lifetime cost of the loan according to currently available refinancing arrangements. If he decides to go ahead with a new loan, he can apply directly by filling out a brief form and authorizing the transmission of his relevant financial information to the most attractive lender. He can expect on-line notification of loan approval sometime tomorrow.

The personal dimensions of his son's semester off and his father's health care needs will take more than the Web to resolve, but at least he can check the financial implications easily. Insurance and tuition planners are already linked to his personal site, and some quick adjustments to policy and time parameters will give him updated information on cost and payment impact of adding an insurance policy and pushing back the college graduation date. While he is at it, Bill can transfer some cash to his son's college bank account in response to that not-too-subtle hint attached to Bill Jr.'s e-mail.

Creating a new profile for his wife's self-employment income and tax-deductible retirement options is a bit more time-consuming, but once the template is in place he will be able to plug in new employment scenarios and additional earnings as they come along. Plus, this gives him a chance to try out some of the new features of the retirement/portfolio management package that was added to his site recently. Only 11:30 and he is almost done with the list. Plenty of time to research a few potential stock picks and sell off some disappointing performers before printing out the entertainment industry data for his daughter's class. Bet they do not know how many motion picture studios lost money last year, or what the average return is for their favorite record labels.

Bill Bates, of course, is a fictional character. But meeting his combined financial, investment, and information needs is high on the agenda of managers and strategists with responsibility for electronic commerce. In fact, Bill's behavior, and the assumption that an increasing number of people like Bill will turn to the Web to manage their finances, has captured the imagination of banks, software companies, mutual funds, and investment services providers of all types and sizes. The desire to capture Bill's loyalty is driving the rapid development of advanced, integrated personal financial products for the Internet.

Bringing It All Together on the Web

One of the contenders for Bill's business is Scott Cook, chairman of Intuit. Cook explained his company's plans to "reshape itself into an on-line bazaar for financial services" as follows: "We believe there's a huge business opportunity in providing the marketplace where buyers can meet sellers of financial services." Cook envisions that this new marketplace will include not only financial planning and management tools like Quicken, Intuit's current flagship product, but also direct sales of insurance, stocks, loan applications, credit cards, and other financial services traditionally associated with different industries and institutions.[1]

Many executives at banks and investment houses have come to the same conclusion—and are looking for ways to defend against further inroads into their core business by software companies such as Intuit and Microsoft. An analysis of the Bill Bates scenario helps to explain why. In the course of a 90-minute session on the Web, Bill used the following types of financial services:

- ▷ Banking
- ▷ Insurance
- ▷ College and mortgage loan planning

  ▷ Loan application
  ▷ Bill payment
  ▷ Financial planning
  ▷ Retirement planning
  ▷ Stock trades
  ▷ Investment portfolio management
  ▷ Financial and investment research

All of these services are available somewhere on the Web, but certain vital links between them are still missing. One missing piece is the integration that puts every type of transaction just a click away from the user. Another is the ability to securely combine confidential financial information from different external sources with a personalized profile of financial activity and recurring service needs. Whoever controls these and other vital links in the digital value chain will be well positioned to develop new products and revenue sources as on-line commerce expands. Competition for that front-end integrator position is one of the significant drivers of the current scramble for partnerships, strategic alliances, and Web-based technology solutions among large and small companies. Once these services are available in an integrated Web site, they are no longer necessarily seen as separate products from providers clearly labeled as banks and brokers and financial planners. In fact, the better the user interface of the future, the more transparently all these providers and services would blend into one.

Front-end integration is just one of the key electronic commerce roles that remains in contention. The opportunities for profit and growth are even greater in the less visible but more pervasive layers of interaction that underpin activity on the Web. This means that the consumer market for Web financial services and banking applications represents only one component of the shifting relationships within the banking and finance industry.

Merchants selling their products on the Web require a different set of integrated services, including secure digital payment and identity verification to protect them and their customers. Behind the scenes, they need to integrate credit card processing, check clearance arrangements, and vendor payment with legacy financial functions, supply-chain management, accounting, and audit and financial reporting requirements. Individual agents and brokers moving onto the Web are looking for on-line trading and investment support services, along with the ability to manage client portfolios and channel value-added financial information while tracking their own investment performance and managing a variety of business services.

As diverse as these different on-line markets and customers are, they are all participants in the emerging digital value chain. They all need the integrated, network-accessible banking and financial services that are still in an early stage of development. The realignment of banking and financial services through Web commerce, therefore, begins with behind-the-scenes processing and clearance functions and includes all value exchange transactions from multinational payment systems to corporate credit transfers to small businesses as well as individual consumers.

Mapping the Competitive Landscape for On-Line Financial Services

This book provides a business perspective on the shifts taking place in the competition for market share and customer loyalty on the Web. Subsequent chapters describe in more detail the strategies different industry players have developed to meet on-line market demands. This chapter identifies the core areas of electronic commerce that define the digital value chain and provides a framework for interpreting the current competition for digital advantage. Table 1.1 illustrates some of the major battlegrounds for integrating financial services on the Web today, and it indicates the unresolved issues still in contention.

A more detailed discussion of each of these core areas helps to illustrate the ways in which the 'Net is changing traditional relationships and services within banking and finance, shifts in the overall competitive landscape, the technical and standards infrastructure, and the requirements of individual and business users.

TABLE 1.1 **Digital Competition for On-Line Financial Services**

Competitors	Domain	Issues
FRONT-END INTERFACES		
Software and access providers; banks and mutual funds	Consumers, small businesses, and business-to-business agents and brokers	Integrated standards for seamless access; enhanced connectivity; use of push technology
PAYMENT AND TRANSACTION SYSTEMS		
Technology and software providers; banks and credit card companies	Credit cards, smart cards, electronic checks, and digital cash	Acceptance and deployment of common standards; integration with trust functions
INTEGRATED INFORMATION ACTION AND RETRIEVAL		
New Web-based companies; brokers and financial-service providers	Personal profile information and follow-up; banking and investment transactions and data; planning, managing, advising, and forecasting; accounting, auditing, and clearing processes	Requires back-end integration and real-time access to secure personal information and public external/product information cost and pricing variations
TRUST BROKERS AND SECURITY SERVICES		
Banks, brokers, telecommunication and access providers	Secure access and identity; transaction security and privacy; settlements and clearance functions	Technical and regulatory issues; responsibility for creation of secure trust infrastructure; assessments and legal tests of liability
DATA MANAGEMENT AND INFORMATION MINING		
Back-end service providers; access providers	Tracking macro and micro data; trends and market intelligence	Privacy and international restrictions; development of new business models

Prime Real Estate: The Front-End Interface

At the top of the digital value chain is a hotly contested struggle over desktop control and branding of the *customer interface* for the delivery of financial services. It is a prize worth fighting for, because whatever platform captures the loyalty and the personal financial information from on-line customers is going to be in an ideal position to benefit from product extension, strategic alliances, and e-commerce growth. The bad news, from the viewpoint of established banks and financial institutions, is that the Web has driven the competition for customer eyeballs (and pocketbooks) into the open. Still chastened by the lukewarm consumer response to proprietary PC banking software and the rise of financial management programs like Quicken and Money, bankers were initially slow to embrace the Internet as a prime delivery channel. Now they are confronting the prospect that other companies with a head start at implementing Web interfaces and secure services have already staked out a claim to the desktop.

The *competitors* actively contending for market share in this space include the following:

> ▷ Financial management software developers
> ▷ On-line banks
> ▷ Mutual funds and on-line broker Web sites
> ▷ Bill payment and check processing service providers
> ▷ Web browser developers
> ▷ Integrated financial services providers

The investment that banks and other competitors have made in developing their own proprietary software to manage the user interface is turning from an asset to a liability as the Web becomes a universal channel for information access and establishes itself as a secure location for financial transactions. As some of the world's largest software and computer companies have already discovered, competing with Internet standards is an expensive and ultimately futile battle. Providing on-line compatibility with other offerings on the Web has become a competitive necessity.

As more financial services organizations come to terms with the need for Web-based products, a new round of strategic alliances is blossoming. Many of the companies focused primarily on electronic payment and secure transaction solutions for the 'Net have also shifted their tactics to move away from direct marketing to the end user in favor of cobranding or infrastructure-only roles. CheckFree, for example, one of the largest providers of on-line bill-payment software, has shifted its emphasis from individual consumers to licensing its service to banks that offer it under their own brand as part of a cluster of on-line banking services.

No matter which user interface comes to dominate the financial services industry, a few fundamental issues remain:

▷ How soon will a significant percentage of consumers and businesses adopt the Web as their prime vehicle for financial activity?

▷ Which applications will capture customer attention and create loyalty?

▷ Do different demands and expectations distinguish the consumer market from the business-to-business market for financial services?

▷ Will future services rely on Web access as we know it today, or will the next step for financial services be the adoption of push technologies such as Webcasting and channeling that promote a more proactive customer relationship?

A recent FIND/SVP survey indicated that consumers, at least, are more ready to take advantage of on-line financial services than their banks may expect—but only if they can access a variety of services in one location and be assured that their interactions will be kept confidential. Table 1.2 summarizes the March 1997 survey reported by FIND/SVP.

FIND/SVP Emerging Technologies Research Group estimates that more than 16 million households will be banking on line by 2001, and it predicts that integrated financial services will provide the motivation that gets them there. That integration may take place

TABLE 1.2   Consumer Opinions of On-Line Banking

FIND/SVP reported that

▷ Eighty-eight percent of the potential market for financial services would like to see their bank bundle additional services such as brokerage and credit cards.

▷ The fear of losing privacy is greater than the fear of losing funds to on-line fraud.

▷ More than 46 percent of PC owners and intended buyers said they would be willing to pay for electronic financial services that include on-line banking.

Source: FIND/SVP News Release, March 25, 1977. Http://etrg.findsvp.com

at the back-end banking level, as discussed in more detail later in this chapter, or it may be generated in real time by a standards-based interface that interacts on demand from the user with other authorized sources of financial information and transaction services. This approach is especially attractive to the smaller, nonbanking companies that fill more specific niches in the digital value chain.

Business-to-business consumers of on-line financial services and individual agents and brokers turning to the Web as a combination resource and service delivery channel for their own customers are more focused on services that will boost performance and productivity by reducing their time requirements, consolidating and streamlining transactions, and providing access to essential resources. Business users are especially concerned about reliable, high-speed connectivity and end-to-end security in moving more critical transactions and financial information activities to the Web.

Cashing in the Chips: Payment and Transaction Systems

Once money becomes another form of networked bits, and the majority of financial transactions move on-line, industries from publishing to retail to telecommunications can contend for a piece of the banking pie. Whoever launches the digital dollar of choice and provides the best infrastructure for access will establish new channels for value exchange and settlement that could bypass banks altogether. The implementation of SET, the standard for secure electronic transactions on the Internet, is already under way with the support of MasterCard and VISA. Widespread adoption of the SET protocols, which include security measures like encryption, digital authentication, and verification of on-line identity, will increase consumer confidence in credit card transactions on the Web.

Digital currency, or electronic cash, has some advantages over typical credit card transactions, especially in cases where small amounts of money (under $10) are involved or where the buyer wants to ensure anonymity. A number of digital currency solutions are already available, and some software companies with digital solutions such as Digicash's Ecash have established partnerships with traditional banks to attract consumers and establish trust.

MarkTwain Bancshares, a medium-size bank with total assets of $3.1 billion in 1996 and 120 locations in three states, has partnered with Digicash to become the first bank to offer Ecash to its customers. Since the Ecash offering was launched on the MarkTwain Web site, about 2,000 customers have signed up to receive digital currency tokens on line. The total amount of digital currency in circulation on the Web, however, is infinitesimal compared with one day's volume of credit card purchases or checks written. MarkTwain bank managers, in fact, have concluded that significant growth of Ecash will require alliances with nonbank companies such as Internet service providers and leading browser providers such as Microsoft and Netscape.

Larger banks are less concerned about the start-up purveyors of electronic cash than about the well-established companies such as General Electric Information Services (GEIS) and Motorola that are now investing substantial resources in establishing smart card and digital-payment products. A number of the contenders for market share and recognition as Web payment standards are described in more detail in subsequent chapters, including secure, multifunction smart cards.

Many companies are convinced that the security features and flexible applications of multiapplication smart cards will define a new standard for secure on-line payments. One of the major issues is the lack of infrastructure for connecting smart card readers and terminals to the Web, especially in the United States. While the rest of the world has adapted smart cards for millions of vending-machine systems, telephone calls, bus and train fares, tolls, and other small denomination cash disbursements, U.S. vendors have just started to deploy smart card readers built in to computer keyboards, Web TVs, bank kiosks, and other Web-connected locations. Even optimistic proponents predict that it will be several more years before smart card connections to the Internet are universally available. In the meantime, Web payments and on-line financial transactions using SET-protected credit cards are expected to increase dramatically, giving credit card companies an edge in the competition for Internet payments.

All-in-One Services: The Integration Layer

The development of *integrated, customized financial services* is an active area of competition for start-up, Web-based companies and established financial institutions alike. It has finally dawned on leading banks and brokers that consumers do not want to navigate from Web site to Web site to keep track of their finances. Nor will they necessarily pay a premium to access accounts on line. Web-based services have to be more convenient, easier to use, and less expensive than the alternative to win the loyalty of consumers like Bill Bates. Some of the integration can take place at the user's end by providing a well-designed, standard software interface to the different providers of relevant financial information. This type of real-time integration of distributed resources is, after all, one of the greatest advantages of building on a standards-based Web platform. It is not that easy, however, for many of the key players in banking and finance today to provide the necessary links to the back-end systems that create the essential customer data.

Banks and investment companies typically have already devoted enormous resources to creating and operating proprietary back-end processing systems that are not easy to integrate with the Web environment. Such systems limit their flexibility for providing integrated financial information and real-time integration of services and also prohibit adopting more streamlined processing methods to reduce costs and take full advantage of the Internet to streamline user-initiated transactions. Chapter 2 describes in more detail some of the barriers that must be overcome to move bank transaction data more flexibly onto the Web.

While banks grapple with the challenge of redesigning back-end systems, other industries are looking for ways to leverage their information systems and Internet connections to establish an edge in this lucrative part of the digital value chain. A February 1997 Killen Associates study, "On-Line Value-Added Financial Services: The Next Revenue Generator," predicts that nonbank companies will begin to compete for banking's customer base by offering valued-added, integrated financial services via the Internet. The Killen study surveys the landscape for all potential banking competitors and comes up with the list shown in table 1.3 from outside of the core banking and credit card companies.

Not all of these potential competitors will be successful in developing a new line of value-added financial services, but the availability of a Web delivery channel, a standard infrastructure for security and transaction services, and a growing appetite among businesses and consumers for integrated financial services certainly creates an environment that invites ventures into traditional banking territory. Awareness that outside companies may launch major competitive

TABLE 1.3 **Competitors from Nonbanking and Credit Card Companies**

▷ Leading financial information and content providers such as Dow Jones and Bloomberg

▷ Suppliers of telecommunication, software, and hardware services for banking and credit transactions such as ATM and Point of Sale systems

▷ Nonbank companies with identifiable brands and large customer bases, such as Century 21, Virgin Atlantic, and Sainsbury

▷ Connectivity providers and on-line networks such as AOL and CompuServe

▷ Leading Internet software developers such as Netscape and Microsoft

▷ Major consulting and system integration firms such as Anderson, Ernst & Young, and KPMG

Source: www.killen.com/studies/study.olfs

initiatives has in turn motivated banks and investment companies to move more aggressively in seeking alliances and establishing joint ventures to maintain their claim to this part of the electronic commerce infrastructure.

Whom Do You Trust on the Web?

Another domain of the digital value chain, and the one that provides an essential foundation for the functions that have preceded it, is the role of on-line *trust broker*. In essence, this function allows all the participants in electronic commerce transactions on the Web to identify each other with an appropriate degree of certainty. In addition, the trust broker ensures a direct link between established digital identities and the contents of the messages that have been exchanged—at least to the extent that the receiver can be confident that the message has not been altered in transit and that the person who signed it cannot deny having been the one who actually sent it. These may seem like very simple steps toward establishing trust on the Web, but in fact they are at the heart of a viable digital trust infrastructure. The critical step of establishing identity, which we tend to take for granted in the day-to-day exchange of other types of commerce, has to be re-created on the Web to take into account the special nature of digital exchanges.

Senders and receivers of on-line financial information cannot rely on any of the familiar methods of identifying themselves. It is far too easy to tamper with standard electronic mail to assume that the plain-text signature is a reliable, legal indicator of who sent the message. Recent episodes of rogue Web servers set up to intercept and redirect traffic between servers and browsers on the Web illustrate that on-line identity can never be taken for granted.

Other commercial transactions, such as face-to-face cash purchases, credit card payments, phone orders, standard bank checks, and so on, may seem to function without such a complex broker support system, but they actually do have their own well-established and embedded trust infrastructures. The digital trust broker must replicate these functions in a way that makes sense in a totally networked environment.

On the Web, a customer cannot see all the trappings of a going business such as aisles filled with products or a rented space in a mall or a thick catalog with toll-free numbers and reply envelopes. Indeed, one of the most compelling features of the Web is that anybody can set up shop there. How does a customer on the Web establish trust in the identity of a merchant on the Web? Similarly, a merchant on the Web cannot ask for a customer's driver's license or conclude the person placing an order is old enough to enter into a commercial transaction by looking at him or her. Nor does a business have any more information than a customer does in dealing with another business.

Commerce on a purely digital medium requires a purely digital means of establishing identity. Merely digitizing nondigital means of identification will not suffice, because on the one hand some of what gives the means validity will be left behind, and on the other the means will be subject to forgeries not possible in the nondigital world. To wit, typing in a credit card number on the Internet does not result in as secure a transaction as presenting a credit card at the point of sale.

A way is needed for one set of bits to associate identity—a person, corporation, merchant, or service—with another set of bits in a manner that satisfies three basic requirements for trust and identity establishment. In a commercial transaction, the trust each party places in the other participants is a function of the knowledge each has about the identity of the others. When business is conducted between people or organizations that do not have firsthand knowledge of each other, the necessary identity information is provided by a third party—a trust broker who authenticates the identity of the participants in a commercial transaction and may guarantee the trust placed in the established identities by fully or partially guaranteeing the transaction itself.

A digital trust broker has two primary tasks: The first is to establish the identity of the participants in the transaction in a way that will be legally binding in case of dispute. Second, the trust broker has to communicate this information to the participants securely. As we have seen, most of the mechanisms buyers and sellers use to establish and communicate identity for nonelectronic commerce do not adapt readily to electronic commerce. Opening a World Wide Web outlet has forced many businesses to analyze their requirements for trust and identity and to look for ways to satisfy these requirements in e-commerce. Banks, which have played a central role in traditional commercial transactions, must now integrate their services with the alternative structures established by digital certificate authorities and software solution providers in order to retain a place in the on-line trust environment.

As the requirement for trusted digital identity becomes more central to on-line transactions, more companies are exploring the possibility of establishing their own certificate authority (CA) infrastructure to register and verify the identity of employees and customers. Liberty Financial Companies, for example, has started to issue digital certificates to mutual funds customers who want to conduct secure transactions and received customized financial planning services on the Web from the Stein Roe Mutual Fund Web site. Liberty is also establishing a secure digital trust relationship with its independent broker agent channel by providing certificates for its Keyport Insurance company agents as described in chapter 4.

Businesses have to implement standardized and widely accepted solutions to create the infrastructure needed for secure electronic commerce in this new environment. Digital certificates pave the way for establishing trust and identity on open public networks such as the Internet and open the competition for the role of trust broker to a wide variety of established and start-up companies.

Turning Data into Dollars:
Information in the Digital Infrastructure

As more consumers and transactions move to the Web, the function of capturing and mining the data associated with on-line user behavior, preferences, and purchases increases in value. Providers of the front-end user interface can obtain in-depth personal profile information as part of creating customized service options. As the FIND/SVP consumer survey revealed, however, many consumers are even more concerned about the loss of privacy for this type of data than they are about on-line fraud. Without clear-cut guidelines for how such personal profile information will be protected and who will have access to it, there seem to be limits to user willingness to divulge preferences. This concern for privacy is not the only limitation to front-end data collection. The European Union has promulgated regulations that prohibit on-line storage and network transmission of individual personal data on any European citizen outside of European borders. If these regulations are enforced in their present form they will conflict with the current data gathering practices of a large number of companies using the Web for international business.

Less problematic are the multiple opportunities for data aggregation and generic user profiling associated with the back-end processing of Web transactions. Companies that are already in business to provide back-end processing services, such as credit card authentication, check clearing, and mutual funds transaction services, are natural beneficiaries of this new product and revenue opportunity. The desire to obtain direct access to valuable market and user trend information also provides a motivation for other companies to ally with existing processing providers or to integrate this function into their own Web business models. The CEO of VISA, for example, recently characterized the customer profile information associated with commerce on the Web as a form of "infomoney" and predicted that consumers and innovative companies will find an increasing number of ways to realize concrete value from this new form of digital currency.

The Next Steps:
From Realignment to Real Revenues

Every layer of the new digital value chain offers opportunities for banks and financial services companies to expand their core business models and increase revenues. But they are far from alone in moving to take advantage of the growth potential of electronic commerce on the Web. With electronic commerce moving quickly in the direction of customized, integrated financial services and standard solutions for digital trust, the traditional advantages of banks and well-established investment companies are being challenged by more flexible business models. Banks themselves are experimenting with new approaches to customer service and product extension based on the one-to-one, interactive capabilities of the Web. A number of these evolving business models are represented in subsequent chapters. The most promising can be summarized as follows:

▷ **Virtual companies.** Banking and finance on the Web do not require red bricks and mortar or a prestigious address on Wall Street. Many start-up ventures are taking advantage of the relatively low cost and unlimited global reach of Internet connectivity to forgo physical location and conduct business directly on line. The experience of Security First Network Bank, the first full-service bank to open on the Web, is described in more detail in chapter 3, while the first year of operation for WallStreet Electronica, an innovative international Web brokerage and investment services company, is discussed in chapter 9.

▷ **Hybrid models.** Well-established banks and brokerages that open Web sites typically regard them as additional marketing and distribution channels rather than substitutes for traditional outlets. One disadvantage of this approach is that the Internet becomes another cost center without offering significant revenue growth or opportunities for cost reduction. In this situation there is little incentive to move aggressively in developing value-added Web services and therefore little likelihood of keeping ahead of nonbanking competitors in the digital value chain.

Some banks, such as First Union and Wells Fargo, have developed advanced on-line services as part of a hybrid model that includes a wide range of value-added products for individual customers as well as support and secure infrastructure for associated merchants to do business on the Web. The model leverages the investment that banks have already made in establishing a secure financial infrastructure and opens the door to significant growth and revenue extension.

▷ **Strategic partnerships.** Many financial services companies and banks have developed individual or consortial partnerships with key software and Web solutions companies such as

Microsoft, Netscape, and Intuit, as well as with bill payment and processing providers such as CheckFree and First Data Corporation and digital trust brokers such as Verisign. These partnerships allow the financial and banking sector to move ahead with electronic commerce strategies while retaining a focus on their core business activities.

Conclusion

The realignment of banking and financial services on the Web is already under way, and the pace of change is accelerating. In the near future, the major impact will be seen in terms of new products and services, alliances and preemptive strategic moves, and rethinking of the traditional roles of established players in the face of virtual competitors on the Web. The longer term competition for leadership and market share in the digital value chain is still in flux.

Banking is certainly not what it used to be, but no matter what form it takes in the digital world the exchange of value continues to play a critical role in shaping and enabling commerce. Fundamental changes in the mechanisms for representing the exchange, safekeeping, and accumulation of what we simplistically call money, from coinage to merchant letters of credit and from checks to consumer credit cards, have always underpinned and foreshadowed transformations in business relationships and the growth of new financial institutions. It is no wonder, then, that the convergence of secure electronic payment systems, digital channels for credit and investment, and the massive growth of the Internet as a multipurpose, multifunctional network reaching millions of homes and businesses around the world has given rise to a frenzy of entrepreneurial and competitive activity that is shaking the foundations of traditional financial services.

References

1. "One Stop Financial Shopping," Interview with Scott Cook, *Reuters,* March 10, 1997: www.news.com

2

Frontiers of On-Line Financial Services

RAVI KALAKOTA AND FRANCES FREI
UNIVERSITY OF ROCHESTER

Introduction

"Banking is vital to a healthy economy. Banks are not." This statement succinctly captures the turmoil in the financial services industry.[1] Before we examine the implications of this statement, it is necessary to define which segment of the banking industry is being most affected by the Internet. Banking as a business can be subdivided into five broad types—retail, domestic wholesale, international wholesale, investment, and trust. Of all these types, retail banking is probably the most affected by technological innovations brought about by electronic commerce.

On-line retail banking (also referred to as PC, remote, or electronic banking) has instigated a desperate positioning battle among competing companies from all different sectors of the financial services industry. The number of "strategic" alliances among banks, software companies, on-line services, telecommunication firms, and credit card companies is surpassed only by the number of consultants ready to help orchestrate these alliances.

The momentum of on-line banking has picked up considerably for four reasons:

19

1. **New distribution channels.** Financial institutions now have a variety of technological means to initiate on-line banking programs without incurring the heavy capital investments needed to develop their own systems. The reach and delivery capability of computer networks such as the Internet far exceeds any proprietary bank network ever built and makes it continually easier for customers to manage their money anywhere, anytime.

2. **No barriers to entry.** Technology is creating a level playing field where fast-moving nonbanking firms can easily provide banking products. This trend can be seen in the area of bill payments, where recent innovations have provided an opportunity for nonbanks (e.g., CheckFree and Intuit) to break into the banking business, threatening one of the most profitable services provided by banks. The present nature of on-line payments is a clear indication that if the banking industry fails to meet the demand for new products, there are many industries that are both willing and able to fill the void.

3. **Changing customer expectations forcing the need for agility and flexibility.** New technology has not only enabled an ever-increasing range of products, it has also had far-reaching effects on consumer expectations. Financial institutions understand that to meet consumer expectations, they need to be flexible by separating the content (financial product) from the distribution channel (the branch). The traditional model of one-stop integrated financial shopping has outlived its usefulness and is keeping banks from being agile enough to meet new consumer demands.

4. **Digital convergence of financial management transactions.** Technology has enabled a convergence of a broad range of financial management activities that previously were considered disparate. Only recently has software been written that makes it possible to perform diverse transactions such as bank, credit card, brokerage, and mutual fund statement download, including transaction history, current holdings and balances, consumer and business payments, and funds transfer for recurring

payments through one common interface. This convergence of transactions is a remarkable milestone. However, a precondition for convergence is the need for communication among a wide range of financial institutions (FIs), including merchants, banks, brokerage houses, payment processors, and government agencies.

It is clear from these trends that the primary impetus for drastic change in the banking industry does not come from forces within banking but from competitive pressure outside the industry. This chapter will address the origins of this competition and ask three questions that are particularly relevant to banking and financial services managers:

1. **What are the business dimensions of this nonbank competition?** These dimensions include new products, new delivery channels, and better customer service.
2. **What are the technological dimensions that impact the business dimensions?** These technology dimensions include the World Wide Web, Internet, and open transaction standards such as Open Financial Exchange (OFX) that enable an open framework for electronic exchange of financial data, transactions, and communications.[2]
3. **What are the organizational/process dimensions that impact the business and technological dimensions?** These dimensions include process design, performance measurement, and organizational structure. A fundamental question influencing on-line banking implementation that is rarely asked is: What is the optimal organizational structure that banks have to adopt in order to be agile enough to meet new customer demands?

How bankers respond to the preceding questions will have a big impact on what the industry will look like in the next decade. Financial institutions recognize the potential benefits of being first movers into what will inevitably be an important but crowded market. To avoid being left behind, banks are going directly to the market with on-line banking programs rather than running lengthy pilot tests with focus groups.

However, few managers have a clear vision of tomorrow's banking environment. In fact, few financial institutions have strategic plans in place today that anticipate the future of on-line banking. The challenge for the banking industry lies in creating the right products and providing the right incentives for consumers to use PCs regularly for banking. Figure 2.1 highlights the overall infrastructure of retail banking in the United States today and provides an overview of the relationship among the issues that will be discussed throughout the chapter.

The remainder of the chapter is organized as follows: In the next section we discuss the *changing dynamics* in the banking industry. These include changes in consumer preferences and demographics, increasing importance of cost reduction, regulatory reform, and new use of technology for delivery of financial services and products. This is captured in figure 2.1 by *External Environment* and *Institutional Response*. In the following section we discuss the technological issues of on-line banking including the types of products and services offered, the various implementation strategies available, and the back-office implications of these offerings. This is captured in figure 2.1 by *Systems Requirements* and *Actual Practice*. In the next section we discuss the *management issues* surrounding the offering of on-line products and services including pricing and differentiating strategies, marketing issues, and building customer loyalty.

Changing Dynamics in the Banking Industry

Traditionally, banking has had the attributes of the classic oligopoly: risk avoidance; product uniformity; buttoned-down managerial conformity; standard interest rates and pricing; limited cost control and market innovation; relatively undifferentiated customer service and—surprisingly, considering the lack of competition—lackluster financial performance.[3] These attributes made it possible for savings

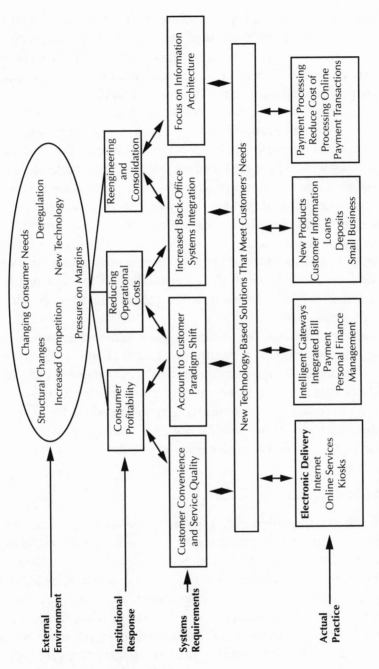

FIGURE 2.1 **The Retail Banking Framework**

23

and loan competitors to begin their attack on commercial banking during the 1970s, both in terms of receiving deposits and lending. Such encroachment is happening again in the 1990s as software companies such as CheckFree, Intuit, and Microsoft attempt to replace banks as the intermediaries in retail banking.

In recent years, there has been a major change in the way banks strive for increased profitability. In the past, the banking industry's chief concerns were asset quality and capitalization; if the bank was performing well along these two dimensions then it would likely be profitable. Today, performing well on asset quality and capitalization is not enough. Banks need to find new ways to increase revenues in what can, at best, be called a mature market for most traditional banking services, particularly consumer credit. This is complicated by the changing structure of the competitive environment for most banking products. A thorough understanding of this competitive environment is needed before individual banks can determine their best strategies.

We have identified five distinct factors that have conspired to create the new competitive environment, each of which will be described in detail: changing consumer needs; changing demographic trends; deregulation that is encouraging cross-industry competition; the drive to reduce costs by optimizing branch networks through institutional consolidation; and the use of technology to create new financial products and attractive product bundles.[4]

Changing Consumer Needs

Many consumer requirements are based on a simple premise: customers and financial institutions both seek more multifaceted relationships with one another. Customers want to be able to bank at their convenience, including over the weekend or late at night, and they want banks to provide more interesting financial products. Likewise, bankers want more stable and long-term relationships with their customers. From the bank's perspective, customer relationship management is difficult, even though financial institutions are highly automated and their products are essentially information products.

Changing consumer needs can be seen in the trend of buying investment products (managing the future) including mutual funds, annuities, and trust services. For the last decade, investment products have been one of the fastest growing industries. For a perspective on the change consider the following: Since 1989, bank deposits have grown 8 percent, while mutual funds grew 63 percent.

Demographic Trends

More than any other factor, demographic trends, such as an aging population, will influence the retail banking strategies of the future. Today we have close to 77 million baby boomers driving our economy, and they represent only part of the economic picture. America also has 44 million retirees with savings and incomes who need financial advice, counsel, and products. When these two groups are considered simultaneously there is a market of more than 100 million potential investment product clients, an enormous market of people who will be seeking sound investment advice for several decades.

Social and economic changes in the United States have altered the way Americans value their time and money. Americans spend more time than ever working and therefore place a higher premium on their leisure time. Thus they can be a receptive audience for time-saving products and services. In addition, the reduced level of job security and the need to plan for the future have heightened concern over personal debt, retirement planning, tax planning, and saving for college. As a result, consumers are increasingly careful in dealing with their personal finances.

Companies that take advantage of this window of opportunity by targeting the appropriate customers with the products and services especially right for them will surely have a lasting competitive advantage. Electronic delivery of these products and services certainly will be one of the means of achieving this edge because it provides convenience and the ability to customize products and services on a mass level.

Institutional Consolidation

Since 1984 the banking industry has been consolidating at a rapid pace. The central goal of most mergers is to reduce operating costs. In 1980 there were more than 14,400 commercial banks in the United States. At the end of June 1994 there were fewer than 10,200 banks. The key to that decline was bank mergers, which outpaced losses of banks due to failure by 4 to 1 and offset the establishment of new banks through de novo charters and the conversion of thrifts to commercial banks by a wide margin. More than 67 percent of the merging banks represented bank holding companies combining affiliated institutions, and nearly 71 percent of the acquired banks had total assets of less than $100 million.[5]

Just as banks have disappeared, so too have individual banking companies—multibank holding companies, one-bank holding companies, and all banks that are not affiliated with a holding company. There were more than 12,000 separate banking companies in 1980 but fewer than 8,000 by the middle of 1995. Much of that decline reflects mergers among bank holding companies, which typically involve a large company acquiring a smaller one that serves a different geographic market.

As banks merge to reduce their operating costs they are obviously growing in size. However, even their increased size is dwarfed by many of their new competitors. Consider the following: Merrill Lynch manages more than $500 billion in financial assets and expects to top $1 trillion by the end of the decade. Merrill Lynch also manages more retirement funds—$71 billion worth—than the 100 largest banks combined. Likewise, assets managed by the Fidelity Group in the United States have grown from $4 billion in 1972 to $40 billion in 1985 and up to $400 billion in 1994.[6]

Similarly, the top issuer of credit cards in the United States is not a bank but rather Dean Witter (Discover Card).[7] The GM and Ford finance companies are bigger than most of the banks in offering installment finance to their customers. If banks are going to compete with these larger competitors they must address their traditional banking overhead structures and existing retail strategies. Providing on-line financial services addresses both of these needs. Consider, for instance, branch delivery economics. Brick and mortar branches, on average, cost $1.5 million each and branch ATMs are also expensive when labor, setup, and maintenance costs are taken into account. In contrast, on-line technology can deliver some services more economically than existing service delivery channels because the infrastructure costs (e.g., personal computer) are shared with the consumer.

Regulatory Reform

Recent years have brought about far-reaching regulatory changes that have removed many of the competitive protections previously enjoyed by commercial banks.

The passage of the Riegle-Neal Interstate Banking and Branching Efficiency Act of 1994 (the Riegle-Neal Act) has created new opportunities for banks to serve customers across state lines—from accepting a deposit in any branch to combining all of a consumer's banking products into one total relationship. The Interstate Banking Bill will let banks take the final steps to become truly full-service financial providers. This ability to provide complete financial services is necessary if commercial banks are to survive increasing competition from mutual funds, brokerage firms, and insurance companies.

A bill pending in Congress will dismantle Glass-Steagall, the last remaining barrier between banking and securities firms. The Glass-Steagall Act was part of the Banking Act of 1933 passed during the Great Depression. Reform of the Glass-Steagall Act is expected to allow investment banks to broaden their product lines.

Technology-Based Financial Services Products

Another factor complicating predictions about the future structure of banking is the growing application of computer technology to banking. Some observers believe that additional development of electronic cash, such as smart cards, could stimulate further banking consolidation. They point to the fact that the start-up costs associated with electronic payments technologies can be high, in part because electronic cash requires large investments in computer software and other resources to establish a network of secure electronic transactions. Those large fixed costs have led observers to warn that a few financial services providers—those with the resources to absorb the costs—could come to dominate the payments system.

By contrast, the development of electronic banking might actually increase competition in banking markets and decrease bank operating costs. Electronic banking offers an inexpensive alternative to branching to expand a bank's customer base, and many banks are using it to increase service to their current customers. Many banks have set up Web sites, and some plan to offer banking services over the Internet. Many banks are already offering certain banking services over the telephone. Smart cards and other forms of electronic cash could be the key to consumer acceptance of home banking, eventually allowing banks to reduce their physical branches.

The use of technology in banking and corporate finance is not a new phenomenon. Large businesses have been using computers to handle electronic funds transfer (EFT) and other financial accounting tasks for years. The past two decades have seen retail banking deploy a substantial number of automated teller machines (ATMs) and point-of-sale (POS) terminals. It is estimated that by the year 2000 there will be 200,000 ATMs in such high-traffic locations as supermarkets, airports, shopping malls, and universities. More recently, the use of PCs as a retail banking interface has been gaining momentum.

Home Banking History

The recent hyperbole around home banking is not simply the latest Wall Street fad. Financial institutions were interested in turning the home banking concept into a reality as early as 1970. Many banks invested millions of dollars in R&D, certain that home banking was going to take off. *American Banker,* in October 1981, published a series of articles promoting the virtues of home banking. To the question of whether home banking would become a major force in the market by 1985, an executive vice president of First Interstate Bank replied, "Absolutely! And I want to be there."

The most popular approach of the 1970s was home banking via a Touch-Tone telephone, which enabled customers to check account balances, transfer funds, and pay bills. With telephone banking, customers use a numeric password on a push-button telephone to access banking services. The telephone was believed to be the ideal home banking technology since most people already had phones. Despite the initial optimism, results were very disappointing. The telephone was an awkward technology for home banking, since it does not provide visual verification, which is important to customers. Also, push-button phones were not yet common in the 1970s.

In the 1980s cable television was also considered as a possible medium for home banking. Although this approach solved the graphic limitations dilemma of the telephone, it had other drawbacks. The primary obstacle was that the necessary two-way cable was virtually nonexistent, since only a small percentage of Americans had two-way cable TV. Since the personal computer has both the visual display and two-way communications, it has always been considered a leading contender for the home banking crown.

During the 1980s and early 1990s, several banks offered home banking services and invested hundreds of millions of dollars into home banking. Just like the telephone and cable systems of the 1970s and early 1980s, home banking from a PC was initially a failure—the absence of a critical mass of PCs and a PC-friendly population stunted the growth of the concept and resulted in the failure of efforts such as Chemical Bank's Pronto System.

Why Will It Be Different This Time?

Several factors lead us to believe that home banking has a reasonable chance of success this time.[8]

Consumers Decreasing the Learning Curve

Consumers are becoming increasingly computer literate and are able to interact more fluently with their on-line financial services providers. Over the years, consumers have demonstrated a high level of acceptance of basic electronic services. The banking industry expects

that PCs will eventually replace ATMs and POS terminals as the crucial method of consumer-bank interfacing. However, the use of technology is not restricted to ordinary consumer-bank interface (or retail banking). Evidence indicates that banks and software companies
are beginning to find a receptive audience among PC users wanting
to simplify bill paying, checkbook balancing, credit management,
and tax-related tasks.

Increasing Consumer Awareness

Advertising and media attention have never been stronger. Mainstream magazines are dedicating and increasing the amount of coverage given to computer-related topics. The result of this can be seen
in consumers being more aware of the alternatives. As consumers
understand what is out there, they will become more demanding in
terms of expectations. Banks that do not meet expectations face the
distinct possibility of mass exodus.

PC-Installed Base Is Quite Large

First and foremost, there is a critical mass of PC-using households
with modems. Today there are more than 30 million PCs in America's homes, and, for the first time in history, consumers are now
spending more money on PCs than on TV sets. For a long time
home banking was a classic chicken-or-egg problem; without a large
enough sample of potential users, there was no urgency for the financial institutions to provide services. Conversely, without a wide
array of services, there was little consumer interest. This problem is
resolving itself. Computers today have CD-ROMs, high-resolution
graphics, sound, and modems, which make it easy to get on line. Modem penetration is a key issue for home banking, because the current services do not work without a modem. Clearly the technology
exists to make home banking a reality. Whether it will happen via the
Internet, a proprietary service, or both is yet to be determined, but
the infrastructure is in place.

The Alternative Is Too Expensive

In 1995 more than 30 billion checks were processed in the United
States. The cost associated with writing, mailing, and processing

these checks is staggering. The typical firm expends an estimated $9 per customer (in processing and infrastructure overhead) just to get paid. Moreover, the process usually begins and ends on a computer system, albeit with numerous steps in between. As the world economy grows, the current system reveals itself as too costly, inefficient, and susceptible to fraud. Sooner or later it will need to be changed.

Fierce Competition

While home banking offers a great deal of promise, it also carries above-average risk. First and foremost, the likely competitors for home banking customers (Intuit, Microsoft, Charles Schwab, and AT&T) are faster moving and better capitalized than most banks. Given the potential profitability and strategic importance of home banking, competition is likely to intensify. Second, while we believe in the promise of home banking and think that consumers are ready, it may be years before anyone makes money in home banking. The investments required to build the service infrastructure are significant and must be made today.

Changes in Institutional Perspective

One of the major issues driving changes in the way financial institutions view technology is the movement from a cost- to profit-centered perspective. With significant competitive pressures on profit margins, one of the few ways to make a profit on a product or service is to become the low-cost provider. Because banks have a shrinking pool of (traditional) revenues to cover the costs of operations, many seek competitive advantage in their ability to process transactions and serve customers more efficiently.

Five key issues that will influence the movement toward a revenue-oriented perspective of banking operations are (1) developing cross-functional business processes; (2) coordinating operational support such as capacity management with changing business plans; (3) organizing the people, equipment, and systems to provide operational support; (4) moving the customer service function from pure support to a mix of sales and support; and (5) improving management reporting systems in operations.

Maximizing revenue growth requires a holistic look at the set of processes a bank uses to serve its customers. Institutions are examining every component of their operating structures to find more effective ways of creating and delivering products and services. Technology will play a key role in redesigning business processes as banks upgrade from 20- or 30-year-old information systems to new systems and ways of attracting and serving customers. To make the shift from account- to customer-based services (see figure 2.2), banks must invest in process reengineering of an unprecedented scale.

The business objectives driving most of the decision making in the back office can be characterized by a migration through three stages of culture: product, market, and relationship (see figure 2.2). Most financial institutions began as a product-oriented organization and have now migrated into a market culture. These institutions have yet to move to a relationship-oriented culture, although virtually all of their Web pages and brochures indicate that this is the goal. The product culture offered no differentiation of market—the view was a single, homogeneous unit with the same product sold throughout. Supporting this culture was a host-legacy architecture of independent applications that performed account posting on a host mainframe. In a market culture, rather than a homogeneous unit, the market is segmented. By far the most prominent segment-

Product-Oriented Management	Market-Oriented Management	Relationship Management
Independent Accounts and Services	Fixed Product Bundles	Customized Product Bundles
Performance Measured on Share of Product	Performance Measured on Market Share	Performance Measurement
Account Information Centrally Managed	Centralized Market Sector Profiles	Integrated Profiles of Customers at the Point of Sale
Mainframe-based Systems	Mainframe-based Systems with Limited Integration	Client/Server Systems
		Electronic Commerce

FIGURE 2.2 **Evolution of Retail Banking Strategies**

ing scheme is by age and income, even though this is widely regarded as inadequate. Today many organizations have taken steps to segment by lifestyle characteristics as well. For institutions involved in data warehousing, developing extensions to customer information systems, and marketing customer information systems, segmentation analysis is critical. Selecting the appropriate segmentation criteria and accurately managing the divides is the linchpin for developing good customer profitability analysis and segmentation strategies.

Categorizing On-Line Banking Product Offerings

To put on-line banking into perspective, realize that an estimated 835,000 consumers have already signed up with 150 different financial institutions for on-line checking account access. That is 610,000 more, or four times, the number eight months ago. But still, even after a year of intense media hype, it is less than 1 percent of households, or just 4 percent of the 19 million Internet users identified in the 1995 CommerceNet study. The reasons for this gap include limitations in the types of services currently available, the approaches banks have taken to implement on-line banking products, and the back-office challenges of providing fully integrated on-line products.

Types of On-Line Financial Services Products

Let us review our definition of on-line financial services, which we define as those providing the ability to conduct bank transactions from the comfort of home (or office) using a telephone, television, or personal computer. Examples of the transactions include reviewing checking and savings account balances, transferring funds among accounts, paying bills, reconciling checking accounts, ordering duplicate bank statements or new checks, viewing and downloading bank and credit card statements, opening new accounts, applying for loans, and possibly in the future taking out "cash" in the form of a debit or smart card.

These transactions fall into three categories: basic (the need to manage the past, for example, access to bank statements and bills); intermediate (the need to manage the present, for example, funds transfer, access account-related information); and advanced (the need to manage the future, for example, download data for use with personal finance software products). This classification is useful when analyzing and categorizing the product offerings of various institutions.

1. **Basic products and services** are those involved in personal finance such as checking and savings account statement reporting and 24-hour account management. Basic services also include a growing array of home financial management services, such as household budgeting, updating stock portfolio values, and listing most recent transactions.
2. **Intermediate products and services** add to the basic services such offerings as account reconciliation across several products (balancing checkbooks); paying bills, status of payments, or stop-payment requests; and consumer and mortgage loan management. Increasingly, these services will be complemented by a broad array of activities such as obtaining loan applications, historical performance data, prospectus download, and stock and mutual funds information.
3. **Advanced products and services** include stock and mutual funds trading services, foreign exchange currency trading and cash management, letters of credit management, tax return preparation, and other sophisticated services such as electronic submission and acknowledgment of income tax filings and payments for individuals, proprietorships, partnerships, and corporations to state, federal, and international taxing authorities.

Basic Products and Services

On-line banking, which allows consumers to avoid long lines in both teller and toll-free service queues, as well as giving them the flexibility of doing their banking at any time, clearly has potential in the area of personal finance. In addition, on-line banking offers the industry cost-cutting potential in both office expenses and physical buildings because it is estimated that processing an electronic transaction costs six times less than the cost of processing a check.

The personal finance software currently available ranges from simple (e.g., software that keeps up-to-date check registers) to sophisticated (e.g., software that tracks assets, liabilities, loans, and credit cards). Software products such as Microsoft's Money can calculate mortgages and loans, estimate interest, make automatic adjustments for inflation, and even determine the monthly savings necessary to meet retirement goals. Automated activity is a key benefit of this software. For example, the first time the consumer completes a bill payment, the financial information, including the name and address of the payee, date of the transaction, budget category, and amount of the check, is recorded. For subsequent payments, the consumer need only enter the first few letters of the payee's name and the software recalls and fills in all of the information from the last check, allowing for amount and date adjustments. For regular check transactions, such as mortgage and auto payments, users can also automatically schedule payment reminders.

Automated account management is also currently available with credit card statement management as an example of how electronic banking can help consumers manage their finances at a sophisticated level. Quicken, a personal financial management program made by Intuit, can connect to VISA and provide access to monthly financial statements. Quicken will even have a modem call a consumer's computer and periodically dump statements directly onto the hard drive, allowing for the credit card transactions to be seamlessly integrated with the consumer's check transactions. The incorporation of both checking and credit card expenses into the family budgeting software obviously allows consumers a more thorough understanding of their finances. Irrespective of the software package, the underlying principles and capabilities remain the same.

The creation and monitoring of personal budgets is a key feature of most personal finance software packages. All of the programs provide initial budgeting categories and can automatically create budgets based on past spending habits. By using the budget plan to compare expected versus actual expenses, the consumer can obtain a picture of where money is going and how to economize to achieve long-term goals. The software creates reports based on consumer-specific budgets and delivers different views of financial information in the form of charts, graphs, and tables. Additional modules make it easy to determine the effects of compound interest and inflation rates on personal loans and savings plans, such as mortgage payments, retirement planning, and tuition.

Intermediate Products and Services

Intermediate products go beyond the basic personal finance capabilities listed earlier and include direct bill payment and accounting functions (table 2.1). Bill payment is by far the most mature service in this category.

The on-line payment of bills was developed in the early 1980s and has become of increasing interest to consumers. Bill payment works in the following manner: A customer establishes a file of certain merchants with his or her bank and regularly uses either a telephone or personal computer to direct the bank to make payments to these merchants. The bank transfers funds through an automated clearinghouse when possible or else actually creates and mails a check to the specified merchant when electronic payment is not an option.

CheckFree offers on-line bill paying as an intermediary through third-party software packages (and recently has offered its own software package for direct bill payment). Once the software is loaded— and the customer registers his or her bank account number with CheckFree—writing checks takes only seconds. To provide an example, if Jane Consumer owes the local telephone company $75, she

TABLE 2.1 **Summarizing the Key Basic and Intermediate Services**

Banking Account Data Management	Statement data, balance inquiry, and funds transfer from checking, savings, and money market accounts, including year-end summaries and tax notices.
Bill Payment	Electronic check writing from any demand deposit account to electronic payees (such as large billers) and nonelectronic payees (such as individuals).
Bill Presentment	Electronic delivery of bills and invoices by billers to consumers and small businesses, including receipt certification and promotional inserts.

clicks on the check-writing feature and a picture of a check appears. She fills in the name, amount, and date she wants the bill to be paid and then instructs her computer to transmit the check. This final step is accomplished by modem, which dials the CheckFree computer with payment instructions.

Each evening, CheckFree processes all payments it has received from consumers, verifies that money exists to cover them, and then either electronically notifies the Federal Reserve Board to transfer that amount from the customer's account in Bank A to the merchant's account in Bank B or mails the merchant a check. More sophisticated options, in which the user can actually program the computer to pay certain monthly bills automatically at specified intervals (say, once per month), are also possible. The computer keeps track of these bills and never forgets to record payments. The cost for this convenience in addition to the one-time software expense of approximately $29.95 is $9.95 a month for the first 20 payments (checks), and $3.50 for each additional batch of 10 payments. The price, in comparison with the cost of the stamps required for traditional payment, is not much of a premium for the customer.

Clearly, home banking services for individuals are becoming fairly ubiquitous. However, similar on-line banking services for small businesses are not yet as prevalent. Very few banks offer on-line accounting functionality, even though it is something every business requires. Although full-fledged accounting programs are more sophisticated for small businesses than for consumers, typically providing general ledgers, invoicing functions, and inventory management, personal finance software also has the potential to handle payroll functions and track accounts receivable and payable. This could be a lucrative opportunity for banks in extending their product offerings to accounting-related activities by offering business software in the form of Java applets or more traditional software packages.

Advanced Products and Services

There is a growing push in the banking and brokerage community to develop systems that support the important financial decisions people make concerning their savings including investments, retirement planning, college savings, insurance decisions, home buying, home financing and refinancing, and more. These financial decisions are not new but are much more complex today than they were 30 or 40 years ago.

The goal of many financial services firms is to offer their customers complete portfolios of life, home, and auto insurance, along with mutual funds, pension plans, home financing, and other financial products. However, not only are customers reticent, but the systems in place at many financial services firms are not interoperable. Even within companies that offer a range of financial products, each line of business typically has separate accounting and customer record systems. Further fragmentation results from various systems acquired through mergers that have not been integrated. To offer comprehensive services, banks must integrate all of this information to make it accessible by the customer from a single access point.

Retirement planning in the United States is a good example of this need for integration. Changes in pension and Social Security benefits have moved the burden of funding retirement onto the consumers' shoulders. Yet only 5 percent of consumers have retirement plans, largely because of the complex nature of financial planning. Consumers are unable to make plans without aid, and yet professionals do not always provide appropriate answers. Further, the services of a truly unbiased financial adviser are too expensive for all but the very rich. Books are helpful, but they cannot provide the precise solutions to individual needs and circumstances that often require customized plans.

Figure 2.3 illustrates the range of advanced services already being offered or planned for the near future. These services range from on-line shopping (e.g., Wells Fargo) to real-time financial information from anywhere in the world. While some of these services may appear simple, they require extraordinary integration of computer systems at the branch, central office, and strategic-partner levels.

Implementation Approaches to Home Banking

Pushed by growing consumer demand and the fear of losing market share, banks are investing heavily in home banking technology. Collaborating with hardware, software, telecommunications, and other

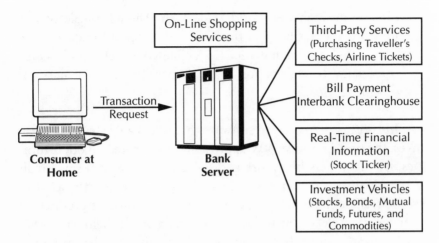

FIGURE 2.3   **Advanced Services and Home Banking**

companies, banks are introducing new ways for consumers to access their account balances, transfer funds, pay bills, and buy goods and services without using cash, mailing checks, or leaving home. The four major approaches to home banking (in historical order) are

1. **Proprietary bank dial-up services.** A home banking service, in combination with a PC and modem, lets the bank become an electronic gateway to a customer's accounts, enabling him or her to transfer funds or pay bills directly to creditors' accounts.
2. **Off-the-shelf home finance software.** This category is a key player in cementing relationships between current customers and helping banks gain new customers. Examples include Intuit's Quicken, Microsoft's Money, and Bank of America's MECA software. This software market is also attracting interest from banks because it has steady revenue streams by way of upgrades, updates, and the sale of related products and services.
3. **On-line services based.** This category allows banks to set up retail branches on subscriber-based on-line services (e.g., Prodigy, CompuServe, and America Online).
4. **World Wide Web based.** This category allows banks to bypass subscriber-based on-line services and reach the customer's browser

directly through the World Wide Web. The advantage of this
model is the flexibility at the back end to adapt to new on-line
transaction processing models facilitated by electronic commerce and the elimination of the constricting intermediary (or
on-line service).

In contrast to packaged software that offers a limited set of services, the on-line and WWW approaches offer increased opportunities. As consumers buy more and more in cyberspace using credit
cards, debit cards, and newer financial instruments such as electronic cash or electronic checks, they will need software products to
manage these electronic transactions and reconcile them with other
off-line transactions. In the future, an increasing number of paper-
based, manual financial tasks may be performed electronically on
machines such as PCs, handheld digital computing devices, and interactive televisions and telephones, and banking software must have
the capability to facilitate these tasks.

Home Banking Using Bank's Proprietary Software

Robert Spicer, Vice President of Chevy Chase, a federal savings bank,
wrote an interesting article detailing the origins of home banking:

> Home banking began in the mid-1970s with the desire to reduce
> back-office check processing costs through bill payment by
> touch-tone telephone. The first home banking system I worked
> with offered consumers the ability to pay anyone at any time of
> the day and used voice response technology to minimize per-
> sonnel costs. We were convinced that consumers would respond
> to this service and that back-office check processing expenses
> would drop off dramatically. However, after a heavy investment
> of time and money, we found that the check processing savings
> produced by the system were offset by the costs of a new back-
> office bill payment department. The services also failed to gen-
> erate enough consumer interest to achieve the economies of

scale that would have made it cost-effective. In hindsight, we believe the basic problem was consumer unfamiliarity with the technology. Consumers were too accustomed to writing checks, and as a financial institution we did not have the resources to educate people about the value of home banking.[9]

On-line banking was first introduced in the early 1980s, and New York was the hotbed of home banking. Four of the city's major banks (Citibank, Chase Manhattan, Chemical, and Manufacturers Hanover) offered home banking services. Chemical introduced its Pronto home banking services for individuals and Pronto Business Banker for small businesses in 1983. Its individual customers paid $12 a month for the dial-up service, which allowed them to maintain electronic checkbook registers and personal budgets, see account balances and activity (including cleared checks), transfer funds among checking and savings accounts, and—best of all—make electronic payments to some 17,000 merchants. In addition to home banking, users could obtain stock quotations for an additional per-minute charge. Two years later, Chemical teamed up with AT&T in a joint venture called Covidea meant to push the product through the second half of the decade. Despite the muscle of the two home banking partners, Pronto failed to attract enough customers to break even and was abandoned in 1989.

Other banks had similar problems. Citicorp had a difficult time selling its personal computer–based home banking system dubbed Direct Access. Chase Manhattan had a PC banking service called Spectrum. Spectrum offered two tiers of service—one costing $10 a month for private customers and another costing $50 a month for business users, plus dial-up charges in each case. According to its brochure, business users paid more because they received additional benefits such as the ability to make money transfers and higher levels of security.

Banc One had two products: Channel 2000 and Applause. Channel 2000 was a well-received trial personal computer–based home banking system available to about 200 customers. Applause, a personal computer–based home banking system modeled after Channel 2000, attracted fewer than 1,000 subscribers. The trial was abandoned before the end of the decade because the service could not attract the critical mass of about 5,000 users that would let the bank break even. In each of the mentioned instances, the banks discovered that it would be very difficult to attract enough customers to make a home banking system pay for itself (in other words, to achieve economies of scale). Figure 2.4 describes a traditional proprietary system of banking.

On-line banking has been plagued by poor implementations since the early 1980s. Home banking services lost too much from concept to reality. In a scathing critique the Yankee Group cites Bank of America's home banking as an example. That service, it says, "was designed initially to operate entirely online on their central processor, with difficult sign-on procedures, slowly drawing graphics at 300 baud for each single entry screen, and such slow response time has to be confusing and cause errors."[10] This service later evolved into a menu-driven service with no graphics that operated at either 300 or 1200 baud accessible from any personal computer via Tymnet. It took a few more years before users could use the Dollars & Sense*

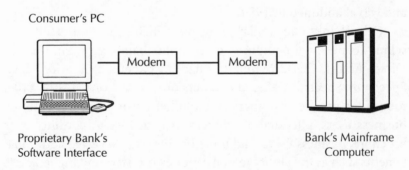

Consumer's PC

Modem — Modem

Proprietary Bank's
Software Interface

Bank's Mainframe
Computer

FIGURE 2.4 **Proprietary Software Method**

---

* In 1985, Dollars and Sense cost $119.95 for the Apple version and $179.95 for the IBM version.

financial management software to integrate personal finance with on-line banking activities. The problem with this gradual evolution was that consumers who initially used the service and left could not be coaxed back.

Most home banking services were anything but easy to use. They were basic terminal emulation systems[*] that worked at 300 and later 1200 baud and had complex menus that reflected more about the way banks keep their books than the way consumers spend their money. Typically the services were designed to run on the least-powerful PC possible (Pronto, for instance, was geared to the Atari 400), which had the effect of lobotomizing more powerful PCs. They nearly lobotomized the user, too, with mind-numbing repetition of menus and torturous verification procedures, which, combined with the crawl of remote communications to the bank's mainframes, made home banking seem extremely slow and even painful to use.

Recently Citibank revamped its Direct Access product to allow consumers to dial in to Citibank's system and transact bill-payment services. This new service, while using an outdated interface, is promising in that consumers can check their account balances, transfer money among accounts, pay bills electronically, review their Citibank credit card accounts, and buy and sell stock through Citicorp Investment Services. Although the underlying systems run in batch mode, Citibank has put together a middleware piece that makes the consumer think he or she is operating in a real-time environment. Although this can work in a setting where Citibank is not interacting with third-party systems, there are potential difficulties with this batch/real-time mix if Citibank offers outside products and services (e.g., insurance products). In addition, because the consumer is interacting directly with Citibank's system, he or she has no way of performing household budgeting functions on the financial data. Clearly Citibank will need to either provide this functionality itself or offer easy interface to the popular personal finance packages. However, it is important to point out that the new Direct Access represents the first major improvement in proprietary software home

---

[*] Terminal emulation systems presented a remote window that allowed access to all the functions on the mainframe. Two popular terminal emulation packages are Kermit and NCSA Telnet.

banking in 15 years, which is demonstrated by its explosive growth from 40,000 subscribers to 190,000 in the past nine months.

Banking via the PC Using Dial-Up Software

The main companies working to develop home banking software are Intuit, the maker of Quicken, Microsoft, the maker of Microsoft Money, Bank of America and NationsBank, which acquired Meca's Managing Your Money software from H&R Block, and ADP, which acquired Peachtree Software. In this section, we will examine Intuit in great detail because it is the leader among home banking software companies and exemplifies the overall strategy in this area of software development.

Intuit

Intuit is the leading provider of home and small business financial software, supplies, and services for PC users. It pioneered computerized personal finance management with the introduction of the Quicken program in 1984.* Intuit has been in the forefront of new on-line financial services, launching bill-payment services in 1990, IntelliCharge credit card services in 1993, and Quicken Quotes, a portfolio price update service, in 1994. In recent years the company has benefited from the personal computer boom and by giving consumers a diverse product breadth and a software bundle (or suite) focus, including offerings that focus on personal finance, small business finance, financial planning, tax preparation, and bill payment and transactions.

Quicken was introduced in October 1984 and has since been enhanced and upgraded several times. Quicken allows users to organize, understand, and manage their personal finances. Designed to look and work like a checkbook, Quicken provides users with a method for recording and categorizing their financial transactions. Once entered, the financial information can be analyzed and displayed using a set of reports and graphs. Quicken also allows users to reconcile their bank accounts and track credit card purchases, in-

---

* Suggested retail price for Quicken in 1986 was $79 for the Apple version and $99 for the IBM version.

vestments, cash, and other assets and liabilities. The software enables users to make payments by printing computer checks or initiating electronic payments via modem. Several factors, including good design, affordable pricing, and availability of new features and services, have contributed to Quicken's success.

As a complement to its personal finance software products, Intuit offers value-added services such as on-line banking, bill payment, and credit management that further automate users' financial transactions. On-line banking is a new feature of Quicken 5 for Windows, which was released in the first quarter of fiscal 1996. Intuit's on-line banking services, in conjunction with the services of Intuit's financial institution partners, allow users to download and automatically categorize savings and loan account activity, brokerage activity, and charge account activity, thereby reducing data entry and providing an easily accessible view of their financial portfolios.

Intuit believes that it can expand its competitive position by extending its business into the electronic commerce market. In its annual report, the company defines electronic commerce as "electronically-enabled financial transactions and electronically-enabled marketing and sales of financial products."

How Intuit On-Line Banking Works

To take advantage of Intuit on-line banking, customers will sign up with local banks and then use the Quicken software to access the desired information from their banks. The software will dial the local number using AT&T's 950 access service. (The 950 service covers 90 to 95 percent of the country and users simply dial 950–1ATT). On-line connections among the financial institutions and Quicken users are the responsibility of Intuit Services Corporation (ISC), which Intuit sold to CheckFree in 1996. ISC gets Internet access from Concentric Network Corporation, which has more than 200 local points of presence (POPs). ISC also currently provides the on-line banking and bill-payment services for users of Microsoft Money.

ISC is basically an intermediary between the Quicken software and the financial services. Figure 2.5 illustrates the structure of this network. ISC's network design is what is known as "burst and disconnect," which simply means that the user receives the requested information quickly and then is logged off of the system.

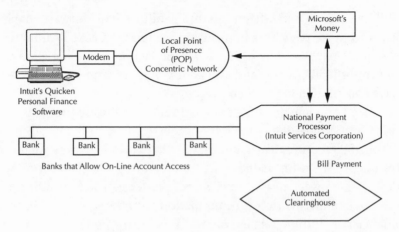

FIGURE 2.5   **Intuit Services Corporation Architecture**

This strategy allows for a maximum number of users in a short period of time. In contrast, services like America Online or Compu-
Serve earn money by keeping the customer on line and billing for
time spent. These traditional on-line services have lots of menus
and graphics that take time to traverse and thus provide for additional revenue if consumers do not have unlimited-usage accounts.

Intuit is selling specific information and wants users on and off
the system quickly. Intuit's banking partners download all the relevant banking information (bank balances, statements, and so on) to
Intuit's servers (ISC). The banks send information for every customer signed up for the service. When a customer requests information, the Quicken software dials the ISC servers in Downers Grove,
Illinois. Since the data have already been transmitted to ISC, the requested information is simply downloaded to the local Quicken
user. The total on-line time is about 15 seconds.

Although the banks transfer data in batch mode once a day, this
procedure is not practical for credit card processors such as American Express. Credit card users want to check on recent transactions
and want real-time data. For instance, in the case of American Express, ISC will simply pass the transaction request on to American
Express. The requested statement information then is passed back to
ISC and to the Quicken customer. Currently, American Express is In-

tuit's only partner set up to handle real-time data transmissions. Today the banks work in batch mode (as dictated by their legacy systems), but over time many of the banking partners will have to move to real-time mode.

On-line banking enables users to check current account balances, transfer funds among accounts, determine the clearance of given transactions, and reconcile accounts. Each financial institution sets its own fees for on-line banking services. The compensation Intuit receives from the financial institutions is based on that institution's consumer usage.

Intuit's Bill Payment

On-line bill payment enables users to pay bills by transmitting payment instructions via modem. Bill payment works differently than the other banking services. For example, assume a Quicken user needs to pay three bills: Bell Atlantic, Macys, and Fred's Auto Repair. The user would open Quicken and "write out" the three corresponding checks, indicating the names of the payees and amount paid. After the consumer hits the transmit key, the Quicken software dials Intuit Services Corporation. ISC looks at each payee and determines the correct method for handling the transaction. The first bill, Bell Atlantic, is tied to the Federal Reserve's Automated Clearing House (ACH) network. Thus, the bill is paid electronically using the ACH system, which happens almost immediately. The bill is cleared at midnight central time.

In the case of the second bill, Macys, which is not tied to the Federal Reserve ACH system, Intuit will print a physical check, batch it with other Macys payments, and then express mail it. In the third instance of Fred's Auto Repair or any individual payee not likely to have multiple incoming checks, Intuit will print a check and mail it. These payments take only a few seconds to process. The network then tells the local Quicken user how long it will take to pay each bill and sends back a confirmation number.

This service is offered through financial institution partners and directly from Intuit. Again, each financial institution sets its own prices for on-line bill-payment services and Intuit receives compensation from the financial institution based on consumers' usage. For its customers who do not bank at a partner institution, Intuit provides an on-line bill-payment service for a monthly fee of around $5.95 for 20 bill-payment transactions.

Clearly, with a diversified product base, Intuit is well positioned to exploit the next big electronic wave in on-line banking. Other reasons that make Intuit a formidable competitor include

Multiplatform strength. Unlike some of its competitors that have concentrated solely on the Windows market, Intuit established itself as the personal finance software leader for the DOS, Windows, and Macintosh platforms.

New revenue opportunities. Intuit is developing new software products and electronic services that complement its main products, Quicken and QuickBooks. Recently Intuit announced an expansion of its plans to offer electronic statement delivery in conjunction with VISA.

Recurring revenue opportunities. By offering services such as electronic credit card statement delivery and supplies such as checks, invoices, and envelopes, Intuit adds to the attractiveness of its software products. These additional services pave the way for additional revenue opportunities with relatively more stable revenue streams than those commonly associated with packaged software.

In addition to the prospects of benefiting from the strong PC growth among consumers and small businesses, Intuit is in a strong position to benefit from strategic alliances with financial institutions.

Banking via On-Line Services

Although personal finance software allows people to manage their money, it only represents half of the equation. No matter which software package is used to manage accounts, information gets managed twice—once by the consumer and once by the bank. If the consumer uses personal finance software, both the consumer and the bank are responsible for maintaining systems that do not communicate, giving a whole new meaning to double-entry bookkeeping. For example, a consumer enters data once into his or her system and transfers this information to paper in the form of a check, only to have the bank then transfer it from paper back into electronic form. Where an electronic check is issued, the systems that receive the information rarely communicate automatically with the bookkeeping systems.

Unfortunately, off-the-shelf personal finance software cannot bridge the communications gap or reduce the duplication of effort described here. However, a few home banking systems that can help are beginning to take hold. In combination with a PC and modem, these home banking services let the bank become an electronic gateway, reducing the monthly paper chase of bills and checks.

Computerworld published an article that illustrated how early on-line services–based banking worked.[11] Shawmut was reportedly one of the few U.S. banks offering such a service to small business (called Business Arrive) and individual accounts (called Arrive). Once customers signed up for Arrive or Business Arrive, they accessed the system through either 300 or 1200 baud modems, dialing a local CompuServe number. Shawmut transmitted to the CompuServe database daily updates on Arrive customer accounts and received from CompuServe reports on customer transactions. Service fees were $8 for Arrive, $35 for Business Arrive. Access time was extra, ranging from $7.50 to $18 per hour, depending on the modem speed and time of day.

The general structure of the on-line services banking architecture is shown in figure 2.6.

Intuit and America Online

Intuit announced an agreement with America Online (AOL) on November 13, 1995, in which AOL offers Intuit's home banking services to its 6-million-member customer base. AOL users do not need to use off-the-shelf Quicken software to access the banking services. Rather, Intuit has a Quicken-like forum (see figure 2.6) application into America Online that provides basic banking functionality (transferring funds, bill paying, downloading bank statements, checking

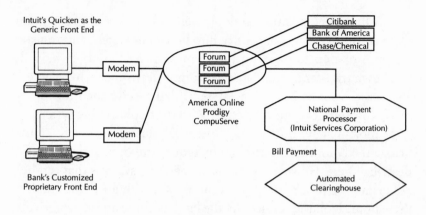

FIGURE 2.6   **On-Line Services Banking Architecture**

account balances, and so forth). The banking service is provided through Intuit Services Corporation, the same entity that links Quicken to Intuit's 21 banking partners. To use this service, AOL customers must have an account with one of Intuit's partner banks.

AOL is offering this service free of charge to its customers. The payment to Intuit is structured the same whether the customer chooses to use Quicken, Microsoft Money, or AOL. The financial institutions charge the customer a fee for the banking services (though some banks have opted not to charge customers); money is then paid back to Intuit. One can think of the AOL relationship as another access point to Intuit Services Corporation and a further cementing of Quicken as the premier personal finance software product. A customer can walk into a bank and be offered three home banking choices: Quicken, Microsoft Money, or AOL. All three use ISC as the back end and either Quicken or Money as the front end.

In sum, this offering gives customers more choices for home banking. Clearly, Intuit wants to get the banking service into as many hands as quickly as possible. AOL customers are a preselected group of potential early adopters; obviously they have modems and are users of on-line services. The more customers that sign up, the more financial institutions will enter the home banking arena, bringing with them more potential customers.

Banking via the Web

With the explosive growth in Internet use, banking via the World Wide Web will undoubtedly catch on quickly. The goal of this approach to banking is to provide superior customer service and convenience in a secure electronic environment. The competitors in this segment are banks that are setting up their Web sites and firms such as Intuit that can easily move their products to the Internet.

How is Internet banking different from on-line banking? This is an important and often misunderstood distinction. Banking on the Internet is not the same as banking via on-line services. Internet banking means that

1. Consumers do not have to purchase any additional software (the Web browser is sufficient), store any data on their computers, back up any information, or wait months for new versions and upgrades, since all transactions occur on a secure server over the Internet.
2. Consumers can conduct banking anywhere as long as they have computers (not necessarily their own) and modems—whether it is at home, at the office, or in a place outside the United States. Banking via on-line services can be restrictive, because the customer has to install a software package that resides on his or her computer. This limits banking transactions to only that computer and requires making a call to access a separate network and working with a separate software company and bank that may limit their hours of operation.
3. Consumers can download their account information into their favorite programs, which means that they do not have to follow the dictates of the service provider.
4. Internet banking allows banks to break out of the hegemony of software developers. If bank customers (end users) install personal financial management software on their PCs, they become direct consumers of software publishers. By controlling the software code behind these programs, publishers control the kinds of transactions end users make and with whom these transactions occur. By maintaining a direct relationship with end users

via the Web, banks can offer additional services and provide a personal feel to the interface—without seeking the cooperation of a software publisher.

If banks choose to offer home banking via personal financial management software, they lose control over the end-user interface and the relationship they have with customers. This loss of control has tremendous long-term implications. The history of the software industry offers compelling proof of the importance of a direct relationship with consumers. In the early 1980s IBM decided that operating systems were not central to its business strategy. As a result, IBM licensed DOS from a small software company called Microsoft. IBM called this operating system PC-DOS and allowed Microsoft to market this same operating system to competing computer manufacturers under the name MS-DOS. IBM's seal of approval made DOS an industry standard. However, the company was unable to move the industry to a new operating system called OS/2 in the late 1980s. Microsoft controlled the customer relationship and was able to convert most end users to the Windows platform. Likewise for banks, losing control over the interface can have dire consequences.

Intuit's Internet Strategy

Intuit realizes that the Web could be a big factor and is working to provide a version of Quicken that uses the Web's capabilities. The future success of Intuit depends on its ability to integrate its software with different systems from several institutions. New software features allow users to integrate Quicken with Web browsers such as Netscape Navigator and the Internet access module. For example, a single click in one of Quicken's banking screens lets the user connect to the Internet, launch Navigator, and move directly to a site on the Web dealing with banks.

Today Quicken can store a wealth of information on a consumer's PC, but that information is static. Intuit plans to use the Internet as an extension of its core products. If a user wants information about a topic and it is not available on the CD-ROM, the product can dial the Intuit Web page, which contains additional financial information. The information will range from stock information to advice and technical support. "Cruising" the 'Net requires a browser, and Intuit opted to bundle the market-leading Netscape Navigator with Quicken for 1996.

The difference between Intuit's service offerings on the 'Net and on ISC is that confidential information will be handled through ISC, and the Internet will be for browsing and obtaining general information. This separation will remain until Internet security issues are resolved. The Internet also may help Intuit sell more software. For instance, a user working on a tax return can be alerted to the availability of a state tax program from within the software. The user can download the software and unlock it with a code from Intuit after supplying a credit card number separately. Intuit believes that the Internet is a great way for the company to offer superior customer support. The company has designed a system in which customers use the Internet to reach Intuit's customer service facility.

Intuit will provide free access to the Web using a third-party provider, Concentric Network Corporation. The concept is that any time a customer needs help, he or she can, from within the software, dial the Internet and access the Intuit Web page, where help is available. If the user wants to browse Internet sites other than Intuit's, then the customer must pay a fee. Concentric is charging $1.95 a month for one hour of access, which is competitive with other access providers.

Security, a crucial component of Internet banking, is handled in one of two ways, depending on whether the network in question is public or private. For a private network, Quicken contains a communications module that connects directly to customers' financial institutions for the transmission of confidential data and financial transactions. For a public network, all such transactions are secured by end-to-end encryption utilizing RSA's Public-Key Cryptosystem technology combined with triple DES.[12]

Security will be transparent to users because these transactions are performed from within Quicken; the communications will happen in the background and the information will be integrated seamlessly into the user's Quicken files. For interactive use of the information available on the Internet, Quicken users will have integrated

access to the security mechanisms built into Netscape Navigator. In addition, Intuit is working with Netscape and others to encourage the development and availability of secure protocols for electronic commerce such as secure electronic transactions and open exchange.

Security First Network Bank

The first Internet bank to provide electronic banking services to Internet users was Security First Network Bank (SFNB). Figure 2.7 shows SFNB's model user interface. (See chapter 3 for a more detailed discussion of SFNB.) In an effort to help expand Internet banking SFNB made its software available for licensing to other financial institutions. SFNB had to jump through some regulatory hoops before getting permission from the regulators to become a Web bank.

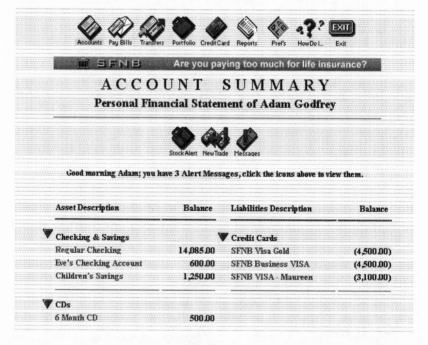

Figure 2.7   Model for Integrated Account Access at Security First Network Bank on the Internet

Before going on line, Cardinal Bancshares, the holding company for SFNB, applied to the Office of Thrift Supervision (OTS) in September 1994 for approval to change the business plan of its subsidiary, First Federal Savings Bank of Pineville, Kentucky, to include banking on the Internet. The application also requested that the bank's name be changed to Security First Network Bank. After careful review and a detailed analysis of the security architecture, the OTS granted approval on May 8, 1995, and SFNB went on line October 18, 1995. SFNB made history by conducting the first-ever Internet banking transaction with a donation to the Red Cross.[13]

SFNB expects to strengthen its ties to consumers by selling more services and making it more difficult for customers to switch. By brokering new financial services, banks can become one-stop shops for upscale customers. Most important, they can significantly increase fee income. SFNB is also attempting to provide backward compatibility. For instance, SFNB provides compatibility with personal finance software such as Quicken by allowing the exchange of information via Quicken Interchange Format (QIF) files. This is a much-needed feature for customers who want to migrate.

Models of On-Line Banking: Open versus Closed Systems

While it is clear that electronic commerce and banking are inevitable, the technology models to provide these services may not yet be fully understood by the banking industry at large. Two technology models of on-line banking are *open* and *closed* systems. Briefly, an *open* system is one in which content changes can occur easily because of the use of standard technology and components. For instance, a banking interface developed around the World Wide Web (WWW) is an open system that is easy to customize to a bank's changing needs. On the other hand, a *closed* system is one in which the changes are difficult since everything is proprietary. For example, a banking interface developed around a package such as Intuit's Quicken cannot be modified unless the vendor comes out with a new version of its software.

Banks need to be familiar with both models when offering products and services on line. With the high level of customer interest in
PC banking and the emergence of the Internet as a vehicle for doing
business, many banks have announced plans to offer Internet banking
services. Hundreds of banks have already set up home pages on the Internet to provide existing and potential customers with information
about upcoming services (static information). Approximately one-
fifth of these banks provide the ability to interact with the bank by
offering on-line applications or financial calculators. A much smaller
percentage offers the ability to view account balances and transaction
history. With the exception of SFNB, few banks are offering any actual
banking transaction services because they do not yet have the necessary technology or expertise.

Internet banking differs from traditional PC banking in several
ways. In most home banking ventures, the bank provides the customer with an application software program that operates on the
customer's PC. The customer then dials into the bank via modem,
downloads data, and operates the programs that are resident on his
or her PC. The customer is able to send the bank a batch of requests
such as transfers between accounts. Any software upgrade has to be
incorporated into new releases and redistributed to the customer periodically; as more functionality is added to the software, more and
more space and speed are required from the customer's computer.

With Internet banking, on the other hand, potential customers
may already have all the software they need to do their banking,
since the only requirement is a Web browser. The actual banking
software resides on the bank's server in the form of the home page.
This software can be updated at any moment with new information,
such as new prices or products, without having to send anything to
the customer; it can also continue to expand and become more sophisticated without becoming difficult for the customer to operate.

With traditional PC banking interactions, if the customer has
more than one account or other financial products, the data are
downloaded from multiple sources and then plugged into the appropriate places in the software. A bank server on the Internet, however, can perform this function for the customer and provide an integrated snapshot of his or her financial portfolio. It becomes much

easier for the bank to outsource a product such as a brokerage account and have that information appear on a customer's bank statement as if it were an internal bank product.

Another difference between the two models is that in PC banking, although the customer can work on his or her finances off line and then make a quick call to download new data, it would involve a long-distance or toll-free call for customers outside a metro calling area. Banking with a browser, on the other hand, involves a continuous, interactive session, initiated by a local telephone call to a local access provider or on-line service.

An *open* system such as the World Wide Web offers two additional key benefits: control of the user interface and intermediation. With an *open* system, such as the application designed for SFNB, the bank designs the user interface and is therefore able to incorporate its own look and feel. This authority allows the bank to enhance its brand awareness and maintain direct access to its customers.

The *open* system also allows banks to offer an expanded array of financial services and to choose their business partners when offering additional services such as brokerage accounts and mutual funds—all of which lead to stronger customer relationships and increased revenue.

In a *closed* system using proprietary financial management software such as Quicken or Money, the software publisher acts as intermediary between the bank and its customers. In managing the customer relationship, the software provider controls the interface design, thereby diminishing and even eliminating any reference to the bank itself. The software provider also controls the selection of financial providers and determines the choice and availability of services.

Management Issues in On-Line Banking

The challenge facing the banking industry is whether management has the creativity and vision to harness the technology and provide customers with the new financial products necessary to satisfy their continually changing financial needs.

The immediate question facing the banking industry is how to deliver high-quality products at the customers' convenience with high-tech, high-touch personal service for the right price. To achieve this, management has to balance the five key values that increasingly drive customers' banking decisions: simplicity, customized service, convenience, quality, and price. These values vary in levels of importance to customers, but together they represent a synergy of buying values. On-line banking will realize its full potential when the following key elements fall into place:

▷ The development of an interesting portfolio of products and services that are sufficiently differentiated from competitors' and create value in the eyes of the consumer.

▷ The creation of on-line financial supply chains to manage the shift from banks as gatekeepers to banks as gateways (see figure 2.8).

▷ An emergence of low-cost interactive access terminals for the home, as well as interactive home information services offered at an attractive price.

▷ The identification of new market segments with untapped needs such as the willingness to pay for the convenience of remote banking.

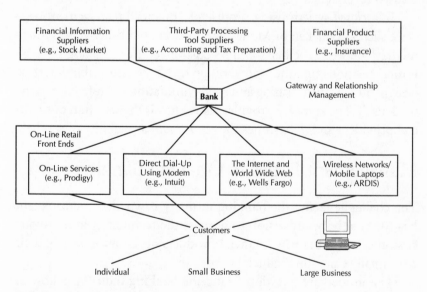

FIGURE 2.8   **Emerging Financial Supply Chains**

▷ Good customer service on the part of banks. Because technology increases the ease of switching from one bank to another, banks that do not offer superior customer service may see low levels of customer loyalty.

▷ The development of effective back-office systems that can support sophisticated retail interfaces. Back-office systems must be given due importance in the on-line banking area.

However, banks that wait to be adept at all of the mentioned elements before offering on-line banking services may be least likely to reap the rewards. Since on-line banking is attractive to a wealthy segment of the population initially, the banks that move first will be increasing their share of the most profitable customers. And, assuming they do their job well, these first movers will have a rather effective hedge against competing services that will inevitably follow.

Differentiating Products and Services

Characteristics that will differentiate winners from losers in the competitive on-line banking industry are the willingness to take risks in terms of being a first mover, the strategic choices involved in deciding whether to partner with a software provider, the products and services to offer on line, and the ultimate aim of on-line banking in terms of profitability, customer loyalty, customer satisfaction, and so forth. Early entrants into the Internet banking market may benefit on multiple fronts from the notion of differentiation. These banks will appeal to a new potential market that represents the attractive demographic segment of educated, professional, and affluent consumers.

Strategic decision making needs to take into account the changing market structure. Intuit and other vendors see a growing demand for their products and are setting themselves up as intermediaries in the personal finance marketplace. In other words, Intuit is creating an interface between desktop software (Quicken) and a third-party network processor that will serve as a switch to any bank that wants to participate in home banking. Similarly, Microsoft wants to serve as the front end for customers banking over the Internet through Microsoft Money. Microsoft and Intuit would charge

banks every time a customer comes through the third-party processor's switch.

To offset the increasing power of these intermediaries, some
banks are forming cooperative partnerships with banking-software
companies or writing their own software. Banks seem wary of letting
other parties control the interface, even if such an opportunity appears convenient and economical at the outset. Banks rightly fear that
once customers set up Microsoft or Intuit software, it is easier to
change the bank than it is to change the software (which may increase
the cost). More seriously, banks may all look the same to Quicken
users and thus would be viewed as providing interchangeable services. A particular bank would have no way to differentiate itself from
the other, no way to add new products to its offering, and no way to
build brand identity with customers banking over the Internet.

The alternative is for banks to bypass these intermediaries and provide customers with bank-developed software. The problem with this
approach is that banks do not know how to develop consumer software
and, worse yet, do not have the resources in terms of software expertise
to continually improve it. Ultimately, competitiveness will depend on
ease of use and low fees, as well as well-devised banking services.

An appropriate strategy for banks must take into account methods to prevent customers from migrating to banks with competing
on-line offerings. Banks may find their current customers switching
from branch banking to PC banking, allowing a more efficient use
of the bank's resources. The true challenge for each bank lies in
strengthening the loyalty of this group of customers to the bank itself.
The ultimate market leaders will be those that enhance their images
as customer-driven banks, even with customers who do not use home
banking. More importantly, by developing internal expertise today,
banks can position themselves to react quickly to competitive moves
and consumer trends as the financial services industry evolves.

Managing Financial Supply Chains

A new model of twenty-first-century banking is emerging. In this
model, banks are no longer gatekeepers but rather gateways to finan-

cial products (see figure 2.8). In the old gatekeeper model, the bank functioned as an inhibiting intermediary that restricted the customer's product choices. In the new gateway model, the bank functions as a flexible intermediary that provides access to an entire spectrum of products and delivery channels. Some of the products—insurance, entertainment, travel, and investment management—may not even originate from the bank but from a third-party provider. In other words, the bank acts as a gateway and provides its customers with access to value-added service providers anywhere in the world.

Banks and other financial services firms are not the only ones acting on the gateway model. On-line technology such as the Internet and World Wide Web (WWW) allows software companies including Intuit and Microsoft to become gateways also. These firms are working overtime to address the demand for financial gateways based on the premise that financial products are software and information commodities. The challenge to banks is real: most of the software companies are used to product life cycles of 12 to 18 months versus the years it often takes banks to develop and deploy new products. Although the current focus of these software companies is primarily on developing gateways for financial transactions and simple account management tasks, the threat is imminent because the model can be extended to encapsulate other types of financial products.

Thanks to deregulation, financial institutions are now able to offer a wider variety of financial services. However, if they choose to let nonbank intermediaries control the relationship between them and end users, these intermediaries can choose banks' business partners in the financial supply chains. In fact, a savvy brokerage provider would rather negotiate with a personal finance software company or a service provider than with an individual bank. Signing a deal with Intuit or Microsoft would give the processor access to all Bank1, Bank2, and Bank3 end users. Signing a deal with Bank1 would allow the processor access to Bank1's customers only. Clearly, design of financial supply chain relationships is a matter of great import.

If nonbanks see an opportunity they will move very quickly. To gain advantage in this potentially lucrative market, banks seem to be following three strategies:

1. Invest an unprecedented amount of capital in building information and technology infrastructures and on-line banking products and services that will counter the threat from nonbanks and fundamentally change the way banks service retail customers.
2. Seek partners in the on-line financial supply chain that links customers, intermediaries, banks, and third-party service providers. With the partnerships in place, banks expect to provide much better value than the disjointed chains that predominate today (see figure 2.8). These financial supply chains seek to provide the best price and value to the end customer (where the battle for the market share is ultimately won or lost). It should be noted here that a primary bank competitor in this instance is the customers themselves because the Internet makes gathering information through these disjointed chains easier than ever before.
3. Move from a product-dominated model to a customer-centered model. The objective is to capture customer loyalty by providing an ever-increasing number of consumers with the luxury of more convenient, customer-centered (relationship) services that until now have been available only to those with major accounts.

Probably the single greatest challenge is the lack of holistic strategic dimension to management of the stated objectives. The gateway model requires banks to develop a strategy that provides both a macroeconomic underpinning and workable policies and objectives for the range of functions along the financial supply chain. Additionally, the burden falls on the banks to take a lead in integrating all the supply chain functions and installing the information and control systems increasingly required for on-line banking. We examine why banks need to think of on-line financial supply chains as the basis for providing the gateway and relationship management functions in a working paper.[14]

Product Development Strategy: Good Product Mix

If banks offered only checking, savings, and lending services, remote banking would not have great market potential. But the product mix today includes an array of CD accounts, access to mutual funds, and brokerage and insurance services. There will be even more products available as banks vie with nonindustry competitors in the race to become financial supermarkets. In turn, consumers are faced with the complex challenge of keeping their money working most productively as economic conditions change. On-line banking gives consumers the ability to monitor the performances of their investments and shift funds among various accounts.

Good product mix and product development strategies will raise the entry barrier and increase the competition's cost of doing business. Banks that choose to wait and see how technology evolves before embarking on a product development strategy will find themselves investing defensively a few years down the road simply to hold onto their existing customers. These banks will not enjoy the economic benefits of being early players or the momentum that comes from being a market leader.

Pricing Issues in On-Line Banking

Perhaps the single most important issue driving consumer acceptance of on-line banking is pricing. Once equipped, a user confronts high connect charges, high subscription fees, or both. Data have shown repeatedly since 1986 that PC owners have an interest in home banking services but are very price sensitive, with significant drops in interest when fees rise above $10 per month.[15] Yet most pricing is above this level; it seems banks are ignoring the lessons that history is trying to teach them.

Pricing is a complex issue that has implications in terms of cost recovery, profitability, and short-term objectives such as market penetration. A number of objectives have to be balanced when establishing pricing strategies. For example, when Citibank dropped all fees for electronic banking services in 1995, its objective was to achieve market penetration among existing and future customers. This strategy is based on the premise that market share and long-term profitability are correlated.

Pricing can also be used as a behavior-modification mechanism. Take, for instance, First Chicago, which penalizes customers by charging them $3 each time they use a teller for a transaction that could have been performed at an ATM.[16]

Pricing affects on-line banking at three levels: initial software pricing, financial product pricing, and usage pricing.

1. **Initial software pricing.** To gain market share and achieve a critical mass of customers, banks and software companies will have to bundle their respective personal finance products with new PCs. This is not just a variation of the old "give away the razors, make money on the blades" marketing approach; it is a reformation of the way in which software and networks are tightly linked or loosely coupled that creates far greater flexibility in pricing for market share and profit.

2. **Financial product pricing.** The pricing of financial products has to balance three major costs. The first are *developmental* costs, which include costs associated with the design, implementation, testing, and commercialization of a financial product. The second set of costs are *marketing* costs, which include costs of launching the new product and maintaining it throughout the early growth stage. Finally, there are *support* costs, which include the costs of providing and delivering the product and maintaining it via back-office systems.

3. **Usage pricing.** Home banking services can be expensive to implement and operate, yet consumers are rarely willing to pay much more than $10 or $15 per month. Thus the usual pricing method is to look at the bank's volume of transactions and charge accordingly. Companies offering these services have to be careful to provide incentives, such as low fees, to get customers to use the service in the first place. The ultimate consideration in setting prices is the marketplace. If the target audience perceives the cost of new products as too high, it will resist adopting them.

Marketing Issues: Attracting Customers

The benefits of on-line banking are often not made clear to the potential user. Questions such as the following often arise: How is balancing the checking account on line superior to doing it on paper? How is paying bills on line superior to the familiar process of writing checks? Where is the consumer gaining value? Perhaps the answers to these questions are not clear to the bankers themselves. Regardless of how banks choose to answer these questions, it is clear that they make a mistake trying to sell on-line banking services on the basis of convenience. While short-term convenience is important, consumers are more interested in the long-term ability to control and organize their finances.

Banks must also look beyond home consumers for on-line banking. Many regard small businesses as the next target for these services. The increasing use of personal computers by small businesses presents a solid opportunity for banks to build a profitable base of small businesses until a broader consumer market evolves. There are thousands of small businesses with annual sales ranging from $250,000 to $5 million. Many of these firms have PCs and modems. New services including interactive cash management services will potentially generate significant revenues. Industry studies indicate that 20 percent of small businesses are immediate prospects for on-line banking and are willing to pay more than individual consumers for the service—up to $100 a month. Thus banks have the opportunity to earn a comfortable markup on delivery costs for this market segment.

Retail customers are becoming an increasingly critical source of funds for most banks, even though these customers traditionally have been the least profitable. Similarly, small- to mid-sized businesses, which many banks historically have not courted with special services, will be a new source of profitability for banks. Despite this reality, few banks are sales oriented in these areas apart from their advertising, especially at the branch level. On-line banking provides not only a new sales tool but also the opportunity to generate additional revenues from value-added services. Just the offering of remote banking capabilities automatically enhances a bank's image as a progressive institution. There is no documentation as yet, but it would be surprising if this service did not also have value in attracting new customers who are not current prospects for on-line banking.

Customer Service Issues: Building Customer Loyalty

Building customer loyalty is based on a simple premise: customers and financial institutions both seek closer relationships. On the customer side, several factors are working for loyalty. Customers are increasingly familiar with using technology to access bank accounts and to handle financial affairs, and this familiarity increases interest in additional services. However, the switching costs of moving from one software platform to another will help keep customers with one bank. The oft-cited time squeeze—from long commutes, heavy workload, family obligations, and household management—on consumers is also pushing them toward integrated services that can speed up financial procedures.

The benefit for financial institutions lies in cementing relationships with current customers, as well as the prospect of gaining new customers. There are also positive cost implications for the long-term value of building customer loyalty. In the world of electronic commerce, there is not a big difference in cost between serving one or one hundred thousand customers. Such a trend can only help banks become more competitive in a financial services market that is truly global and increasingly competitive.

Back-Office Operations Issues in On-Line Banking

Today, back-office operations technology is a crucial and misunderstood element of on-line banking. Although we are making great strides in developing the front-end interface, much thought needs to be put into the reengineering of back-office operations and systems. Given the front-office needs outlined in previous sections, the back-office computer systems used by financial institutions today will be inadequate for many future on-line banking requirements. We will see a major restructuring of banks' back-office systems in the coming years. This will push back-office improvement to the forefront because it will require major investment.

But before any technology or systems change, there needs to be a shift in attitude. Managers often think of back-office systems and operations as a subordinate function, one that should respond to their needs and desires without question and go quietly about handling all the boring details and back-office drudgeries that a manager should not have to worry about. This attitude may have its roots in the historic role of clerks, whose job was to support the manager. For too long operations functions in banks have been viewed as cost centers with a vague customer linkage. This thinking will have to change to reflect the strategic nature of back-office systems and will need management commitment to keep up with new demands on it.

Emerging Questions in Back-Office Operations

Figure 2.9 illustrates the complex structure of back-office systems. The complexity arises from the fact that many business units, accounting, financial reporting, marketing, and so on use separate

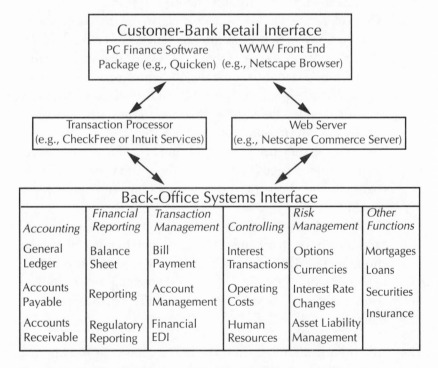

FIGURE 2.9 **The Elements of the Back-Office Interface**

mainframe systems for their processing. With the advent of electronic commerce, and the need for customers to be able to access their consolidated accounts, banks will now have to find ways of integrating the information stored in these various mainframe databases.

Clearly banks have to address some basic questions in building back-office support infrastructure:

> ▷ How to create (or buy) a common platform that enables any transaction initiated on any device (phone, screen phone, PC, ATM) to be instantly acknowledged at all other points of delivery. This is especially challenging if the bank mixes proprietary legacy systems with new systems from outside providers.
> ▷ How to create an information architecture (e.g., customer information files) that is portable across a variety of platforms. Given that this information architecture is network based, it must address the myriad security concerns (authentication, confidentiality, integrity) that networking typically raises.
> ▷ How to create platform-independent content (text, audio, graphics, video, hypertext markup language [HTML], or 3D virtual reality modeling language [VRML]) that can be translated into text-only terminals, Web browsers, multimedia kiosks, Braille interfaces, or even audio versions of the bank products. Given the variety of content types, banks need to understand information content quality from the customer's perspective; they need to provide quality information to service customer needs. This raises the related issue: How do banks define, measure, and benchmark information content quality?
> ▷ How should this financial content be structured, organized, and mined to attract and retain customers? Financial institutions are flooded with data but have little process knowledge. The usefulness of being on line will reach a point of diminishing returns if the data are not carefully structured and organized.

These questions need to be addressed in the context of whether the goal is to provide real-time or batch-oriented functionality.

Real-Time versus Batch Operations

Consider the following problem in bill payment. A bank's system interfaces with the third-party transaction processor CheckFree, which provides a common interface for Microsoft's Money and Intuit's Quicken transactions (see figure 2.6). Several questions highlight the complexity of the back-office situation. If a customer pays a bill by Quicken in the morning, can the result of that transaction be seen that evening when the customer attempts to balance his or her checkbook? Can a consumer call a bank customer service representative to put a stop-payment request on a payment the same day it was initiated? Can the customer who transfers money by PC see that transaction when he or she goes to the ATM later that day? The answer to these questions is no for many banks and the reason is simple: The back-office systems were not meant to work in real time.

In addition to the real-time difficulties, on-line banking is further complicated because most existing back-office systems are batch oriented. For instance, if $300 is withdrawn from an account at an ATM, the account balance will not be changed until the next day. The delay results from the third-party transaction processors handling these transactions by automated clearinghouse in batches to accommodate economies of scale. Until banks and other payment processor systems go real time, customers will see a timing disorientation between PC service and the bank's pay-by-phone, telephone, branch, and ATM services, which are all posted in real time to the bank's host computer. This problem is further exacerbated when you cross and try to integrate product lines.

This integration will require a fundamental change in the database design and architecture, with information integration as the goal. In addition, banks need to phase in new data types such as standard generalized markup language (SGML) to deal with structured documents and active document architectures (e.g., OLE and OpenDoc) to deal with objects rather than individual data elements.

As a note of caution, it must be stated that many institutions, instead of working from the root problems (i.e., addressing process deficiencies), often tackle superficial symptoms in back-office operations. This is evidenced by either surrounding outdated mainframe-based systems with intelligent front ends or replacing batch-oriented technology with more real-time banking solutions that provide integrated customer information. Without a sound business case, neither of these enhancements by themselves will provide the necessary gains for institutions to remain competitive in the twenty-first century.

Consolidation of Back-Office Systems

To industry outsiders, systems consolidation is perhaps the most visible business issue in banking. Over the past decade, institutions have merged at record rates, striving to achieve favorable economies of scale or better market penetration. Lines of business have been sold or discontinued, and unprofitable or poorly located branches have been closed.

For consolidation to succeed in achieving the anticipated economies of scale, banks must eliminate redundant systems, integrate remaining legacy systems, reengineer business processes for a consistent touch and feel across products and channels, and plan for further consolidation. However, banks must accomplish this while paying close attention to the preservation of technology investments in either existing computer equipment or personnel training. Without this strategy, the industry will see lower than anticipated cost savings as a result of these mergers and acquisitions.

To enable better consolidation, many institutions have developed independent subsidiary service corporations that house and manage all information technology (IT) assets. These organizations typically have four areas: data-processing operations, item-processing operations, system performance and support, and telecommunications and network operations. Data- and item-processing operations are losing the political power they once had. The power is shifting to the telecommunication and networking operations area as host-centric systems are replaced by distributed architectures. With more distributed systems, the focus has also shifted from hardware to software. Today, the central question is what the solution can deliver with regard to software capabilities. The software focus also includes network management, systems configuration, and data-management issues.

Within this organizational structure, the decision-making process needs to occur at an enterprise-wide technology planning committee level. This committee should ideally consist of IT and business unit executives. Traditionally there has not been good linkage between business and technology strategies and objectives. This failure can, in part, be traced to the lack of dual control of a technology infrastructure. There are many war stories that range from business objectives that failed to understand the technology functionality to technology capabilities not meeting business expectations. A list of management objectives from a business perspective must be matched with a technology strategy that enables those objectives to be achieved within a certain period of time. It is virtually impossible to achieve this in today's complex environment without senior representatives from the business and technology functions working in tandem (and thus sharing the success as well as the responsibility) to reach their common goal.

Relationship Banking and Data Warehousing

It is fair to say that banks today are as much in the business of managing information as in that of accumulating and managing wealth. Harnessing the untapped value of customer information is critical to banks fully realizing their relationship banking strategies. Yet to fully utilize information, banks must be able to route, analyze, and integrate data into meaningful patterns using data-warehousing technology.

Relationship banking requires new ways to apply technology for customer management. Each transaction a customer undertakes with a bank constitutes a trail. If that transaction is aggregated with the customer's other transactions and analyzed, it may yield invaluable historical information about consumer preferences and how the bank may cater to and influence those preferences. If the customer's transaction history is analyzed along with that of other customers, the bank may discover a segment preference that can be satisfied by new products and services.

The challenge becomes greater because back-office systems must also manage transactions over time and integrate them across products. Banks incur costs and generate income through frequent, one-on-one interactions with their customer base over a long period of time. To determine accurately whether the entire relationship with an individual customer is profitable, banks must examine the bundle of products provided and the amount of services required, per customer, to maintain these products. Unlike most other businesses, in which each sales transaction typically produces a specific, measurable profit (before overhead), banks must examine the combination of products and usage of those products to determine profitability of a product for each individual. For example, a checking account does not have a set profitability figure but rather its profitability is dependent on a particular customer's use of that account. If one checking account customer goes to the branch every day and another goes to the ATM once a week then the checking account profitability will be different for each customer. This remains a difficult undertaking for virtually every bank because most, if they calculate consumer profitability at all, calculate it with a fixed component per product.

Banks, like enterprises in every industry, have been awash in data for years. In effect, they have focused on accumulating data (a collection of facts) rather than managing information (data endowed with meaning that enhances its usefulness). New technology can help banks achieve a more sophisticated understanding of customers in their various transactions. Traditional mainframe environments have made it difficult for institutions to capture, process, and assimilate this diverse information. The evolution of banking systems driven by integrated customer information files (CIFs) and real-time on-line transaction processing (OLTP) can help banks assess the true value of a particular customer by providing an accurate, comprehensive picture of the total relationship across all product lines. However, the change from collecting data to managing information using data warehousing requires not only technological enhancements but also a change in the value-added activities—data acquisition, data aggregation/consolidation, and data organization.

Conclusion

In this chapter we presented an overview of changing dynamics in the banking industry that, together with technological changes, are creating the need to rethink the existing paradigm of financial services.

Fifteen years ago, commercial banks were indistinguishable from one another. Today, the strategic options of these banks are quite varied. The retail banking industry is entering a period unlike any in its history—a period of unbridled competition that will call for all the creative ingenuity, innovation, and entrepreneurial skills that bankers possess.

Financial institutions today have reason to worry that if they do not offer on-line banking services, affluent customers will be stolen away by software companies, on-line access services, brokerages, or global entertainment companies. The current situation presents both opportunities and risks. In addition to wanting to protect their existing franchise, financial institutions can look to on-line banking and related services to expand their product offerings and win new business.

In sum, financial institutions must not lose sight of the fact that on-line banking is in their best interest and that it is up to them to market the idea. They need to market on-line banking as the ability to organize in an increasingly complex and confusing world. The term *organization* encapsulates the ideas of control, timeliness, time savings, and easy access to more information. This is not a major shift; this is the goal customers have always had in their banking activities.

References

1. Andrew E. Serwer, "The Competition Heats Up in Online Banking," *Fortune* (June 26, 1995).
2. Open Financial Exchange Specification, Final Draft, January 20, 1997. Available at http://www.intuit.com/ofx/techspec.html.

3. Terri Dial, "Differentiate Strategies for Future Success," *Bank Management* 71 no. 5 (1995): 20–22.
4. Ravi Kalakota and Andrew Whinston, *Electronic Commerce: A Manager's Guide* (Reading, Mass.: Addison-Wesley, 1997).
5. Federal Reserve, "Banking Industry Consolidation," unpublished presentation.
6. Kurt F. Viermetz, "The Strategy of an Investment Bank" (speech delivered to the Association of French Bankers). Available at http://www.jpmorgan.com/CorpInfo/Perspectives/IssuesPersp .html
7. See note 6 above.
8. See note 4 above.
9. Robert Spicer, "Commentary," *The Magazine of Bank Management* (April 1987).
10. Yankee Group Comments, *The American Banker* (February 10, 1987).
11. *Computerworld* (July 2, 1984).
12. Ravi Kalakota and Andrew Whinston, *Frontiers of Electronic Commerce* (Reading, Mass.: Addison-Wesley, 1995).
13. James S. Mahan, testimony before U.S. House of Representatives Subcommittee on Domestic and International Monetary Policy of the Committee on Banking and Financial Services, March 7, 1996.
14. Ravi Kalakota and Frances Frei, "Managing Online Financial Supply Chains," working paper, 1996.
15. See note 10 above.
16. See note 1 above.

3

Banking on the Web

Security First Network Bank and the Development of Virtual Financial Institutions

KIM HUMPHREYS
SECURITY FIRST NETWORK BANK

Introduction

On October 18, 1995, Security First Network Bank (www.SFNB .com) opened to the public as the world's first Internet bank. At a moment when many observers were still questioning the security of on-line financial transactions, SFNB laid claim to a place in Internet and financial services history as the first full-service bank doing business on the Internet. In retrospect, Internet banking was clearly an idea whose time had come. SFNB was a pioneer in this new delivery channel, but innovation is a daily event on the global network. By 1997 thousands of banks around the world had at least opened informational Web sites, and increasing numbers were moving to offer a variety of on-line financial transactions. Banking on the Internet may still represent the frontier of financial services, but a lot of settlers are staking their claim to the territory.

As of October 1996, one year after SFNB was launched, 28 financial institutions, including 23 in the United States, allowed their customers to conduct various forms of banking on the Internet. Although hundreds of financial institutions provide at least a home page on the World Wide Web, less than 1 percent offer complete interactive banking. However, 87 percent say they plan to expand the size and capabilities of their sites within a year. And by the year 2000, more than 1,500 institutions project they will offer some form of Internet banking.

Even as more and more banks acknowledge that Web-based financial services will have a major impact on both consumers and the entire banking industry, a number of questions are still being debated. How have customers responded to a completely virtual bank? Are their expectations and interactions different in the on-line environment? What business model is best suited to banking on the Web? What impact will electronic banking have on an institution's personnel, branch integration, information systems, and technology? What are the most viable security solutions available? How can banks best demonstrate to customers that their assets will be safe and their transactions private on the Internet? In the context of such rapid growth, it seems especially appropriate to analyze the experience of the earliest practitioner of full-service Web banking to gain some perspective on these and other questions.

After more than a year of operation, a continuous stream of new products, and an evolving relationship with customers, SFNB can provide some concrete answers to issues looming in the future for many financial institutions. This chapter provides an overview of the early development of Security First Network Bank and analyzes its marketing and customer-retention strategies, its security infrastructure, and its role in creating the new delivery channel of Internet banking.

Founding Vision and First Steps

Although SFNB's debut on the Web caught many in the industry off-guard, its founders considered Internet banking to be a natural progression from the home banking systems based on modems and personal computers first introduced to Americans in the mid-1980s. The difference, however, is that today's home banking, based on the Web, offers the convenience, functionality, and low cost lacking in the home banking options of the '80s. Consumers remained cool to

PC banking because it did not provide the same fast, easy access to transactions and account information as they found at the ATM or even in the traditional local branch.

Nonetheless, banking executives needed to find more cost-effective delivery channels to overcome limitations of labor-intensive, high-cost branch banking models. The World Wide Web, with its ubiquitous browser-based access, offered a completely different delivery model for banking, one in which customers could tap into their accounts from home, office, dorm room, hotel, library, or café to conduct transactions at any hour. Under siege by nonbank competitors, the Web also presented the banking industry with an opportunity to regain much of its control of the payments system by strengthening customer relationships through greater convenience, better service, and comprehensive product offerings. Imperative to the fruition of this concept was the right combination of vision and operational know-how, a melding of technology, business savvy, and tenacity.

The idea of putting a financial institution on the Internet was first conceived during a family gathering in June 1994. Michael C. McChesney and James S. Mahan III began to consider the idea seriously after McChesney presented his brother-in-law with several articles regarding innovative businesses thriving on the Web. The first concerned a flower shop that had doubled its business within a month of going on line. Another related the experiences of two attorneys who received more than 30,000 responses to an advertisement placed on the Web for U.S. green cards.

The complementary backgrounds of both men also played a major role in the realization of this endeavor. At the time, McChesney served as chief executive officer of SecureWare Inc., Atlanta, a computer and network security firm he cofounded in 1986 to develop highly secure operating system technologies primarily for the government market. SecureWare's technologies had been used to protect some of the world's most secure network computer platforms, including projects for the U.S. Department of Defense such as the B2 Bomber program. Mahan was then chair and chief executive officer of Cardinal Bancshares, an innovative $650 million bank holding company he had cofounded several years earlier in Lexington, Kentucky.

In addition to the alchemy of their respective expertise, the timing could not have been better. The recently introduced World Wide Web was already burgeoning as an information resource and a tool for electronic publishing. However, relatively few companies had yet recognized its potential to fundamentally transform the business environment. McChesney and Mahan saw great potential in using the Web commercially to simplify people's lives through the delivery of goods and services. A natural first step would be to provide banking products and financial services on line, available at the customer's convenience. So, after conducting consumer focus groups in five major metropolitan areas around the country and thoroughly investigating the security requirements and regulatory constraints, McChesney and Mahan set out to create the first electronic national bank.

Initially hesitant to mix business and family, they approached a number of organizations, including newcomers Netscape Communications Corporation and Open Market, seeking a deal to outsource the development of the necessary software to put their bank on line. Unable to come to terms on cost and ownership rights, the pair determined that McChesney's software development company would undertake the project.

In the spring of 1995, however, their plan took a dramatic turn. At the request of a friend, Mahan gave a brief, nine-minute speech regarding the fledgling Internet banking project to attendees at the Montgomery Securities' Annual Financial Institutions Conference in Pasadena. Overwhelmed by the immediate interest of some of the country's largest financial institutions to purchase their Internet banking software, Mahan and McChesney quickly expanded the business plan. It was clear that they had stumbled onto something more significant than they had originally envisioned. They were not simply creating the first on-line bank but in effect establishing the Web as a channel for the delivery of financial services. It was important that they proceed with development of the Internet banking solution not only to accommodate a small Internet-only thrift but also to satisfy the requirements of the financial services industry at large. This would require the full attention of a dedicated team. Thus, the plan evolved to create not only Security First Network Bank but also a software development company, both of which would ultimately become subsidiaries of a new holding company.

In addition to operating as the world's first Internet bank, SFNB would offer proof of concept and provide a real-life example of the utility of the software. It would also expand the value of McChesney and Mahan's venture by creating a market for the software and security solutions developed for SFNB. In turn, paving the way for more banks to go on line would lend credibility to the Internet as a viable delivery channel and convince consumers that Web banking was the wave of the future, thereby driving a growing number of early-adopter consumers to SFNB. Because of its twofold strategy, SFNB welcomed additional banks to the Web.

Establishing a clear operating entity for SFNB required considerable realignment of existing partnerships, as well as new mergers and acquisitions. To build the first Internet financial institution, Cardinal Bancshares had to do some shuffling of its subsidiaries. The bank holding company first sold four of its five First Federal Savings Bank branches to Mutual Federal, another of its savings bank subsidiaries. The name of the remaining First Federal charter was then changed to Security First Network Bank to clearly reflect the new entity's mission. This move paved the way for part one of the founders' vision and set the stage for launching SFNB in the fall of 1995.

Securing Federal Regulatory Approval

Although banking is among the most highly regulated industries, at the time there were no existing laws governing virtual banking. In order to leverage SFNB as a model to encourage other financial institutions to set up virtual branches, Mahan and McChesney decided to adopt a proactive strategy and approached the Office of Thrift Supervision (OTS) for regulatory approval of SFNB's Internet banking business plan. Ideally the process would help to establish precedent and clear the way for other financial institutions that might potentially license their software to begin offering Web-based banking.

A laborious nine-month process ensued in which SFNB was integrally involved in educating regulators about the new industry. Of great concern was security. In addition to in-depth explanation and demonstration of its security technologies, uncompromised after nearly a decade of use in protecting top secret military operations, SFNB hired a group of "professional hackers" from Georgia Institute of Technology to try to breach its security system. After several weeks, the group was still unsuccessful. On May 10, 1995, the Office of Thrift Supervision set a precedent by granting its approval of Cardinal's plan to operate an Internet bank. Garnering government endorsement of SFNB's Internet business plan was undoubtedly a preemptive move for Mahan and McChesney, but it was also an important step in securing their second mission. By assuaging federal regulators, they had effectively dismantled an obstacle they may have encountered later when offering an integrated Internet solution to other financial institutions.

Just two weeks after securing federal regulatory approval for its Internet banking plan, SFNB received another significant endorsement, this time from the banking industry itself. Two superregional bank holding companies, Huntington Bancshares of Columbus, Ohio, and Wachovia Corp. of Winston-Salem, North Carolina, along with Area Bancshares of Owensboro, Kentucky, agreed to invest a total of $5 million in the project in return for certain licensing rights to the Internet banking software. It was now time to move forward on part two of the venture, marketing the Internet banking and security solutions to other financial institutions.

In May 1996, Cardinal spun off SFNB in order to separate the Internet banking operations from Cardinal's traditional banking business. Included in the spin-off was SFNB's acquisition of Five Paces, developer of the Internet banking software, and the announcement of its intent, upon regulatory approval, to acquire SecureWare, developer of the security solution. Concurrent with the spin-off, SFNB also conducted its initial public offering, successfully raising approximately $60 million. The capitalization would enable the company to focus on the research and development of long-term industry solutions and allow it to increase its staff and expand its facilities to meet growing customer demand.

In less than two years, SFNB's software development arm had effectively created a new channel for the delivery of financial services, facilitating the opening of the world's first Internet bank. During that period, it had also developed a number of commercial products while supporting SFNB's operations. By November 1996, the acquisition of SecureWare was effected, and the company was merged with Five Paces to form Security First Technologies (S1), officially bringing together the core competencies used to launch the world's first Internet bank. The name change allowed the company to capitalize on the significant brand awareness SFNB had amassed in its first year of operation.

S1's flagship product, Virtual Bank Manager (VBM), is the financial services application that enables financial institutions, including SFNB, to offer traditional banking products and services such as checking, savings, and money market accounts and certificates of deposit over the Internet. VBM also allows institutions to offer services unique to electronic banking including electronic bill payment, automatically reconciled check registers and statements, digital images of cleared checks, customized reports, and anytime, anywhere access to accounts via the Web. The S1 solution also provides round-the-clock customer service via e-mail and phone. And, although VBM was originally developed for SFNB, its customizable graphical user interface (GUI) allows financial institutions to distinguish themselves from on-line competitors by designing their own home page bank lobby, leveraging their existing brand awareness.

To effectively market its solution, Security First Technologies devised a three-tiered business model. S1 would offer direct licenses of its software to large financial institutions that could efficiently run the operations in-house. The company also would market its solution, including the software and S1's Internet data-processing and customer support services, to smaller institutions looking to outsource to avoid allocating extensive financial and employee resources. And, S1 would license its software solution to bank data core processors that would then remarket the solution to their financial institution clients.

By year-end 1996, S1 had surpassed its goals by licensing its solution to 13 financial institutions with aggregate assets totaling more than $215 billion. Of the 13 institutions, two are global banks (one domestic and one international) and seven are outsourcing the Internet data-processing and technical support to the S1 Data Center in Atlanta. S1 had also developed relationships with four of the top seven core processors in the United States, including ALLTEL Information Services Inc., M&I Data Services, Computer Services Inc., and FiServ Inc., extending its reach to more than 7,000 potential financial institution clients.

Additional strategic relationships had been initiated with a variety of companies specializing in electronic payment systems and alternative delivery channels. S1 had announced an agreement with VISA Interactive to offer Internet financial services to its 100+ financial institution clients. Through a licensing arrangement with National Commerce Bancorporation (NCBC), its subsidiary National Commerce Bank Services Inc. (NCBS), an innovator in in-store/supermarket banking, signed on to remarket VFM to its more than 200 financial institution clients. To further strengthen its sales and marketing reach, S1 also developed strategic partnerships with Hewlett-Packard Company and Unisys Corp.

Defining an Internet Bank: What Is Different?

Besides being the first to debut on the Internet with full transaction capability and secure financial services, there are a number of factors that differentiate SFNB from other financial institutions. First, SFNB exists primarily on the Web. Whereas other financial institutions are attempting to offer Internet banking as a value-added service, at SFNB Internet banking is the focus. The strategy is to give depositors a secure environment in which to learn and grow accustomed to this new form of banking. Using the most efficient delivery channel available, SFNB predicts that over time, with the appropriate volumes, overhead can be driven down substantially to resemble that of a telephone-based mutual funds financial services firm such as Charles Schwab or Fidelity. A traditional financial institution utilizing the most expensive delivery channel—branches—will have overhead of approximately 350 basis points to average assets. In contrast, an Internet bank can operate at about 100 basis points to average assets, creating a more profitable situation for the institution and a tangible payoff for its customers.

If an electronic financial institution is going to make the same fixed margin on capital as the traditional, nonelectronic institution, that leaves a 2 to 3 percent margin cost savings to take advantage of internally or pass on, in whole or in part, to the customer. The financial institution may elect to offer 2 to 3 percentage points higher interest to depositors. Or, on the other side of the balance sheet, the institution may choose to lend money at 2 to 3 percent lower rates, while still making the same margins. In SFNB's case, decreased operational costs are transferred to customers in the form of a number of free services and higher interest rates on deposits. For example, SFNB consistently offers among the best rates in the country on CDs and money market accounts. In turn, SFNB profits because these offerings drive a higher volume of deposits and customers to the institution.

Another distinguishing feature of SFNB is size. With just more than a dozen employees, SFNB can take a more aggressive and creative approach than traditional, larger institutions, which typically are slower to adapt to technology, incur higher overheads, and operate in a more bureaucratic manner. Conversely, SFNB has developed and deployed new technology rapidly, positioning itself as an industry leader. And due to the nature of the delivery channel, small size does not equal limited services or geographic scope. Because of its position on the Web, SFNB can meet and even exceed the service offerings of larger financial institutions and its customer base blankets the entire country.

These differences help to define the unique qualities of an online bank, but they also raise some challenging issues for the heavily regulated banking industry. From its inception, SFNB has taken a proactive stance in the regulatory arena. Because the field is so new, regulators do not yet have a standard policy on Internet banking. SFNB's approach has been to share with regulators what it has learned concerning the nature of the Internet, so that they are better able to make informed judgments. Due in part to SFNB's efforts, Internet financial institutions can now be insured by the FDIC and therefore are subject to the same federal regulations as any other financial institution.

Federal auditors visit SFNB on a regular basis to verify the physical security of the site and the procedures and processes involved in administration, data management, and programming. The computing and programming components of most financial institutions today are already so broad that internal process regulations have required very little adjustment for Internet-based banks. One of the few new stipulations is that financial institutions must verify every link from their Web sites to any other addresses on the Web to ensure that there are no inappropriate links or implied relationships that do not meet regulatory standards.

Other regulations are being reviewed with respect to Internet banks. Officials at SFNB and other financial institutions have been working with the U.S. House of Representatives Committee on Banking and Financial Services and specifically with its Subcommittee on Domestic and International Monetary Policy to speak to these issues. One significant regulatory issue currently being addressed is Reg E, which stipulates that every electronic transaction must give the customer an opportunity to receive a receipt and be verified by a written statement generated within 30 days. An example would be the receipt received after conducting an ATM transaction, which later shows up on the customer's statement. For a customer using an Internet financial institution, the account register *is* the statement, and it is updated each day according to account activity. A printed statement, mailed once a month, not only costs the financial institution more than it does to maintain the account but is outdated by the time of receipt. The current information is readily available in the customer's account, accessible through the financial institution's Web site. Officers at SFNB have worked to see that the regulation is modified to take into account the dynamic nature of an Internet bank, and recent reports indicate it is being addressed. Congress turned Reg E over to the Federal Reserve to interpret under its designated authority. As a result, the Federal Reserve has proposed an interpretation that allows for the electronic disbursement of statements that are retainable by the customer. The implication of this interpretation is enormous cost savings for financial institutions and customers.

Another regulatory requirement that must be redefined as it relates to networked financial institutions is the Community Reinvestment Act (CRA). This legislation requires financial institutions to actively participate in and support the communities they serve. For financial institutions with a well-defined physical community, this is a valid requirement. Obviously, the term *community* requires a new definition in the network sense. As a national financial institution with customers in all 50 states, SFNB and other Internet financial institutions present a puzzle for CRA enforcement. Thus far, SFNB has satisfied CRA requirements by judging its certifiable lending area around the physical operating center in Atlanta and its newly opened City Office. Since loans currently are only made in Atlanta, SFNB has been able to define its business area as two miles in every direction of its lending office. However, SFNB officers believe there will be a national CRA status for Internet financial institutions at some point.

Customer Response: The First Year

How has the virtual bank worked in practice? At its one-year anniversary in October 1996, SFNB had opened approximately 7,000 accounts with total deposits of more than $20 million, a monumental growth rate. These numbers are especially impressive when considering that the bank opened with no existing brand awareness or physical location, and, at the time of its opening, was accessible only through a computer with a secure Internet browser over an entirely new delivery channel. Add to that the fact that it relied on very limited marketing and advertising efforts and an extremely small staff. Initial marketing efforts were limited and targeted at consumers who were already on line and would therefore have some level of familiarity with the new delivery channel.

Since SFNB outsources its core competencies, data processing, bill payment, and customer service to the S1 data processing and customer service center, the bank operates efficiently with only 12 to 14 people at the operations center in Atlanta. Because SFNB enables anyone with a social security number, a U.S. mailing address, and Internet access to be a potential customer, depositors from all 50 states and all continents have opened SFNB accounts, a claim we have been unable to find from any other traditional or Internet bank.

After launching with basic Internet checking, SFNB has added interest checking and savings accounts, certificates of deposit, money market accounts, and credit cards. The yields for SFNB's CDs and money market accounts have been cited in *Money, Kiplinger's Personal Finance, Smart Money,* and other publications as among the country's highest, and the average balances for these two accounts have surpassed even SFNB's optimistic predictions. Averaging approximately 800 account openings per month over the last six to eight months, customer referral continues to be a leading channel to new customers, speaking highly of SFNB's customer service efforts. Customers can call the 24-hour help desk toll-free or send e-mail from anywhere in the world via the Internet for assistance with questions regarding financial or technical matters.

Arguably, the most profound accomplishment of SFNB's first year of operation is its proof of concept. A new financial services channel was instituted, and SFNB proved its viability. Rather than simply presenting a home page with information about the financial institution, SFNB offered the first true functionality, enabling customers to interact—and transact—with their accounts over the Internet.

SFNB's success in the consumer marketplace has also helped to generate interest in its subsidiary products offered through Security First Technologies. Offering the SFNB experience on the Web as validation, S1 is now positioned to take the infrastructure built for this bank—complete with its foundation of military-grade network security and pillars of on-line financial services applications—and offer a new paradigm for the financial services industry. Drawing on the valuable insight gained into the wants and needs of Internet banking customers, as well as the requirements of merging this new technology with financial institutions' existing systems, S1 offers its clients a comprehensive package including consulting, implementation, marketing support, training, and customer service and data center outsourcing.

The SFNB experience offers a useful benchmark for conducting financial services over the Internet because it has implemented a number of innovative strategies to win consumer confidence in banking on the Web. The major challenges SFNB faces in marketing its services over the electronic delivery channel continue to be consumers' security concerns, consumer access to the bank, consumer education, and customer support. SFNB has responded to these issues by forging a new relationship with its customers based on the advantages of electronic commerce. Rather than allowing the technology to depersonalize the relationship between customer and bank, SFNB is using the technology to improve its personalized service, with the ultimate goal of helping customers gain greater control over managing their money. With this philosophy in mind, SFNB approaches each challenge by dismissing the traditional banking paradigm and replacing it with a model in which the bank can completely tailor its services to individual customers.

Security and the Electronic Commerce Infrastructure

First impressions often dictate future perceptions and, in the case of security, SFNB did not leave anything to chance. From approaching federal regulators to test its security platform to including security in its name, SFNB's strategy has been to address consumer concerns about Internet security head-on. Although SFNB officers could have been satisfied with the success of their proven secure bank operations, they chose also to take on and tackle customer perception of Internet banking security. In designing the Web site, SFNB gave special attention to creating an appearance of strength and safety. As illustrated in figure 3.1, the home page features a security guard icon that, when clicked on, offers a detailed description of SFNB's security architecture and an explanation of how it works.

There customers learn that, in addition to being fully insured by the FDIC just as a physical bank branch would be, depositors have SFNB's full guarantee that their money is safe. The "SFNB No Risk Guarantee" is SFNB's marketing response to security concerns, guaranteeing that it will provide 100 percent reimbursement for any funds removed from an account without authorization, as well as for any bank errors or security breaches. SFNB already provides a multi-layered, military-grade network security system that in many ways is safer than a physical branch.

Three levels of security are required to protect transactions conducted over the Internet. First, information being transmitted across

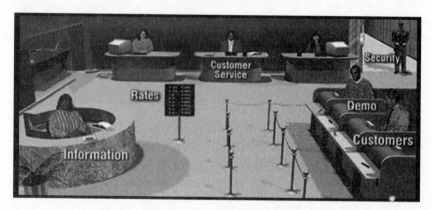

FIGURE 3.1   **Security First Network Bank Home Page**

the public network must be encrypted for privacy and to ensure the information has not been altered en route. Most Web browsers, such as Netscape Navigator, support an encryption standard called Secure Sockets Layer (SSL), which provides two-way capability to ensure integrity and authenticity. Encryption provides a protected path for data as they travel across the Internet between the customer and bank to prevent others from viewing or altering the information. In addition to ensuring the integrity of the data, SSL provides authentication through the use of digital certificates so that customers are assured they are talking to SFNB and not some fictitious financial institution set up to impersonate the bank. The financial institution sends a certificate to the browser, which the browser opens and verifies.

While it sounds complicated, the customer is not even aware that these steps are being taken. The browser is able to distinguish the validity of a certificate. If someone is trying to impersonate a financial institution, either no certificate or a fake certificate is sent. The browser would then warn the customer that he or she might be entering an invalid site.

Firewalls and filtering routers comprise the second layer of the security architecture originally developed by S1. Functioning as an armed guard, the firewall forms a barrier between the outside Internet and the internal customer service network. To protect all inside customer service addresses from outside access, all incoming information packet traffic is actually addressed to the firewall. Traffic through the firewall is subjected to a special e-mail proxy process that operates in much the same way as a filtering router, verifying the source and destination of each information packet. The proxy then changes the information packet address of the packet to deliver it to the appropriate site within the customer service network, leaving the structure of the bank's internal networks invisible to outside observers. The filtering router verifies the source and destination of each packet of information received over the Internet and determines whether to let the packet through. Allowing only secure hypertext transfer protocol (HTTPS) traffic to the server, filtering routers deny access if the packet is not directed at a specific, available service.

In addition to encryption, which acts as an armored car, and firewalls and filtering routers, which serve as armed guards, a trusted operating system provides protection for information stored at the bank, that is, the vault. The trusted operating system acts as a proxy server, carrying out actions on behalf of a program. For instance, in a traditional branch the customer does not walk into the vault to get cash. Rather the customer approaches a teller, or proxy, who verifies the customer's identity and carries out the request by counting out the appropriate amount of cash and securing the customer's signature as proof of the transaction. The trusted operating system goes a step further in ensuring the safety of customer accounts by compartmentalizing them, similar to providing virtual lock boxes for each account. For example, if someone were able to "break into" the Internet bank, he or she could only access one account, not the entire vault. In doing so, the nonauthorized person would be forced to electronically forward the funds to a traceable address; to access the funds, it is likely that the person would incur greater expense in breaking in, in terms of time and money, than would be gained from a single account. To date, the S1 security architecture has not experienced any successful security breaches.

Because of its commitment to security, SFNB has had to balance ease of access for customers with control of unwanted prying. From the beginning, SFNB's strategy has been to target technically savvy, early adopters of the Internet technology. These individuals have a proclivity for using the Internet and also are familiar with Netscape Navigator, which at the time of the bank's opening was one of the only browsers to support Secure Sockets Layer (SSL) encryption, the first layer of SFNB's security architecture. When SFNB began operating in October 1995, none of the popular proprietary on-line service providers offered SSL-compliant browsers, presenting an immediate access challenge—lack of customer compatibility with SFNB security standards.

With the Internet's explosive growth, SFNB adapted its strategy by broadening its target audience. Internet service providers (ISPs), often referred to as gateways to the Internet, began cropping up and, unlike their proprietary counterparts, were using secure browsers to provide access to the World Wide Web. SFNB formed alliances with Netcom, MindSpring, Pipeline, and WinNet to promote its products and services. In comarketing with these ISPs, SFNB offered credit for network connection time to ISP customers who opened SFNB accounts. As proprietary on-line service providers became SSL compatible, SFNB opened satellite sites to become a gold bank on America Online (AOL) and the first bank on CompuServe. Additionally, many telecommunications companies are now offering secure Internet access, and SFNB has formed a joint marketing relationship with BellSouth.Net. By teaming with these various access providers, SFNB resolved the issue of how potential customers could access the bank.

Once customers learned how to access SFNB through the Internet, they still needed to be educated on what the Internet bank had to offer. SFNB provides traditional banking products and services that have been adapted to the Internet. For instance, electronic bill payment is a main attraction because all bills can be paid quickly and easily without checks, envelopes, or stamps. It is particularly convenient for recurring payments such as mortgages because after the initial setup information, including payee, amount, frequency, and duration, is entered, the customer does not need to intervene unless he or she decides to stop the payment. As SFNB began introducing services such as electronic bill payment, it was confronted with the challenge of marketing them over an untested retail delivery channel. To further complicate the situation, SFNB had no existing customer base to leverage. SFNB responded by using a best-of-breed pricing model, offering above-market interest rates and low or no fees to promote its deposit-based products.

The primary rationale for banking on the Web is the convenience of anytime, anywhere access. In an attempt to offer a similar level of convenience, many traditional financial institutions have sought relationships with personal finance software providers to offer PC banking. Unlike Internet banking, PC banking requires the customer to install software on a particular computer terminal, limiting account access to one machine. PC banking customers must also constantly input data and install software updates as they are developed, whereas SFNB provides automatic updates to customer accounts and product offerings. And when a problem arises, the PC banking customer is often bounced back and forth between the software vendor and the financial institution.

Open 24 hours a day, 365 days a year, SFNB provides live, round-the-clock customer service support via e-mail or a toll-free telephone number, and SFNB's well-trained customer service support can respond to both financial- and technology-related inquiries. Because SFNB does not have to support hundreds or even thousands of physical locations, it has been able to invest more heavily in customer service and support. Consumers can log onto the financial institution from anywhere in the world with any secure Internet-enabled device and access their accounts to make electronic bill payments, purchase certificates of deposit, review account statements, or track particular stocks. And with an anytime, anywhere, transaction-based system, more than one person can simultaneously interact with the financial data from different locations. For example, college students and their parents in different cities can jointly track spending and expenses.

Also, because SFNB operates over the most efficient delivery channel, it is able to offer its customers free services, low fees, and higher interest rates on deposits. The bank's regular checking account charges $3.95 per month and provides a free initial order of 200 checks, free unlimited paper check writing, 10 free ATM or VISA debit card transactions per month, and 20 free electronic bill payments per month. The monthly fee is waived for customers with direct deposits, a minimum daily balance of $1,000, or total deposits of $10,000, excluding CDs. Interest checking offers unlimited electronic bill payments each month for a nominal fee of $4.50, while other financial institutions are charging $7.95 a month on average for bill payment. A customer with a $500 minimum balance earns 2.50 percent on deposits in the interest checking account, and interest savings offers 2.60 percent with a $200 minimum balance. Classic and Gold VISA cards are available with no annual fee and competitive interest rates. SFNB's money market accounts offer a range of options, including 3.50 percent annual percentage yield for balances between $2,500 and $9,999, and six-month certificates of deposit yield 5.90 percent, both among the best rates in the country.

Because today's consumers are more interested in managing their finances than managing another software program, an additional SFNB benefit is the personal financial management tools available through the Internet interface. SFNB, for instance, automatically updates account information and provides customers with the tools to chart their budgets, categorize bills, and generate customized spending reports, providing an up-to-the-minute on-line assessment of their personal finances. Therefore, the customer does not have to wait for an outdated paper statement to arrive in the mail. Convenience, cost savings, and financial management tools provide good incentives for attracting and retaining a loyal group of consumers to Web banking.

On-Line Marketing to On-Line Consumers

To convey the benefits of Internet banking, SFNB tackled educating the consumer about its products through a progressive advertising campaign. Because SFNB was interested in consumers already familiar with the Internet, it chose new advertising channels to reach these potential customers. Rather than focusing on traditional print advertising, SFNB placed banner advertisements on various popular Web sites, including Web search engines and Internet access provider home pages, to reach an Internet-enabled audience. Through the banner ads, similar to electronic billboards, SFNB hit high-volume sites in an attempt to brand the financial institution on the World Wide Web. Later, SFNB segmented its on-line audience, for example, targeting the university market with an SFNB satellite on the Tripod Web site, designed specifically for young adults.

The content of SFNB's ads was also innovative. Interesting graphical images, provocative slogans, and product contests offering bathrobes and other leisure items were used to highlight the convenience and technology of banking on the Internet. SFNB supplemented its on-line advertising strategy with mechanisms to garner customer feedback, including on-line surveys regarding fees and interest rates, beta testing of services, and an on-line guest register to determine demographics, such as age, gender, income, and time spent on line. SFNB strengthened its brand awareness by educating consumers not only about the value of its products and services but also about the concept of Internet banking in general.

Another significant challenge to SFNB was the absence of branch support. SFNB responded by offering its customers a new financial services support model proving that the emerging delivery channel allows an Internet bank to be more accessible and personalized than a traditional bank. SFNB offers customer support via real, live customer service representatives who can be reached 24 hours a day, 7 days a week, providing customers with an up-close-and-personal relationship via the Internet. Photos and biographies of each customer service representative are available on line, fostering a sense of connection. In fact, many customers have developed relationships with particular representatives, which will be further enhanced through full-motion video as that technology becomes widely available.

SFNB's innovative marketing strategies have been designed to take advantage of the fledgling delivery channel. By tapping a technically attuned customer base with a propensity for home banking, SFNB discovered a niche market that, given the right education and equipment, could help lead the financial services industry into the forefront of cutting-edge electronic commerce.

Customer Response

During its first 18 months of operation, trend analysis indicated that most SFNB customers initially maintained a small account balance until they felt more comfortable with Internet banking. In fact,

SFNB facilitated this trial period by offering free basic checking accounts so customers could sample Internet banking without risk. SFNB even recommended that customers maintain their current accounts with other financial institutions until they were comfortable with the new form of banking. During a two- to four-month sales cycle, customers will typically deposit $100 (the minimum requirement to open an account) and pay a couple of bills. Once they see how easy it is, many set up direct deposit, making SFNB their primary financial institution, and begin to take advantage of different account offerings. Studies support this trend, indicating that on-line banking customers have an average of more than three banking products—checking accounts, CDs, money market accounts, and the like—compared to the average traditional financial services customer with two products. Once comfortable with the delivery channel, SFNB usage and deposits increase dramatically. The number of e-payments is steadily increasing, and the average checking account balance for SFNB customers has almost doubled since the bank came on the scene. These rates of deposit are expected to continue rising for SFNB and other financial institutions that take advantage of the Internet. A study by Forrester Research reported that assets managed on line are expected to grow from $5.4 billion to $46.9 billion in the next five years.

SFNB's customer demographics underscore the Internet's leading-edge appeal. The SFNB customer base exceeds the U.S. average banking customer base on a number of key consumer indicators—educational level, percentage of home ownership, employment status, and income level. More than half of all SFNB customers own a home and have household incomes greater than $50,000, while the average U.S. household income is $42,000. The majority of SFNB customers are also employed in professional and managerial positions, and 80 percent are college graduates.

Based on recent studies, the future of Internet banking looks even brighter. Currently about 12 million people are estimated to use the Internet. Forrester Research predicts that by the year 2000, 22 million households will have Internet connections in the home. And projections are that 14.6 million of those households will participate in Internet banking, according to the Tower Group, a bank technology consulting firm. One indicator of why Internet banking has become so popular is revealed in a recent study by Booz, Allen, Hamilton, and Co. comparing the transaction costs of different delivery channels. The findings show that a transaction conducted through a full-service branch costs the bank $1.07, whereas a transaction conducted over the World Wide Web costs $0.01. Even telephone, full-service ATM, and PC banking or third-party software cost more than Internet transactions. As illustrated by SFNB, the cost savings of operating on the 'Net can benefit both the financial institution and the consumer.

Perhaps the greatest testament to the effectiveness of the Internet banking model is the relationship that SFNB has built with its customers. Naysayers predicted that personal relationships would not develop because electronic commerce is inherently depersonalized. In fact, just the opposite has proven to be the case at SFNB. Customers often request to work with particular customer service representatives with whom they have developed a rapport. Also, SFNB customers are integrally involved in the success of the institution because they are encouraged to, and often do, provide constructive feedback and suggestions of how the financial institution might better serve their needs.

The remarkable response can be attributed to several factors, but perhaps most importantly, SFNB creatively finds ways to connect with customers through the new delivery channel. For example, a regular column on the SFNB Web site called "Tales from the Vault" provides customers with valuable information concerning personal financial management, including a list of no-fee ATMs around the country that is continuously updated by customers located throughout the United States. The column also highlights individual customers and discusses the various ways Internet banking has been useful for them. For example, one column discussed a customer who uses his SFNB account to manage his finances while attending school in the Virgin Islands. The column even included a photograph of the man using his laptop on the beach. Additionally, the SFNB staff sends periodic e-mail notifications to customers concerning new features, functionality, and product offerings. Finally, SFNB has proven to its customers that secure transactions are possible and convenient if the right technology is used.

A Functional Business Model

SFNB's business model has evolved along with the fledgling delivery channel, specifically in the areas of marketing, customer service, and development. By maintaining a close watch on customer desires and industry requirements, SFNB is able to adapt and expand its activities to satisfy its constituents. From the outset, SFNB's goal was to emulate and improve upon the efficient and highly successful telephone-based mutual funds business model within the banking and financial services industry and to offer the services using the new, more efficient delivery channel. Additionally, it planned to target these products and services to the niche market of Internet users. The assumptions driving the idea were that people wanted self-service banking, because they did not have time to waste in teller lines at branches. SFNB held focus groups in major metropolitan areas around the country to query people about whether they would be interested in banking on the Internet. From these sessions, SFNB decided to target early adopters to the Internet, based on the belief that only people who trust and use the technology first will decide to do their banking on the Web. It was determined that more mainstream users would want to rely on a physical presence, at least early on. In addition, SFNB would have an easier time conveying its benefits to these technologically savvy people who already understood concepts such as real time. Before opening for business, SFNB's Web site provided a survey for prospective customers to help determine how SFNB would scale its fees. Users were asked to send in their preferred choice out of five options of different combinations of interest rates and fees. By letting customers decide how they wanted the services priced, SFNB began early on to cultivate the strong relationships it now enjoys with customers.

SFNB also discovered that in many ways Internet customers tend to be more demanding than the average financial services customers. For example, Internet customers hate fees. Accustomed to using their browsers to find the best deals on anything from cookbooks to new motherboards, these customers expect the financial institution to make it not just convenient but also less expensive to bank from home. SFNB responded by pricing services so that customers saved money in comparison to traditional banking costs. As explained earlier in this chapter, customers are offered basic checking with low or no monthly fees, as well as a number of other free services including 24-hour customer service support and higher interest rates for deposits. Together these offer a powerful incentive for people to bank on the 'Net.

The second thing Internet users expect is quick response. If they send e-mail requests for help or information, they expect responses within a few hours, not a few days. It is important to meet these expectations to avoid attrition. To help SFNB and other financial institutions make the adjustments necessary to meet the Internet customer's expectations, S1 developed a new support call center system. Developed in conjunction with Quintus Corp., Hewlett-Packard Company, and Cambridge Technology Partners, the system provides the financial institution with greater control over support procedures, offering standardized answers to frequently asked questions and improving the overall efficiency of the customer service department.

Through its customer service operation, SFNB is able to respond to its customers' needs by modifying its services. A perfect example occurred when SFNB found that some of its potential customers felt intimidated by the new Internet banking technology and the lack of a physical bank presence. The Internet-only bank responded by developing the concept of a high-tech City Office, a hybrid banking solution that blends the best aspects of a physical presence with all the convenience and power of Internet banking. SFNB opened its City Office in Atlanta in January 1997 to demonstrate its technology firsthand to the consumer, a natural step in the further development and delivery of on-line banking. The City Office also demonstrates a unique approach for S1's financial institution clients who may be considering merging the new Internet technology with their existing branch network.

The Payoff: Consolidated Financial Services

The banking industry stands to benefit by becoming the primary provider of consolidated financial information because of its strong relationship with the customer and its access to customers' data. The S1 solution is being developed to facilitate this move by the banking industry by placing the financial institution in the center of the relationship with its customers, a position that has been threatened by the popularity of proprietary software for financial planning and bill payment that resides on customers' PCs. The proprietary software model is not strategic for financial institutions because the software company maintains the interface with the customer, allowing it to influence decisions and limit choices concerning banking and other service providers.

A consolidation engine is the heart of the S1 solution. Maintaining data on the financial institution's server rather than the customer's PC provides customers with automatic and current account updates, enhanced services, and increased ability to effectively manage their finances at their convenience. While the Internet is an excellent vehicle for this centralized proposition, the concept is not completely new. Financial institutions have typically stored all their data centrally on a mainframe system. When networks started developing, data storage moved out to local area networks. Today, S1's server-centric model brings data back to one central location for better manageability and functionality.

What is unique about S1's strategy for electronic financial services is its building of an infrastructure in which the financial institution will not necessarily be the original provider of some of the products and services it offers. S1 is publishing its message sets so that any number of service providers can link to the system, thereby presenting multiple options for financial institutions utilizing the S1 solution. The financial institution can make its own choice from various back-end service providers (such as brokerage, insurance, electronic bill payment, and so on) while presenting a tightly integrated appearance to the end user. For example, SFNB has begun to offer its customers portfolio tracking services through Macro*World, a third-party provider.

In the future of electronic commerce, financial service providers must be able to work together and share information within a standard interactive platform. For example, when a customer goes to the Ford Motor Company Web site to shop for a car and then applies for a loan from his or her financial institution, the institution should be able to quickly gather the appropriate customer and vehicle information to provide the customer with insurance quotes.

S1 is positioned to take advantage of this fundamental change in the way people conduct financial business through its three-tier system, currently under development. Virtual Financial Manager consolidates data from various sources and provides them across the Internet to the customer in the form of a consolidated financial statement from the financial institution. Not only is S1's Internet solution able to access data from a variety of back-end legacy environments but it also incorporates business logic to present the information in useful formats.

Electronic Commerce Strategies and Open Systems

Financial institutions should consider several strategic issues when moving forward to offer Internet banking. First, banks need to become more customer driven. In the past, the financial institution has defined the technology and dictated how customers must behave, that is, banking between the hours of 9 A.M. and 4 P.M., Monday through Friday. The Internet provides a vehicle for financial institutions to accommodate the customer by taking advantage of the technology customers are embracing. Through this new delivery channel, the industry can tap into customers who are demanding conveniences that branches are unable to provide. The Internet will allow financial institutions to strengthen customer relationships and broaden their markets for potential customers without investing in additional brick-and-mortar locations.

It is imperative that financial institutions also choose the right partners when forging ahead with Internet banking. Financial institutions may be tempted to take an expedient approach to get on the Web, delaying major decisions about their full-blown Internet strategies and data-management infrastructures. Unfortunately, many of these financial institutions will be forced to start from scratch once their strategies have been refined because the quick and easy

Web-based solutions offer only a temporary fix. They are not scalable or flexible enough to be compatible with emerging technologies and industry growth. To fully appreciate the advantage of offering consolidated financial services over the Internet, the financial institution will require a flexible, open solution that continues to grow with the needs of the institution and the state of the technology.

The financial institution should consider the importance of open standards when choosing an Internet banking solution. If the trend of nonbank competitors usurping business from the banking industry is allowed to continue, banks will simply become commodities. In this environment, the only way to differentiate oneself would be by price. If the financial institutions are turned into commodity producers of check-clearing services, only a select few with the lowest possible overhead will succeed. Instead, financial institutions need to build an environment in which customers can choose their financial services providers based on both cost and added value.

When Mahan and McChesney developed the idea of opening a financial institution on the Internet, part of their strategy was to provide an open system for financial institutions. An open system levels the playing field so that providers with the best technology and products can compete effectively.

If a customer accesses financial planning services through an interface that is totally controlled by the software developer and then moves from this interface to banking transactions, the opportunity for financial institutions to control the relationship and take advantage of cross-selling opportunities is lost. The financial institution will be giving up its position as the intermediary between customers and brokerage firms, insurance firms, and other financial services providers, for example. Customers will identify these services with their financial management software, not with the financial institution. Another implication of allowing a third-party software provider to directly control the interface is that there is no differentiation among the home pages and Web sites of the various client financial institutions.

In developing an electronic commerce strategy for SFNB, the bank's management has identified five points that will strongly influence the future of Internet banking. Other banks should consider these questions carefully before making any decisions concerning electronic strategies:

1. *Is there a mandatory switch that customers must go through or can they come directly into software that we run at our financial institution?* This does not mean that a financial institution should not outsource its front-end processing, if that is its preference. What it means is that financial institutions should have a competitive environment in which to choose from multiple front-end processors and in which the financial institution will always have the option of bringing the processing in-house if the front-end processor is charging unreasonable rates.

2. *Can my customer, even five years from now, get to the financial institution from virtually any type of device and over any network?* Bankers must not limit themselves by being tied into a proprietary network or being accessible solely through proprietary software. Rather than being accessible only through a single network, financial institutions must be sure the technology they are investing in will be supported across all networks. Customers also should be able to reach the financial institution using any number of browser-based devices from any number of manufacturers.

3. *Can I choose my own strategic partners?* If financial institutions are going to combine brokerage or insurance data with DDA data, for instance, can they choose which brokerage firms they work with? Will the technology allow their data to be combined into a single statement for their customers? If financial institutions can maintain that control, they will be in a position of intermediate to other financial service providers. If they lose that control, someone else is going to become that mediator. More importantly, they will have lost their greatest asset—control of the customer's DDA data.

4. *Can I control the interface that my customer sees?* Financial services customers must be able to recognize and continue to identify with their financial institutions of choice. This is a particularly tough question for those that offer a pure client/server-based solution. Because they have large applications that run on various operating systems (Windows or Macintosh) on the user's

desktop, it is almost technically impossible for them to allow Bank1 to have one set of interfaces and Bank2 another.

5. *Is the infrastructure being developed by the provider one that will evolve into an electronic payment system under banking control, or will it be controlled by third parties outside the financial services industry?* This question, relating to the future of the payment system, is a bit more complex. An electronic payment system will begin with simple bill-payment services, such as those offered by CheckFree and VISA Interactive. From there, it will evolve to something more closely resembling an electronic payment system. The software providers of closed systems recognize the value in bill payment and control bill payment for their member banks' customers. With a monopoly on all bill payment done through its switch, mandatory switch owners could easily win control of the new payment system, should financial institutions hand over their customer relationships.

By ensuring that all these questions are answered in the direction of open standards, the financial services community can take advantage of the enormous opportunity presented by electronic banking. An open system changes the nature of the competition on the Internet because it allows financial institutions to become the standard for on-line bill payment, maintaining control of the check-based payment system and garnering control of the coming electronic payment system. In addition to ensuring the financial service industry's future, this strategy will strengthen the customer relationship and open up a variety of new revenue sources.

Conclusion: Moving On-Line Banking into the Future

Just as the Internet has provided a new delivery channel for banking that has widespread implications for traditional institutions, virtual banks such as SFNB can offer a vision of how this channel will develop in the future. The Internet allows financial services to be more tailored. Invariably the Web banking option will pull traffic away from branches, so instead of tellers simply acting as friendly receptacles, financial institutions will have marketing staffs to determine product offerings and tailor them to customers. The consolidation engine that S1 is providing to the industry enhances this ability to individualize and cross-sell products to customers. The more information the financial institution knows about the customer, the better able it is to customize its services to that individual and to provide more value.

A typical community bank, or any financial institution for that matter, manages only about 5 to 10 percent of an individual's assets. The rest of the customer's money has been flowing into money funds, mutual funds, and brokerage accounts for 30 years. Electronic banking with consolidated financial services on the Web provides an opportunity for financial institutions to turn that flow of money around and bring some of those assets back under bank management. The Internet allows financial institutions to compete on a more equitable basis with the cost structure of the nonbank competitors. The advantage the industry has as it moves into this competitive environment is its control of one of the two critical payment systems that virtually everyone uses—the check-based payment system. Very few Americans with any net worth do not have a relationship with a bank-based checking account, yet plenty of Americans do not maintain relationships with nonbank competitors.

The Internet is also changing the way customers behave. Currently, only 1 percent of U.S. banking transactions are accomplished via the Internet. But the boom is on the way. Jupiter Communications, a technology research firm, predicts that number will grow to 6 percent within the year and to as much as 75 percent by the year 2005. In the near future, these transactions will be accomplished through the smart card digital payment system, which identifies the card holder by key pairs, or public and private key cryptography. Financial institutions or some other body will begin issuing smart cards with all the customers' banking information on them. The cards will include key pairs that identify the person and how much money he or she has in the financial institution. Customers will carry these cards around to pay for everything; the money will be transferred directly from financial institution to financial institution, eliminating the need for currency, ACH, or credit cards. In addition to the financial services environment, smart cards may extend to other areas of people's lives, where they have different keys for different things. For instance, a key pair at work will provide access to information, computers, and buildings. If the financial services industry positions itself to issue the smart cards, then the potential is great to attract more business to itself.

Changes in the way financial institutions do business translate into new features for their customers. In the future, these customers can expect new access devices, new payment devices, and new tools to sift through information. The browser devices being invented to access the Internet are quickly being incorporated into other commonplace technologies such as televisions and telephones, and they will serve as vehicles for paging, sending e-mail, placing telephone calls, and providing other functions. In fact, such browser devices already can be found in inexpensive mobile apparatuses such as personal digital assistants (PDAs). With this type of interface, people will be able to do their banking, shop at L. L. Bean, or track a FedEx package while walking down the concourse of an airport. This fast, ubiquitous, dial-tone access will exist in the kitchen, or the study, or the car—anywhere it is convenient. Access rates will also increase to support voice and a reasonable quality video. With that kind of speed over the wire, full-motion video will be available to allow customers to receive personal, face-to-face attention from electronic financial institutions' customer service representatives.

This technology leap is not far off. It will be available before the end of the decade, enhancing the anytime, anywhere feature of a browser-based/Web banking system. And, while it will appear first in larger, metropolitan areas such as New York, Los Angeles, Atlanta, and Orlando, it will quickly spread to midsize and smaller communities because wireless systems will provide access wherever the wired system cannot or will not reach.

In summary, the Web is already driving changes in financial services and this is just the beginning. There is no time for bankers to be complacent or hesitant about emerging technology. While the adoption of a new delivery channel may be difficult for bankers at first, the benefits of operating on the Web through a model that allows financial institutions to maintain control of the interface with the customer is demonstrated by the SFNB experience. The alternative, letting other institutions take charge of the customer relationship by creating a different interface for financial data and management, presents a major threat to the banking industry. Ultimately, SFNB learned that cultivating the customer relationship and providing a human touch is the most important factor in Internet financial services, a lesson that should be taken to heart at traditional financial institutions as well.

4

From Web Strategy
to Implementation
at Liberty Financial Companies

IANG JEON AND WILLIAM P. RICE
LIBERTY FINANCIAL COMPANIES

Introduction

Liberty Financial Companies is a Boston-based asset management organization. At the beginning of 1997, it managed $48 billion of assets on behalf of 1.5 million investors worldwide through an array of fixed, indexed, and variable annuities, private and institutional accounts, and 60 mutual funds. Its operating companies include some well-known names in the business, including Keyport Life Insurance Company, The Colonial Group Inc., Stein Roe & Farnham Inc., Independence Life and Annuity Company, Newport Pacific Management Inc., Independent Financial Marketing Group Inc., and Liberty Asset Management Company. Figure 4.1 is a representation of Liberty Financial's corporate Web site located at www.lib.com.

For an organization as large and complex as Liberty Financial, embarking on a new strategic direction is inevitably complex and far-reaching. In particular, a decision to engage in electronic commerce on the Internet presents a host of issues, challenges, and potential risks that could stand in the way of rapid progress. This chapter examines the factors that led Liberty Financial management to

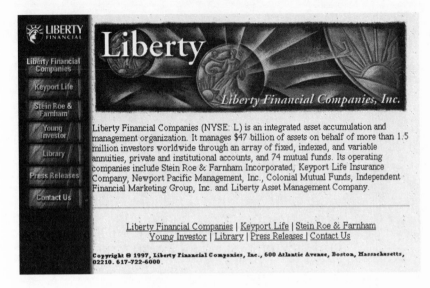

FIGURE 4.1 **Liberty Financial Home Page**

adopt an aggressive and forward-looking electronic commerce strategy and discusses how it combined a versatile system architecture, advanced security solutions, and innovative pilot projects to move quickly from planning to full-scale implementation. In the process, Liberty executives dealt with questions of establishing trust on the Internet, defining the short- and long-term values of moving commerce to the Web, and positioning multiple operating companies within the shifting competitive landscape in financial services and on-line investment. The chapter concludes with some strategic reflections from Liberty's first two years on the Web.

The Trust Factor

Success in the asset management business has always been based on establishing trust between the customer and the company. A customer looking for a financial services product cannot go into a warehouse, kick the tires, or take the product out for a quick spin. A customer buys an annuity or mutual fund based on a combination of objective and intangible factors, including the overall reputation of the company, the past investment performance of the products that company has offered, and the past service the company has provided. It is a relationship of trust—trust that the company will continue to deliver top-notch service, reliability, and performance, and trust that the assets the customer entrusts to the company will be kept safe and grow.

There is also a requirement to build and adapt that trust relationship when financial services companies begin offering products and services through a new technology, be it an ATM at a bank or a Web site on the Internet. Bank customers did not take to ATMs overnight. The technology needed time to gain acceptance; customers needed to learn, over time, that the machines would not lose their deposits, would give them the correct amount of money, and would credit it correctly in their accounts. Similarly, it will take some time for consumers to adapt to the Internet and to learn that they can safely check account balances, make transfers, make purchases, and even redeem shares of financial products over the Internet. To the extent that a financial services company can shorten that trust cycle by offering a compelling combination of convenience and security when introducing its products in an on-line environment, the company will attract a critical mass of customers for these new services.

Liberty Financial has worked over the years to foster a deep sense of trust in the company. The individual Liberty operating companies are some of the most respected names in the business, because they have served their customers with distinction over the decades. Colonial Mutual Funds, which is a mutual funds company that sells its products through broker/dealers, has been serving investors since 1931. Stein Roe & Farnham, which handles Liberty's direct-marketed mutual funds, institutional asset management, and wealth management business, has been, in the words of its slogan, "building wealth for generations." That building of wealth has been going on since Stein Roe & Farnham was founded in 1932. Even this long-standing track record, however, is not enough for customers to automatically shift their trust in Liberty's traditional services onto the new and still largely untrusted platform of the World Wide Web.

A decision to aggressively develop Web products and services carries with it a requirement to demonstrate the highest level of protection for the customer's privacy and assets. It also requires a commitment to customer education and support, especially during the period of market testing and gradual acceptance of the new technology—a period that is in its early stages for Liberty and may last for several more years. The infrastructure required for effective support of secure Web commerce is expensive, and the gradual pace of consumer acceptance almost guarantees that expenditures will outweigh revenues derived from the Web in the short term. In addition to the expense of establishing a secure system on the Web, organizations need to make changes in their in-house, back-end processing to begin providing more integrated statements and services. This helps to explain why most banks and financial institutions have focused their use of the Internet on marketing, publication, and internal applications rather than on offering financial transactions on line.

Balancing Resources and Returns: A Strategic Decision

Liberty Financial executives recognized that the requirements for success in implementing secure electronic commerce programs were rigorous and resource intensive while the short-term rewards would be difficult to quantify. At the same time, they saw that Internet access and the ubiquity of the Web was driving change in all areas of personal and business life. Their conclusion was that the risk in not jumping onto the Internet and developing secure applications was greater than the expense of staking out a leadership position. Companies ignoring the Internet's potential or waiting for someone else to address all the problems will soon scramble to catch up. The real risk is in missing this great revolution in communication and technology and being left behind with an outmoded product. Kenneth R. Leibler, President and CEO of Liberty Financial Companies, summed up the corporate attitude this way: "The Internet may become the most important development in the financial services industry this decade. Liberty Financial is integrating the Internet into its existing business model."

Two members of Liberty Financial's electronic commerce team use their personal experience to underscore the increasing importance of electronic commerce and communication via the Internet in every area of business and personal life. Porter Pierpont Morgan, the Senior Vice President of Marketing at Liberty Financial, took his son Neal to college at Duke University in the fall of 1996 to find that the college of 12,000 students processes 60,000 e-mail messages each day. Every dormitory has a resident technical adviser, who is on call to help students with their computers and Internet connections. E-mailing is the preferred mode of communication for everything from reminders by professors about assignments and upcoming tests to reservations for library books. Some Duke students even use e-mail to set up dates. E-mail is also the way that Porter Morgan, who is in his mid-50s and whose preferred method of communication is by ballpoint pen or telephone, communicates with his son at Duke.

But electronic communication is not being practiced only by college students and adults. It is also becoming increasingly commonplace for grade-school students. Iang Jeon, the Vice President of Electronic Commerce at Liberty Financial Companies, came home from work one day to learn that his second-grade daughter Anna was using a personal identification number, or PIN, instead of lunch money at the school cafeteria. When the students at Anna's school go through the cafeteria lunch line, they enter a four-digit PIN. Every two weeks, they bring in a check from home to pay for the meals. So by the time students now in school and college reach the workforce and become investors, electronic transactions will be second nature to them. Well before then, others will become a lot more comfortable with communicating and getting things done using their computers.

This permeation of the Internet and electronic transactions across age groups coincides with the characteristics of investment and financial services to create a compelling rationale for a strong and early commitment to Web commerce. Why does the Internet seem to lend itself to financial services information? In essence, the financial services industry is not constrained by physical limitations in the delivery of goods and services in the same manner as is a manufacturing firm or a service operation such as a restaurant. Financial services is an information business. A financial services firm such as Liberty Financial Companies provides its investors with information about investments and transactions. Because that delivery of information can be conducted electronically, it is an ideal match for the Internet and the Web. The challenge, in addition to meeting the requirements for security and trust, is in organizing all the financial data in a way that really adds value to individual customers and increases their loyalty to particular business relationships.

The amount of information on the Internet about investing is heartening for a financial services company because it means that the populace is interested in investing. But that same information is likely to represent overload for most people. You could probably find 10 recommendations on the Internet on why to buy and why to sell the same mutual fund. Who do you trust? How do you sort out the information? What information do you accept, and what information do you reject? How does an individual investor determine what information is relevant to his or her situation? What consumers really need is a trusted financial relationship with a brand such as Stein Roe or Keyport or Colonial and a financial adviser or broker/agent who represents such a company and can give an individual investor advice that is relevant to his or her situation.

However, a good brand name, in tandem with a good broker or adviser, is not always enough when offering a service on the Internet. To stand out on the Internet, to cut through all that clutter, a financial services company has to offer information and services that others do not offer or do not offer as completely and competently. A financial services firm also must provide service and information about investing that is tailored to the individual investor with whom it is dealing. Designing Web-appropriate products and services that would distinguish Liberty Financial Companies from the crowd was a fundamental requirement for achieving a competitive advantage through electronic commerce. Providing such products in a secure, customer-responsive environment well ahead of the competition was another. The following sections describe two Liberty Financial initiatives, WebSaver Annuity and LEAPS, that exemplify the company's approach to Web product development and implementation.

Launching the WebSaver Annuity

Liberty Financial was one of the first financial organizations on the Web when www.lib.com opened in early 1995. In keeping with the overall strategy of developing electronic commerce capabilities and learning from pilot projects, managers immediately began looking for opportunities to move beyond the typical information-only, "brochureware" Web site. The development of a new product called WebSaver Annuity created one such opportunity.

WebSaver was conceived and developed by William P. Rice, Director of Corporate Marketing at Liberty Financial, and Jacob Herschler, Vice President of Strategic Marketing at Independence Life and Annuity, one of Liberty's operating companies. Rice was working on developing Liberty Financial's overall corporate Internet presence on the Web and was searching for applications that would demonstrate the potential of the Web to support business growth as well as marketing communications. Herschler was developing a direct-marketing annuity program with Montgomery Ward to market annuities to holders of Montgomery Ward credit cards.

This program represented the first foray of a Liberty Financial company into direct marketing of annuities. The more Rice heard about the Montgomery Ward market annuity, the more he could see the benefits of designing a similar product to market directly on the Web. Such a product would clearly indicate that Liberty Financial Companies, which already had Web sites for itself and several of its operating companies, was committed to providing innovative products and services to meet the changing needs of investors and annuity buyers. Rice and Herschler both realized, though, that innovation for its own sake or jumping into Web commerce just to get out in front of other financial services companies would not move the company's electronic commerce strategy in the right direction. First and foremost, WebSaver had to make sense from a business point of view.

How WebSaver Works on the Web

The WebSaver is a fixed annuity that allows customers to order policies on line from the WebSaver Web site. In the product launch phase, the customer still funds the policy with a check sent through traditional mail to avoid potential security concerns that might hold back consumer acceptance of Internet commerce. The home page for WebSaver, offered by Independence Life and Annuity Company at www.websaver.com, is represented in figure 4.2.

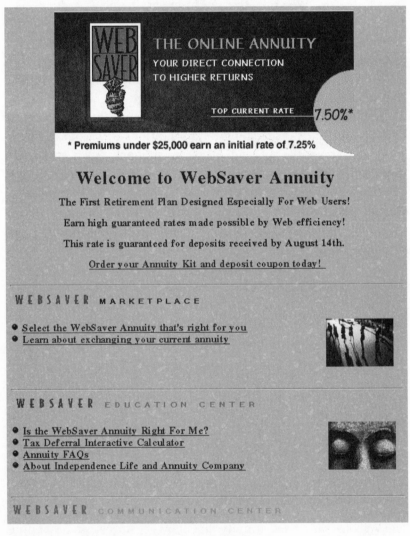

FIGURE 4.2   WebSaver Home Page

The process for marketing and issuing the WebSaver annuity combines Web activity with traditional mail follow-up and payment. Potential customers come to the Web site and, if they choose to purchase the product, fill out an on-line application form and submit it to Liberty Financial. The company opens an account for the customer and sends a payment slip with the contract through the mail. The purchaser then reads the contract, agrees to its terms, signs the deposit slip, and returns it and the payment, again through traditional delivery means. Liberty Financial holds that rate—which was posted on the Web site when the customer sent the on-line application form—for a certain time period, approximately 45 days. The account is closed if not funded at the end of that period. Liberty Financial also takes advantage of e-mail to contact these potential customers shortly before their periods expire. The company also contacts prospects if there is a rate increase; the company will automatically honor the higher rate if the customer's money is received during that time period. So Liberty Financial uses not only the World Wide Web for WebSaver but also electronic mail to market the product effectively.

The WebSaver Annuity cost little to develop and market and could really stand out in the marketplace. That, in turn, allows Liberty Financial to pass those savings on to the consumer. Annuities, which are insurance products designed for retirement savings, are highly price-sensitive products. With a fixed annuity such as Web-Saver, the customer pays an initial premium and the annuity company, which invests that premium, agrees to pay the customer a fixed percentage rate return over a number of years. Liberty Financial found that it could provide an additional 1/2 to 1 percent of income to consumers because of the lower acquisition and servicing costs made possible by the Internet.

The fact that WebSaver was offered directly over the Internet allowed the company to minimize sales and operating costs. For example, WebSaver relies on highly trained annuity specialists who respond to customers by using efficient e-mail instead of the telephone. Liberty Financial worked with its systems staff to integrate the Web page with the company's back-end system to require as little human intervention as possible. Even the design of the Web site discourages phone calls to maximize this cost savings; it offers a toll-free phone number only in the context of getting specific information about exchanging other products to set up a WebSaver annuity.

Since the typical consumer of this product is by definition comfortable using the Internet, most customers seem to prefer the e-mail support option. In the first year of product availability, by far the most popular way of communication from potential customers with questions has been through e-mail. This makes an enormous difference in ongoing support costs for the product. Typically, an annuity company might need 30 or 40 customer support representatives during peak hours. In contrast the WebSaver operation is staffed with only five representatives, who handle the incoming calls but more importantly can turn around a large number of e-mail requests and orders quickly and efficiently.

The Business Advantage

Traditional annuities, on average, cost eight percent to distribute, including commissions to the broker or insurance agent, marketing materials, and wholesaling efforts, which means that a company's cost to acquire $100 worth of premium is about $8. The few traditional annuities that are sold as direct-marketed annuities use newspaper and television advertisements, telemarketing backup, and literature. Those costs can run 4 or 5 percent in terms of acquisition costs. With WebSaver, Liberty Financial attempts to lower the acquisition costs to between 1 and 2 percent. The company has been able to take the savings in distribution costs and put it back into the product in terms of a higher yield. That in turn makes the product more desirable to the consumer.

In addition, WebSaver allows Liberty Financial to expose an entirely new audience to annuities. Roughly 98 percent of annuities are sold after a consumer has a face-to-face session with an insurance agent or broker. WebSaver targeted consumers who typically were direct purchasers and conducted research to determine the best rates. It found that most WebSaver customers already owned annuities and were looking for better rates. The goal of making the product competitive helped the company in writing policies.

There is another advantage of doing annuity business on the Internet rather than by traditional direct methods. The Web gives potential customers the impetus to buy the product, simply by shortening the buying process and presenting essential information to them immediately. Unlike the longer cycle of phone sales followed up by printed marketing materials, on-line customers can access all the information they need directly from the Web site on their own schedules. This means that potential buyers do not lose interest by the time they have the required information in hand.

Since the Web-based marketing, distribution, and support model for WebSaver replaced the traditional large telemarketing force and much of the ongoing cost of maintaining a highly trained customer services force, the investment in the rollout of WebSaver and its annual overhead cost were minimized. A comparison with typical industry costs for bringing annuities to market highlights the difference.

When Liberty Financial comes out with a new annuity program through traditional channels, the company has to create voluminous printed literature to describe it. Liberty Financial can spend hundreds of thousands of dollars to bring out a traditional annuity—understandably limiting the type of offerings that are approved for launch. But the costs do not stop there. With every new piece of literature generated, the company has to train the sales staff to market the product—another major investment in money and staff resources.

In contrast, the total incremental cost for launching the WebSaver annuity (not counting an on-line advertising program and the support staff for the Web site) was about $20,000. This covered the development of graphics for the new Web site, including a WebSaver logo, stationery for correspondence related to the product, and the production of one printed brochure that goes into the fulfillment kit mailed with the contract to new customers. Of course, this low cost also reflects that the complexities of product generation had already been absorbed by the Montgomery Ward model that WebSaver was based on and does not truly account for the many hours that Rice, Herschler, and their staffs put into planning and testing the Web site or the filing procedures required by the regulatory process. Nevertheless, the difference in cost is certainly impressive.

The WebSaver Web site also has an educational function. Through the WebSaver Education Center potential customers can learn about annuities. The Education Center includes frequently asked questions (FAQs) about annuities. An interactive tool at the site allows potential customers to see how the annuity will grow, tax deferred, over the years. Web surfers can also learn how much they will have in retirement if, for example, they put $10,000 in WebSaver. It is a complicated calculation, but the computers behind the scene running the Web site allow Liberty Financial to input different variables. For instance, if a customer wants to retire before age 59 1/2, current IRS rules call for a 10 percent penalty. Liberty Financial is able to show the return, with the 10 percent reduction for early withdrawal. From a compliance standpoint, the computers allow the company to better inform consumers about the different aspects of our products.

Liberty Financial has faced an interesting licensing issue with WebSaver. Since all insurance products must be approved in the state in which they are sold, Liberty Financial has petitioned individual states to have the product licensed or approved by the state's insurance commissioner. The insurance commissioner in some states would not allow WebSaver to go forward without extensive paperwork, simply because the product is distributed over the Internet. From a regulatory standpoint, it has been an interesting exercise. Liberty Financial used the long approval process as a public relations event. Every time WebSaver was approved in a state, the company put out a press release and distributed it to the news media in that state. About three dozen states have approved WebSaver.

Marketing On Line
and Measuring Customer Response

Since the WebSaver was aimed at current Internet users it made sense to focus efforts on on-line marketing of the site, through appropriate newsgroups, posted announcements on the 'Net that Websaver was available, paid advertising on high-traffic financial publication sites, and links from the main Liberty Financial site. A more traditional press release through print and media channels also received a good response. The news releases generated print publicity for the launch of WebSaver in more than 82 publications with a combined circulation of more than 16.5 million subscribers, including the *Wall Street Journal, Business Week,* and *USA Today.* This turned out to be an extremely low-cost way of generating an initial consumer response and attracting traffic to the site, but the growth of traffic was not really dramatic until Liberty Financial invested in direct banner advertising on the Web itself.

Liberty Financial managers saw traffic to the WebSaver site grow gradually, logging up to hundreds of hits daily for the first two months of 1996. To accelerate the amount of traffic and draw more general attention to their product, they decided to experiment with an on-Web advertising campaign with WebSaver banners on a variety of financial sites. One immediate result of this marketing approach was that the number of hits rose 10-fold as soon as the banners began to appear around the Web: from the January 1996 launch to the end of the month, the site attracted 1,264 visitors. In February 1996 this increased to 7,425. Once banner ads started appearing on the Web in March 1996, the number of individual visitors jumped to 48,498 and kept on climbing. Based on these results, the total Web-Saver advertising budget of $150,000 was spent entirely on the Web.

This experience also allowed Liberty Financial to test the value of electronic advertising. Launching a Web product became a multifaceted pilot that allowed managers to learn what worked and did not work in all facets of product presentation, marketing, support, and sales. This generated insights that could be used for planning a more advanced and comprehensive electronic commerce program to follow up on the WebSaver pilot.

WebSaver was positioned and launched as a low-cost electronic commerce pilot program funded on an experimental basis by the corporate marketing budget. But the clear-cut benefits in terms of cost savings, and even the publicity that an innovative Web commerce product generated, were not sufficient to justify the WebSaver business model in and of itself. One of the fundamental questions that needed to be answered was whether this type of product would meet the needs of customers. In terms of evaluation, an important aspect of the program was how well it would sell. In the planning stages it was simply not clear whether prospective customers would be interested in purchasing annuities on the Internet. That basic question was answered quickly. The first customer purchased the product on line within the first 10 days of WebSaver's operation, providing a confirmation of this early foray into electronic commerce by Liberty Financial. WebSaver's success, along with the continuing explosion of publicity and innovation on the Internet, confirmed the senior management view that the Internet offered significant business opportunities that would justify a corporate-wide priority for electronic commerce. This decision was important, because Liberty Financial's next steps were more complex and required an overall corporate investment to create a major advance in security and customer value on the Web.

Trusted Commerce Takes Off: LEAPS

The Liberty Environment for Advanced Personalized Services (LEAPS) was conceived by Iang Jeon, Vice President of Electronic Commerce, as a platform for implementing the company's broader vision of the value of electronic commerce and Web business models for the entire organization. Like WebSaver, LEAPS was implemented as a real business product and also as a prototype for creating a new line of products and services that were intended to take full advantage of the interactive and customization capabilities of the Web. The LEAPS program was designed to place Liberty Financial in the forefront of firms providing the next generation of Internet services by allowing Liberty Financial's operating companies to deliver personalized, interactive experiences to their investors and the intermediaries who serve them.

The first wave of commerce on the Internet involved simply putting information about one's company on a Web site and letting customers respond either by telephone or e-mail. The second wave of commerce on the Internet involves both secure transactions and personalization, and LEAPS builds on the latest technology developments to enable true customer relationship management.

It is important to note that LEAPS is primarily a strategic rather than technology-driven initiative. The goals of the electronic commerce planning team were related to the business rationale and long-term benefits for the entire corporation rather than letting the latest wave of Web technology determine the objectives of electronic commerce. At Liberty Financial, the fundamental business is gathering and retaining assets, and growth opportunities stem from improving customer relationships. As one electronic commerce team member described the strategic thinking that shaped LEAPS:

> The greatest asset we have is our customer base and if we can increase the value of those assets by servicing their needs more effectively and in ways that help them to invest more successfully, then that effort will repay itself many times. If we can combine this with increased efficiency and reduced costs on the operations side, we will become more competitive and increase our flexibility. When you are running a business, you can focus on trying to increase revenues and/or streamlining the business. LEAPS provides multiple opportunities for doing both. The intranet focus is making operations more efficient, and the public Web features improve our relationships with customers and provide support for our traditional distribution channels.

The LEAPS project is based on the fundamental premise that personal computer use and Internet access are going to become mainstream. LEAPS is designed for the early majority, the 35 to 40 million who will be on the Internet in the near future, not the early adopters, the 5 to 6 million who are out there as of this writing. The real opportunity lies in the early majority, those in the mainstream, who are not as willing to learn by reading complex computer manuals or surfing from Web site to Web site to find the combination of information and service that suits them best. In an effort to attract and keep that early majority, Liberty Financial has provided features such as ease of use, ease of navigation, and lower barriers of entry. Because the site is personalized, for example, the user has to enter vital statistics such as age, securities owned, and so forth only once. Most of today's on-line financial planning tools and calculators require this type of data to be entered each time a Web site is accessed. The Liberty sites "remember" these facts and will also reproduce the way the site has been personalized or customized by the user for each subsequent use. "Smart tools" and financial calculators on the site will then use this information.

In addition to serving customer information needs directly through the Web, LEAPS allows Liberty operating companies that use broker/dealer channels to take the same high level of functionality and present it to different channels for a different flavor, making it possible for agents to add more value to their interactions with customers. The underlying architecture of LEAPS allows the server to store the personal interactions with customers and customer records for agents, who will be able to search by the name and account information of their clients—a capability they simply did not have in the former system.

Beyond Secure Transactions to Integrated Financial Services

For a company seeking to establish leadership in electronic commerce today, simply allowing customers to conduct secure transactions on the Web is not enough. As early as September 1996, a report on trends in electronic commerce in "Strategic Insight," a mutual funds industry newsletter, observed, "Transactions on the Internet will become a standard service very quickly, and such capabilities will not provide a differentiating competitive advantage to fund companies over time." While LEAPS definitely supports secure transactions, it looks beyond this function to a broader array of services to leverage the Web for all of Liberty Financial's operating companies and most importantly for the targeted customer and investor. To keep ahead of the Web development curve and address the various distribution channels represented by its operating companies, Liberty Financial needs maximum flexibility in the design and operation of its electronic commerce program. This requirement makes the product-development stage more complex up front, but it also increases the value of the project for the company as a whole and becomes a key way to differentiate the Liberty Financial companies on the Web.

As the number of companies offering secure transactions on the Web continues to increase, a strategy for such differentiation is essential. Even today, a company such as Liberty Financial must cut through the clutter of several hundred thousand commercial Web sites, many of which offer financial services and information, to reach the end user of its services. At last count there were more than 7,000 mutual funds for sale in America. That is more than all the stocks on the New York Stock Exchange. As a result of that clutter, the asset management business is becoming largely commoditized. Distinguishing a brand and capturing mindshare are becoming more and more difficult, not only with investors but also with intermediary distributors such as agents and brokers.

The LEAPS project, which initially was launched on Liberty Financial's Stein Roe Mutual Funds and Keyport Life sites, cuts through the clutter, giving the user a personalized experience, whether that user is a direct-market customer of Stein Roe funds or a broker or other intermediary who sells Keyport annuities. Keyport Life Insurance Company conducts the majority of Liberty Financial's annuity business. The Keyport LEAPS site, represented in figure 4.3, offers a variety of cutting-edge yet user-friendly services for the representatives and insurance agents who sell Keyport annuities.

A Framework for Rapid Project Deployment

The LEAPS team identified key components of the project early in the planning process and also recognized that moving quickly through the planning, design, and implementation stages and getting new products into the electronic marketplace before the competition would itself require an innovative approach. The team focused first on identifying the business applications most likely to advance Liberty Financial's leadership position in the field and then designed functionality around these to avoid being driven by the technology for its own sake. The group considered its primary responsibilities as being the architects of corporate-wide strategic change and the clients who needed to describe exactly what they wanted built to a variety of construction specialists. As long as they could find the right partners and specialists to build the components as specified,

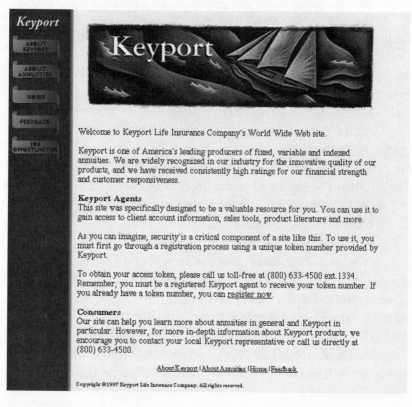

Welcome to Keyport Life Insurance Company's World Wide Web site.

Keyport is one of America's leading producers of fixed, variable and indexed annuities. We are widely recognized in our industry for the innovative quality of our products, and we have received consistently high ratings for our financial strength and customer responsiveness.

Keyport Agents
This site was specifically designed to be a valuable resource for you. You can use it to gain access to client account information, sales tools, product literature and more.

As you can imagine, security is a critical component of a site like this. To use it, you must first go through a registration process using a unique token number provided by Keyport.

To obtain your access token, please call us toll-free at (800) 633-4500 ext.1334. Remember, you must be a registered Keyport agent to receive your token number. If you already have a token number, you can register now.

Consumers
Our site can help you learn more about annuities in general and Keyport in particular. However, for more in-depth information about Keyport products, we encourage you to contact your local Keyport representative or call us directly at (800) 633-4500.

About Keyport | About Annuities | Home | Feedback

FIGURE 4.3   **Keyport Life Insurance Company LEAPS Site**

there was no need for Liberty Financial to carry out every part of the plan directly.

To ensure that the needs of diverse Liberty Financial operating companies were addressed, each of the companies involved in the launch of LEAPS set up internal Internet task forces to discuss the specific implementation of LEAPS and Web commerce within their businesses. At Stein Roe, for example, an operating company that markets a family of 18 no-load mutual funds directly to the consumer, the Internet task force was chaired by a marketing manager and also included active participation from shareholder services, legal, and customer support areas. Combining centralized electronic commerce planning and implementation responsibility with each operating company's ability to specify its priorities in serving a particular market or product group was especially important because of the size and complexity of Liberty Financial and its operating companies. This diversity could potentially slow down the process and make it difficult to reach consensus on particular electronic commerce priorities.

On the other hand, the range of financial services and distribution channels represented within Liberty presented a tremendous opportunity for leveraging successful projects across many different types of business groups and customer relationships. Ensuring that the implementation of the LEAPS project would be modular and flexible increased the efficiency of implementation while serving a broad range of interests and needs among the operating companies to get the most value from electronic commerce. The electronic commerce implementation required participants to figure out how the corporation as a whole should maximize the value obtained from the technology, specify what to do, and assemble solutions in cooperation with outside partners while minimizing the need for slower, in-house development.

The planning process established a number of fundamental decision points that helped to accelerate the timetable for implementation. These included "buy versus build," indicating that the project would integrate off-the-shelf solutions whenever possible in preference to designing applications from the ground up; "parallel efforts," coordination of simultaneous testing and implementation of components such as the user interface, site content development, back-end integration, and security solutions; "iterative development," including rapid prototyping; and "learn by doing" rather than creating elaborate specifications in advance. These decision points also reflected some of the concrete objectives that were established for LEAPS:

 ▷ Start by upgrading the internal IT architecture to enable modular system components
 ▷ Reduce reliance on proprietary solutions and emphasize standardization and integration

▷ Select strategic partners to build and maintain nonfinancial components of the system

▷ Provide the highest possible level of security and flexibility

The first order of business, upgrading internal IT and Web architecture and migrating the Liberty Financial system infrastructure to a modular, flexible approach, provided a new foundation for future project development. This decision reflected the perspective that resolving the problems posed by piecemeal integration of legacy systems and figuring out how to make existing data available in a secure and controlled manner would never be accomplished without rethinking the entire system from the ground up. The mainframe systems simply were not designed for the demands of many thousands of real-time remote access users who required individual, customized responses gathered from a variety of data sources. Rather than continuing to tweak the older systems through retrospective system development, it would be faster to address the entire list of project requirements at once.

As a result of this approach, Liberty now has an object-oriented system environment with the user interface, business rules, and various applications divided into three modular layers, as illustrated in figure 4.4. Adherence to standards and the linking of various components through Web servers provides the glue that holds all the pieces together. This approach allows a much greater extent of plug-and-play implementation of various solutions as they become available. Jeon points out that it is still not perfect but certainly a lot better than the old method. The user interface level of the system shapes the look and feel of each site to fit the needs of the primary customers, while specific business rules can be designed to collect or provide different levels of information. New functionality, for example, an integrated financial planning program that allows customers to track all their investments, can be built into the applications layer where it can also interact with data from legacy systems.

The architecture and system design also free managers to select the best technical solution for a particular application rather than being locked into a particular vendor or software program. Liberty Financial is currently using Sybase for the relational database, for ex-

Project LEAPS

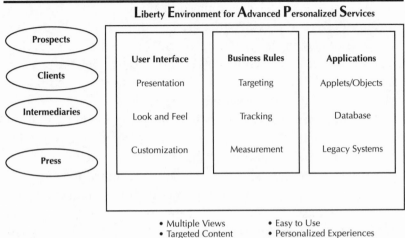

FIGURE 4.4   Liberty System Architecture for Leaps

ample, but it can migrate to any program that may offer advanced features in the future. Especially in the rapidly changing environment of the Web, companies have to look at business-driven technology solutions rather than depending on proprietary products from a certain vendor who then decides when to upgrade. The new corporate electronic commerce architecture addresses major issues including security, personalization, and customization, as well as supporting some of the back-end interfaces that are required to give users the broadest possible access to information and support services.

The need for back-end integration of massive amounts of data embedded in legacy systems has been a major barrier for many financial companies as they contemplate integrated services on the Web. Liberty's system architecture also helps to facilitate this process. It can encapsulate a legacy system with an object and fit it into the environment of the Web. All types of data, services, transaction requirements, and information can be integrated into the new architecture without radical changes in the business rules of the system. Without having to overhaul the underlying database the LEAPS architecture can create personalization and customization of Web interactions with individual customers. Finally, it can provide this function in different ways and with various interfaces on the Web to meet the specific needs of staff and customers at the operating company level.

Another key component of the strategy for rapid LEAPS development was outsourcing parts of the project. The Liberty Financial electronic commerce team identified its core role as defining the business rules that would be applied to the interactions between customers and back-end data. These rules are at the heart of the customer relationship and where opportunities for improving products and services will originate. The other aspects of the project, from managing Internet connectivity and hosting the Web server content to designing the look and feel of the Web pages, could be contracted out.

Based on the ground rule of buying rather than building, Liberty Financial established four partnerships to supply critical project components. The actual design of the Web sites, including the graphics and navigational aids, were provided by Liberty Financial's advertising agency, Cohn Godley Norwood. At the connectivity and systems integration level of the project, the key partner was IDD, which provided the hosting, systems integration, and financial content for LEAPS. California-based BroadVision supplied the personalization system and enabled a customer-tailored interface for diverse users. To ensure the highest level of security, BBN, of Cambridge, Massachusetts, developed and implemented digital certificates for the project. All these activities were under way simultaneously and coordinated by the electronic commerce team to keep the project moving on a learn-by-doing basis.

The final guiding principle for LEAPS was to provide the most secure, most flexible platform for customer and account interactions via the Web. The next section discusses the chosen solution—issuing digital certificates—and explains how it meets Liberty Financial's goal to combine high security with high individual attention.

Inside LEAPS: Certificates for Secure Integration

Security for the LEAPS project is grounded in a system of digital certificates. Certificate authorities on the Internet serve as trusted third parties who can authenticate the identity of each participant in a transaction and issue encrypted digital tokens of such identity in the form of public and private keys. When exchanged and validated by all participants using secure Web standards, these keys link users to messages and also serve to make the transaction legal and binding. If an encrypted message is opened or tampered with by anyone other than the intended recipient, the key will not be able to open it. A number of different companies, including Verisign, GTE, and Cybertrust, have taken on the role of certificate authority. Liberty Financial selected BBN to provide the digital certificates that underpin LEAPS, allowing Liberty to be its own certificate authority.

Customers of the Liberty Financial companies participating in the launch of the LEAPs program have the opportunity to obtain personal digital certificates at no cost. While any user will be welcome to take advantage of the basic information on Liberty Financial company Web sites, the financial planning and other customized information will require initial certification for participation. Once a user has been issued a digital certificate, this identification will allow the Web site to identify and authenticate the user the next time he or she requests access. This in turn provides the combination of security and personal identity that enables a user to conduct transfers, request redemptions, and make purchases of mutual funds.

Figure 4.5 describes the steps involved in obtaining a certificate through a Liberty Financial site. The process starts with an off-line interaction between Liberty and a customer to collect or verify personal identity information that may be used to verify identify later in the process. Once that information is established and recorded at Liberty, the customer receives a temporary identity token, or password, that authorizes him or her to initiate the on-line certificate request process.

When users enter a secure Liberty Financial Web site, they see a message on the screen asking whether they want a digital certificate. There is no obligation to do so, but visitors without certificates will not have access to many of the customized, value-added features of the site. Since the process of certificate registration is fast and simple, the assumption is that regular visitors will eventually decide to register in order to access the full spectrum of services available. To complete the on-line certificate request, the user provides identification and verification information such as account number and the one-time verified access password he or she has already received from the company during off-line interaction.

Public Key Infrastructure

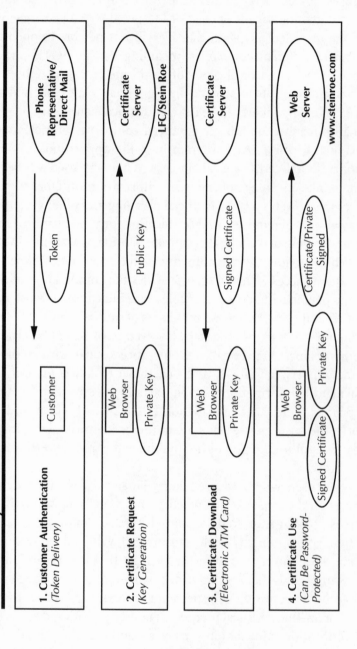

FIGURE 4.5 Digital Certificate Process

The site then conducts an authorization process, which usually takes only a few moments. During that process, the user's Web browser generates two unique encryption keys, one private and one public, that are put on the hard drive of the user's computer. The user's private key encrypts information that can only be decoded by another party with the user's public key. The other party uses the public key to encrypt information that only the user's private key can decode. The private key must be kept confidential.

The user's digital certificate is then officially issued by "signing" the user's public key with a private key that is contained on a secure Liberty Financial Companies server. Once this step has been accomplished, the user is ready and authorized for secure interactions.

Liberty Financial managers believe that the commercial future of the Internet is made far more promising by the perfection of digital certificates. Certificates open up a world of possibilities for expanding electronic commerce. The most obvious application is that deployment of certificates makes Web financial transactions and e-mail exchanges secure by providing a link between the sender and the message that cannot be repudiated, as well as by encrypting the contents of the message while it travels over the public Internet. Because it is based on documentation of identity, possession of a digital certificate also can give users access to other Web servers and services beyond Liberty. Some states, for example, are legislating digital signature laws, which recognize the validity of contracts signed on line with digital certificates.

Ensuring the security of on-line transactions and communication is a fundamental requirement for Liberty's electronic commerce strategy, but since the certificate process is relatively easy to replicate, the higher level of security it provides will not in itself differentiate the LEAPS service from others on the Web over the long term. Nevertheless, this infrastructure represents a significant step in the process of creating truly customized and convenient financial services on the Web. Using the new tools to build a closer relationship with customers and to respond more directly to their needs represents the more lasting added value of LEAPS. The certification process plays a key part in enabling a new level of customization at Liberty.

Personalized and customized Web sites become much more feasible when each user has a unique digital certificate. The Web service automatically checks for the certificate so that the user does not have to enter a long personal identification code each time before entering, as is required by many secure sites. With a digital certificate, the user merely clicks on the certificate that has been downloaded to the computer's hard drive and his or her identity is automatically verified. Because that site cannot be breached by an outsider, the individual can enter confidential account information, such as securities owned and account number, and also begin to take advantage of the responses and advice that are personalized to his or her particular set of circumstances. Clearly this helps users get more from the time they spend on the Web. Behind the scenes, Liberty Financial can keep track of and calculate changes in account balance for users each time they access the site. Each interaction with the Web information will be captured and matched automatically to the appropriate digital certificate so that the company can also evaluate how well the information and other customer needs are being met.

Personalization: The Next Generation of Services

Personalization, therefore, is a key component of the LEAPS sites. It starts as soon as a certificate has been issued. On his or her next visit, a user chooses the site's appearance and features. For the launch of the service, that primarily means adjusting the look and feel of the site—the ability to make the type size larger, to add buttons on the navigation bar, and even to determine what appears on the home page. The user can also choose which news topics he or she wants to keep track of from the news source that comes to the site. The ability to customize the site with larger typeface is just one of the ways in which LEAPS is targeting older consumers who have personal computers—not just the 20-something crowd that is primarily associated with PC use.

Liberty Financial has also developed a series of smart tools and calculators for use on the sites. The retirement calculator can be used either by an individual customer on the Stein Roe site or by a broker or agent accessing the Keyport site.

An important feature of the Stein Roe site is the Portfolio Snapshot. This portfolio tracking tool automatically includes account information for Stein Roe customers, and additional securities can be added. The tool prices those holdings daily. Because the site is personalized and secure, every time the user accesses the Stein Roe site, he or she will have access to that personalized Portfolio Snapshot, which will automatically calculate the value of each individual security, including reinvested dividends.

Liberty Financial has gone to great lengths to provide a full range of support services on LEAPS for the broker or agent in the field. For example, a broker in the field can instantly call up and print any of a dozen forms or brochures a client might ask for or need to fill out during a visit. This could be the difference between closing and not closing a sale during a customer visit. Or an agent might be on a call to a client who bought a variable annuity a while back and cannot remember when. The broker can go on line, tap into his or her Keyport site and discover that the client bought the variable annuity in April of 1986. A broker can find the rate on that variable annuity today and what the client can expect to get when it comes due. Before the implementation of LEAPS, an agent might have been able to get some of the information by calling the home office—if the call was during business hours. By helping an agent attract and retain customers, Keyport will enhance the relationship with the agent and increase business.

This customization becomes the foundation for a number of additional value-added services that can promote growth and revenue and provide a better basis for serving customers and enhancing the quality of their relationships with Liberty Financial Companies. The same is true for existing channel relationships; Liberty managers do not want to replace the existing broker and agent channels at a company such as Keyport, but they see the need to use the Web and the capabilities of LEAPS to make these agents more effective and productive.

The personalization allows Liberty Financial to learn more about its customer base and therefore to be proactive in marketing to those customers. If a Stein Roe site user enters her age as 63 and her status as single, employed, and without children, for example,

Stein Roe will not send her information about saving for her children's college education. But Stein Roe might send target messages to her home page about planning for her retirement. Conversely, a user who is 43, married, and part of a two-income household with teenage children might receive a targeted message that offers him products and advice on how to save for both his retirement and the education of his children.

In the future, individuals will most likely be building their own, completely personalized Web sites. The company will have a single Web page graphic, coupled with a slate of options. The individual user can pick and choose what to put on that page.

Examples from the First Launch Sites

The Keyport and Stein Roe sites include the following:

Account access. Stein Roe customers have secure, private access to their account information on line. Keyport agents and brokers have access to information on their customers.

Transactions. Stein Roe customers have the ability to conduct transactions such as exchanges and purchases from linked bank accounts.

Back-end information inquiry. Representatives have access to up-to-date rate and pricing information.

Interactivity. A variety of interactive financial calculators and worksheets are available, including retirement planning, asset allocation, and college cost calculations.

Customization. Users can select from different graphic treatments, custom navigation views, and different font sizes for readability.

Sales support. Keyport brokers and insurance agents have print-on-demand applications and forms, sales illustrations, and sales literature requests.

Financial content. Users get delayed quotes on stocks, NAVs on mutual funds, news, price charts, and fundamental company analysis.

Measuring the Value for Liberty Financial and Its Operating Companies

The real bottom line of the LEAPS project is, indeed, the bottom line—making sales. This is an electronic commerce endeavor grounded in retaining and attracting clients and assets. This is not an exercise in technology for technology's sake. Key objectives are as follows:

Increasing assets. Our electronic commerce plan is intended to support the fundamental business of gathering and retaining assets.

Serving customers. We must meet the needs and preferences of customers (both direct and intermediary) via electronic delivery of information and services. A key point of the electronic commerce initiative is strong support of our intermediary distribution channels.

Lowering costs. Significant cost savings can be realized over time through effective use of electronic commerce as electronic distribution replaces physical delivery of paper materials, as customer- and broker-initiated Internet access displaces toll-free telephone charges, and as timely availability of appropriate material lowers opportunity cost in terms of missed sales opportunities and shorter sales cycles. The delivery of documents on line rather than through the mail could save Liberty Financial millions of dollars in paper and postage costs. Liberty Financial has 1.4 million investors, many of whom receive quarterly statements plus one prospectus each year, to say nothing of the marketing materials Liberty puts in the mail.

Conclusions from the Liberty Financial Experience

Liberty Financial Companies is just getting started. While Liberty Financial feels it began diving into electronic commerce over the Internet while everybody else was watching from the shore, management realizes that there is a long, arduous journey ahead. Nonetheless, our early plunge into the Internet ocean, we believe, gives us an advantage over other, later entrants. Liberty Financial will have a base of on-line customers it knows well. It will be able to react to the needs of those customers. It can test different strategies. Because of its personalization capabilities and track record, the one-to-one environment gives Liberty Financial a marketing laboratory. It can test an idea or a product or the way it does business with its entire base of LEAPS users. And, consequently, it can be much more responsive to its user base.

A leadership strategy for electronic commerce cannot succeed based on any single capability or service on the Web, but positioning Liberty Financial Companies to be the most advanced, secure, integrated, and value-added financial services provider on the Web is a goal aimed at keeping Liberty at the forefront of new developments in electronic commerce. The lessons from implementing WebSaver Annuity and LEAPS will help to keep the momentum strong.

5

Smart Cards
in Web-Based E-Commerce

SCOTT B. GUTHERY
SCHLUMBERGER ELECTRONIC TRANSACTIONS

Introduction

A smart card is a secure, portable, tamper-resistant data-storage device containing up to 16 kilobytes of personal information. It is the exact size of a credit card and contains a computer with as much power as the original minicomputers. Data stored in a smart card are accessed by placing the card in (contact) or near (contactless) a smart card reader and providing the specific security access codes associated with the data desired. A smart card costs between $3 and $30 depending on its communication features, memory size, processor capabilities, and software functionalities. Integrated-circuit cards, which contain only memory but none of the other features of smart cards, are also available, but the discussion in this chapter applies to cards that contain both memory and a processor.

More than 70 million smart cards worth $500 million were manufactured and distributed in 1996, and their use is doubling every year. The worldwide market for smart cards and associated smart card products and services in 1996 generated approximately $2 billion in sales and is growing at the rate of about 20 percent per year.

The U.S. market for smart cards is roughly 15 percent of the world-wide market.

The personal data stored in a smart card can include *value* (e.g., money, frequent buyer points, telephone call minutes, food stamps, welfare entitlements), *identity* (e.g., GSM cellular phone subscriber identity, RSA private keys, X.509 certificate, name/address/telephone, emergency medical treatment), *authorizations* (e.g., pay TV, bank account, building access, prescriptions, subscriptions, database and network access), *certificates* (e.g., driver's license, passport, amateur radio license, diploma, special training), and *records* (e.g., vaccinations, personal preferences, address book).

Smart cards are already used in a variety of commercial and governmental applications. The biggest programs are GSM telephone subscriber identity and pay TV. The student ID cards at the University of Michigan, Florida State University, and Ohio Old Dominican College are smart cards that can be used to pay for laundry, buy pizza, ride buses, borrow library books, and enter buildings. Mondex and VISACash cards are on trial in a number of U.S. and international cities and can be used in lieu of pocket change for everyday purchases. Smart cards can be used in parking meters in San Francisco and Washington, D.C. The U.S. Department of Defense is rolling out a program of 12 million cards, and a number of states including Wyoming, Ohio, Texas, and Utah are using smart cards for welfare benefits.

Historically, smart card usage has been dominated by banks, bankcard associations, national governments, and other financial institutions. Recently however a number of nonfinancial business segments such as communication, information technology, computer, transportation, hotel, health, entertainment, and retail have begun to experiment with multiapplication smart card programs that contain financial and nonfinancial applications. A common application of these programs is to use part of the capability of the smart card and then sell or rent the remainder to other applications. The income from these "card real estate" sales can merely offset the cost of the card program or actually turn a profit. These multiapplication smart card programs will have the effect of pushing the technology contained in the card. Today's 8-bit microcontroller processors will yield to 16- and 32-bit RISC processors, and 16 KB EEPROM memory will turn into 256 KB FLASH memory before the turn of the century.

Its tamper-resistant and portability features, along with its ability to combine on one secure processor value exchange, identity establishment, and access authorization applications, make a smart card a natural candidate for inclusion in Internet commerce systems. Strong international standards covering the physical form and basic communication protocols of smart cards ensure both system interoperability and healthy competition among smart card manufacturers and service providers. The recent publication of open specifications for using smart cards with personal computers and World Wide Web browsers and the ability to program the smart card's computer using the Java programming language mean that a firm technical foundation has been laid on which smart card–enabled Internet applications can be built.

Chapter Overview

This chapter begins with a brief summary of smart card technology and market segments in the industry. The technical background included will make the rest of the chapter accessible for those who are not familiar with smart cards. The bibliography contains a number of references to excellent and exhaustive treatments of smart card technology and the industry. This section concludes with a discussion of recent smart card developments and applications in the United States, with a special focus on the use of smart cards to support secure electronic commerce and other products and services on the World Wide Web.

The next section details the development of a new technological link between smart cards and the Web: the use of Java on a smart card. One barrier to expanding the use of smart cards in Web applications has been the difficulty of programming smart cards. Creating a smart card that runs Java provides a programming environment familiar to Web builders and opens up a host of new possibilities for integrating smart cards with the World Wide Web. This section includes the Java card's technical underpinnings, its potential applications, and the impact multiapplication smart cards may have on the next wave of e-commerce on the Web.

Smart cards are by no means the only way to facilitate e-commerce, but they have a number of significant advantages over the traditional credit card model and some of the other e-commerce models being fielded. The final section covers the particular contributions that smart cards can make to both anonymous and nonanonymous e-commerce. In the context of nonanonymous e-commerce, this section covers the issues surrounding on-line identity and authentication, why they are needed, and how smart cards can make a unique contribution to their establishment.

Actually, the vast majority of commercial transactions conducted each day are done so without the need to establish an identity. They are conducted anonymously using cash. We will also discuss how smart cards—perhaps even the very same smart card that is used to establish identity—can also be used for anonymous or cashlike e-commerce. Although the contribution of smart cards here is by no means unique—there are a number of anonymous value-transfer schemes discussed elsewhere in this book—smart card cash has the unique property of being useful at the local store and in a soda machine as well as on the 'Net.

After covering the ways a smart card could be used as a payment instrument in e-commerce, we will look at some more prosaic and emerging uses of smart cards. Some of these—such as micromarketing—are linked to the identity issue, and some—such as electronic coupons—simply use the smart card as a new and more efficient way of doing an old job. New technologies are typically used to substitute for old technologies before they find a voice of their own and call us to new possibilities that were simply unreachable from the old technologies. In the emerging uses section we will try to conjecture where smart cards are calling us.

Smart Card Essentials

Smart cards were first conceived of in 1968 by two German engineers, Helmut Gröttrupp and Jurgen Dethloff. They were reinvented in 1970 by Dr. Kunitaka Arimura in Japan and independently redis-covered four years later by the journalist Roland Moreno in France. Through the Arimura Institute, Dr. Arimura holds the Japanese patents for smart cards; and Moreno holds them for the rest of the world through Innovatron. Neither Arimura nor Moreno specified the size or architecture of a smart card computer, and the late 1970s and early 1980s saw much experimentation from very simple memory-only cards to extremely complex dual-processor cards.

Smart cards found their first widespread commercial application as a solution to the problem of credit card fraud in a low-technology setting—French restaurants. By requiring a cardholder to demon-strate knowledge of a personal identification number (PIN) stored in the memory of a microprocessor-enhanced debit card when the card was presented for payment, smart cards in restaurants reduced fraudulent charges by an order of magnitude.

Shortly thereafter France Telecom began using prepaid memory cards in pay telephones. The cards reduced the amount of damage done to pay telephones by criminals trying to steal coins, as well as the expense of collecting, transporting, protecting, and counting all that loose change. But France Telecom benefited financially three ad-ditional ways. First, from the float because the cards were prepaid. Second from the seignorage because the cards quickly became col-lectors' items and many were never used. And finally, from advertis-ing revenues because the surfaces of the phone cards were sold for advertising.

The Japanese and later the Germans were more aggressive in us-ing smart cards for nonfinancial purposes. Japanese applications in-cluded building access, employee IDs, and car maintenance records. The German government provides every citizen with a health records smart card.

The business model initially adopted by organizations running smart card programs was to give the card away for free, charging only for the value that the card contained and not for the card itself. As a result there was constant cost pressure to tailor the card exactly to the application at hand. That is, the smart card should contain just enough technology to accomplish the single, well-defined appli-cation for which it was being designed. The result was a plethora of unique smart card configurations. The spectrum from very cheap 128-byte memory cards used for pay telephones to smart cards containing microprocessors and relatively complex programs was spanned by purpose-built smart cards, each card associated with a single application.

The advent of multiapplication smart cards and the steep economies of scale in microcontroller manufacture have broken down the purpose-built model. Although memory cards, because of their incredibly high volume and overarching concern with price, will probably always be use specific, the number of different application-specific configurations of microprocessor cards has declined as the total number of cards produced has increased. Multiapplication smart cards are also increasing the demand for larger and more capable smart cards with larger data-storage capacity and faster processors.

Technology

A smart card is a tamper-resistant data-storage device with a modest albeit crypto-enhanced microprocessor in a familiar, wallet-friendly credit card form. The primary task of the microprocessor is to guard the data stored in the smart card and to check the identity of any person or computer requesting access to it. After establishing the requester's identity, the microprocessor checks to see whether the person or computer is authorized to receive the data it is requesting. Then it either turns it over or denies access.

Several features of the smart card, including its secure data-storage capabilities and its cryptoprocessing capabilities, have attracted designers of Web commerce systems. In addition, smart cards are network computers in their own right. They are the smallest servers and therefore fit naturally into the Web architecture. They are eminently portable and can be easily associated with the Web regardless of the cardholder's location. Finally, smart cards actively protect the cardholder's personal data by tamper resistance and evidence. They will not release information without the cardholder's permission and require anybody possessing the card to prove he or she is the authorized cardholder before permission can be considered.

A question that must be addressed by any Web commerce system is whether people are who they say they are. When buyers present themselves as merely packets of bits from the Internet, all of the subtle human checks built into face-to-face, telephonic, and postal commerce are missing. The bits may say that they are from Sally Green at 1234 Main Street in Oxford, Ohio, but do the bits lie?

The same question was being asked and answered by smart cards in the French restaurant. There the question was phrased as "Are you the person that goes with this card?" The card created a linkage between a physical person and an instrument of commerce. The same linkage is needed for e-commerce. It is essential to link the package of bits carried over the Internet to a physical person or other legal entity that will be accountable for the outcome of the transaction. What was not necessary in the French restaurant was an answer to the customer question "Are you the waiter that goes with this restaurant?" but in e-commerce the customer has to be assured of the merchant's identity just as much as the merchant has to be assured of the customer's.

The single-chip computer in a smart card is an off-the-shelf 8-bit microcontroller with hardware security features and ever more frequently a modular arithmetic coprocessor for cryptology calculations. The two most popular instruction sets or cores for the smart card computer are the Motorola 6805 and the Intel 8051 instruction sets. Smart card chips are manufactured by a number of companies including ATMEL, Mikron, NEC, Motorola, Philips, SGS-Thomson, Hitachi, Oki, Siemens, and Texas Instruments.

While most 8-bit microcontrollers have the ability to address 64 KB of 8-bit memory, no popular smart cards contain this much. The size of a smart card chip is constrained by the bending it must bear without breaking in the holder's wallet or purse and is thus typically kept to around 25 square millimeters. This limited silicon real estate together with the cost constraints of some large applications mean that the typical smart card contains 4 to 20 KB of memory for both programs and data.

The memory space of the smart card computer is of three kinds: random access memory (RAM), nonvolatile read/write memory (NVM), and write-only memory (ROM). The random access memory holds temporary values such as intermediate calculations when a program is running on the computer. The read/write memory stores cardholder data such as name, credit card account number, Social Security number, or a private encryption key. The read-only memory holds the programs that are run on the smart card processor.

The memory on a smart card is organized this way for a number of reasons. First, roughly speaking, a RAM location takes up eight times more space and an NVM location four times more space than a ROM location. Therefore if you want to get as much information as possible on a smart card you use ROM whenever you can, then NVM, and only as a last resort RAM. Second, a smart card does not carry its own power supply and is only on when plugged into a smart card terminal such as a PC. Consequently any permanent data on the smart card have to be in a type of memory that holds its data where there is no power, that is, NVM or ROM.

The single-chip smart card computer is embedded in a chip carrier that is placed into an indentation in a plastic card and covered by contacts (see figure 5.1). The location of the computer chip on the plastic card and the configuration of the contacts for contact smart cards are set by an international standard called ISO 7816.

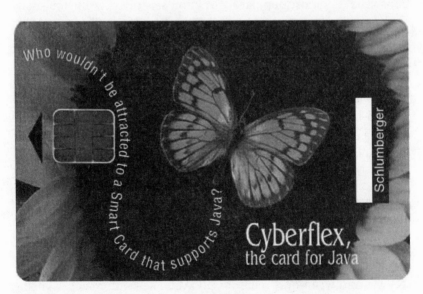

FIGURE 5.1   A Schlumberger Smart Card

There are a number of tamper-resistant and tamper-detection features in the chip itself and in the carrier and its surroundings. For example, the computer may refuse to operate if the clock signal or power being supplied to it is outside of certain bounds. Some memory locations can only be addressed by instructions stored in ROM. The chip may be destroyed by attempts to detach it from the card or the carrier. The particulars of these physical security features vary among chip manufacturers and are closely guarded. It is exactly these features that make smart cards so attractive to the designers of Web e-commerce systems. Fortunately details about them need not be known to make effective and innovative use of smart cards.

The latest generation of smart card chips includes a modular arithmetic coprocessor to help speed cryptological calculations. These modular arithmetic coprocessors perform the following calculation

a * b modulo n

much more quickly than it can be performed on the microcontroller itself. This calculation is at the heart of many of the encryption algorithms used in e-commerce for both private communication and establishing identity.

Analysis of the Smart Card Industry Today

Because of a number of factors including security concerns and domination by large institutional customers, the smart card market has been a closed, almost hidden, market since its inception. The market has been characterized by a small number of suppliers making large runs of purpose-built cards for a small number of large consumers. This insularity has tended to stifle both innovation and application of smart cards. The recent discovery of the general utility of smart cards particularly by the network community and the growing availability of smart card manufacturing equipment are rapidly opening and changing the smart card marketplace.

Figure 5.2 follows a smart card from creation through use and shows the six market segments of the smart card industry.

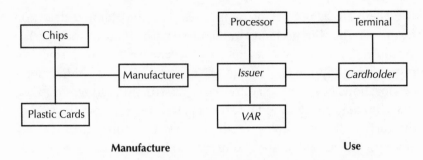

Manufacture   **Use**

FIGURE 5.2 **The Smart Card from Creation through Use**

The smart card industry market segments are as follows:

Segment: Chips
1995 U.S. Size: $10 million
Companies: Philips, Siemens, Motorola, Hitachi, SGS-Thomson, Texas Instruments
Segment: Plastic Cards
1995 U.S. Size: $5 million
Companies: Malso, Kirk Plastics, Golden State Plastics
Segment: Smart Card Manufacturer
1995 U.S. Size: $2 million
Companies: Schlumberger, Gemplus, Orga, US3, Bull CP8
Segment: Terminal Manufacturer
1995 U.S. Size: $80 million
Companies: Verifone, DataCard, Dassalt, Schlumberger, Oki, Toshiba, Hypercom
Segment: Transaction Processor
1995 U.S. Size: $10 million
Companies: CoreStates Financial, First of America, U.S. Data Capture, TransMark, VISA, U.S. West
Segment: VAR
1995 U.S. Size: $35 million
Companies: De La Rue, National Data, Unisys, IBM

The U.S. smart card industry in 1996 showed a gross revenue of approximately $300 million and is growing at a rate of approximately 40 percent per year.

The use of smart cards in the United States accounts for no more than 15 percent of smart card usage worldwide. This is due primarily to an extensive embedded investment in magnetic stripe card technology and a very capable communication network infrastructure in the United States. However, the need to combat mounting magnetic stripe card fraud and the growing use of smart cards in network applications is rapidly turning the United States from a smart card backwater to a market opportunity. In addition, a number of new applications for smart cards are being pursued in the United States including network access, identity, payment, and PCS telephone, where there are fewer embedded infrastructure barriers.

Growth of smart card usage in the United States is also coming from a completely new direction: Web security and commerce. Both Microsoft and Netscape have sponsored workgroups to define specifications for connecting smart cards to personal computer applications (Microsoft) and to Web browsers (Netscape). The Microsoft workgroup is small, consisting of Schlumberger, Bull CP8 Transarc, Hewlett-Packard, Siemens Nixdorf, and Microsoft. This group completed the first version of its specification by the end of 1996 and announced its results at Cardtech/Securtech '96 West in December 1996. The Netscape group consists of more than 50 companies and had not released any specifications by this writing.

The primary thrust of these specifications has been the application of smart cards to general Internet security rather than to e-commerce per se on the grounds that general-purpose security facilities were prerequisites for e-commerce. Applications necessary for e-commerce supported by these security specifications include encrypted and signed e-mail and identity authentication using X.509 certificates and RSA key challenge/response.

To date, three separate application program interfaces (API) for cryptography have been announced: the Cryptography Application Program Interface (CAPI) by Microsoft, Common Data Security Architecture (CDSA) by Intel, and Public Key Cryptography Standards (PKCS) by RSA Security. There are also two cryptography architectures: the Platform-Independent Cryptography API (PICA) by Apple and the International Cryptography Framework (ICF) by Hewlett-Packard. All of these specifications use the smart card as a device to hold cryptographic keys and do cryptographic computations. None of them address writing programs that run inside smart cards.

In an effort to streamline their own software development efforts, almost all smart card manufacturers created what they called card operating systems (COS). These operating systems are in fact little more than resident function libraries and are reminiscent of single-user minicomputer operating systems such as RT-11 and first-generation personal computer operating systems such as CP/M. Furthermore, until very recently smart card applications were written in processor-specific assembly language by smart card manufacturers themselves. As a result these applications were only rarely moved from the card of one manufacturer to the card of another. Thus, although these card operating systems were based on the ISO 7816–4 standard there was no operational way to verify that different smart card manufacturers had interpreted this standard in the same way; that is, there was no industry-wide API for applications of the smart card.

This situation changed dramatically in the fourth quarter of 1996 when Schlumberger announced the implementation of the Java language for smart cards and a standard Java API for smart card applications. This API is the property of JavaSoft and is maintained and evolved by an industry-wide advisory group of smart card manufacturers, smart card issuers and program providers, and smart card application development companies. The implementation of Java on the smart card computer provides a natural and familiar technical foundation for construction of Web applications aware of and enabled by smart cards, including but not limited to electronic commerce applications.

Integrating Smart Cards and the Web: The Java Card

Smart cards have historically been difficult to connect to mainstream information technology systems. Information about the inner workings of smart cards has been deliberately withheld on security grounds, and tools for programming smart cards have been difficult if not impossible to obtain for the same reasons. Smart card technology was a closed entity.

In September of 1996 a major smart card manufacturer, Schlumberger, changed this picture with the announcement of a version of the Java programming language called Java Card for smart cards. Java Card is a subset of Java tailored to run on the modest computer found in a smart card. Java has become the lingua franca of the Web. Putting Java on the smart card not only opens up smart card programming to the software community at large but also provides the technical foundation for multiapplication smart cards without disturbing—and in fact while enhancing—the smart card security story.

A Java program ("applet") is platform independent and therefore can be sent to and executed on any machine on the Internet. The properties of the Java language and the Java run time environment assure the reader that an applet can do no damage to the receiving computer. With the advent of the Java Card, these platform-independence and secure-execution properties are available in a physically secure environment, a smart card. A Java Card applet (sometimes called a *cardlet*) could be a request for identity authentication or for personal information. Not only do the properties of Java prevent the cardlet from doing any damage to the smart card but the nature of the smart card protects the data contained therein and provides to the cardlet only information that its owner chooses to offer.

At the same time as the Java Card specification was divulged, Schlumberger announced the availability of a smart card called Cyberflex that implemented and realized this specification. This implementation was developed by four engineers—Scott Guthery, Tim Wilkinson, Mark Valderrama, and Ksheerabdhi Krishna—in Schlumberger's Austin, Texas, product center. These engineers were part of a small team that had been put together in March of 1996 and charged with breaking the smart card application development bottleneck. Ideas for innovative uses of smart cards were arriving at Schlumberger (and presumably other smart card manufacturers) faster than the few existing trained smart card programmers could implement them. Smart card security needed to be carefully preserved, but smart card programming had to be opened up to mainstream programming.

Almost immediately the team recognized that the problems surrounding security-preserving programming of a smart card were exactly the problems faced by World Wide Web browsers when they received code from the 'Net and were asked to execute it. And it was exactly these problems that a new programming language called Java had solved. Conceptually at least, Java on a smart card was obvious; this had already been recognized by many in the smart card industry. All that remained was the software engineering detail of getting the Java virtual machine and run time support onto a 12-KB smart card.

Why—besides being natural for connecting a smart card to the Web—was Java so obviously the right answer? First, there were clearly a large and growing number of Java books, courses, software tools, and programmers. In fact, the number of Java programmers probably already greatly exceeded the number of smart card programmers. Thus, there was no need to convince programmers at home in modern integrated software development environments that they had to learn 6805 and 8051 assembly language. Java brings smart card programming into the mainstream of software development rather than trying to force the stream to detour through the swamps of microcontroller programming.

Second, the Java safe-programming security model based on a run time bytecode interpreter had been widely discussed and debated. In fact, the smart card industry had also settled on an interpreter-based approach to securely separating applications and operating systems, but the details of what was to be interpreted were still under discussion. The given wisdom in the industry was that while Java was the right answer it would never fit on a smart card. A nontrivial side benefit of the interpreter approach to security is that one also becomes processor independent. A Java cardlet can run without change on a Motorola 6805 core, an Intel 8051 core, a Texas Instruments 370, or a Hitachi H8.

Finally, Java interpreters were being hammered on by thousands if not millions of Internet warriors every day. Holes had been found and fixed. Java security was becoming as good in practice as it was in theory. Clearly, if smart card security could stand behind this wall of frontline experience it would be strong evidence that the critical smart card security story could be preserved—and maybe even strengthened—with the arrival of open-system smart card programming.

Extremely limited available memory means that every instruction in a smart card program has to justify its existence through usage. There are features of Java—double-precision floating point numbers, for example—that simply make no sense on a smart card, at least at present. Including code for doubles in the smart card interpreter for Java would be dead space on the card that could be occupied by more useful code.

Applying this consideration across the entire set of basic Java instructions (bytecodes) resulted in a subset of the bytecodes that can support current and near-future smart card applications. The Java Card—initially—supports only Boolean, byte, and short integer datatypes. It does not support 16-bit Unicode chars, 32- or 64-bit integers, or 32- or 64-bit floats. However, the Java Card supports the full suite of Java programming constructs, including all operators, flow-of-control statements, and object-oriented programming features.

With respect to system services, the Java Card does not support threads, exceptions, or garbage collection. Initially, running one process at a time on the smart card seemed sufficient; if the smart card runs into an unexpected turn of events then the best place to try to handle the situation is probably the terminal and not on the smart card itself. As a result, exceptions can be raised on the Java Card but they are caught on the terminal.

Cyberflex: The First Java Card Implementation

The first implementation of the Java Card specification is Schlumberger's Cyberflex smart card. Cyberflex uses the Motorola SC49 smart card chip, which has 11.3 K bytes of ROM, 4 K bytes of NVM, and 512 bytes of RAM. The Java Card interpreter and its run time support take all of the ROM and 1 K byte of the NVM, leaving 3 K bytes of NVM for user data. The Cyberflex run time library supports on-card file system operations, identity and security features such as PIN handling and file access control, and basic terminal communication functions.

The inner loop of the Cyberflex Java interpreter is roughly 200 8-bit microcontroller instructions long. This loop checks every byte-code every time for conformance to all the safe-computing rules of the Java language. Only if no rules are violated is the bytecode actually executed.

Experience with initial smart card applications written in Java shows that only about 10 to15 percent of execution time is spent interpreting Java bytecodes. Most of the time is spent in the run time library functions. Thus, at least initially, Java can be thought of as a scripting language for the library functions. For the speed and ease of smart card application program development and for the ability to update applications in the field and run multiple applications on a smart card securely, one pays a performance penalty of between 20 and 30 percent over those same applications written completely in assembly language.

Multiapplication Smart Cards

We have talked about smart card applications as if each application had or was resident in its own smart card, which is currently the case. However, as the number of smart card applications expands, this model cannot hold. People are no more interested in carrying a smart card for each application than they are in carrying a different credit card for each merchant. We need to put many applications on the same smart card not only for convenience of use but because there are natural and compelling opportunities for smart card applications to share data and to cooperate in operation. One may purchase an item in store B with some loyalty points acquired at store A plus some digital cash from an electronic purse. The identity certificate used to gain access to an office building may be the same identity certificate used for e-commerce.

A multiapplication smart card must by default enforce bulletproof firewalls between applications so that there is no way one application can interfere with another. One application cannot read another's data or tamper with the execution of another's programs. On the other hand, in particular and well-managed situations a multiapplication smart card must be able to permit—where it makes sense for business and customer convenience—specific and controlled data sharing among applications. For example, you might want all your smart card applications to share the same entry of your home address so that you do not have to enter it for each application.

Ensuring that multiple applications on a smart card cannot interfere with each other leads down the same paths of secure execution reasoning followed in letting Java into a World Wide Web browser or onto a smart card in the first place. The safe-language rules that the Java interpreter enforces are exactly the rules that must be in place on a multiapplication smart card.

What can be added to Java's rules for execution are guidelines about data sharing. Here is where a smart card's historical strengths for identity authentication come into play. Before any of the applications on a multiapplication smart card are activated, an identity for that application must be established—by the presentation of a PIN, for example—either by the cardholder or by the terminal into which the card is inserted. When the application runs, it can only access data and perform operations that have been explicitly allocated to the established identity.

The transition from special-purpose, hard-to-program systems to general-purpose, easy-to-program systems has made the least headway in smart card terminals. This is primarily because terminals are not only replaced far less frequently than the cards but also obviously cost much more to update or replace. Trapped as they are, however, between the Java-powered Internet and Java-driven smart cards, smart card terminals cannot hold out for long before they, like the smart cards themselves, become first-class nonproprietary and generally useful platforms in Web e-commerce.

The Changing Smart Card Business Model

The advent of Java on all network computers—from the smart card in your pocket to the transaction-processing mainframes—is one of the final steps in the shift to open, general-purpose technology for smart card–based systems. This generality and the ability to easily move functionality around in the system are opening up new possibilities for smart card system architectures that were not possible in the era of closed, proprietary systems. It is also causing some radical rethinking of the smart card business model. Who owns the smart card and who determines what applications it contains? Who owns the terminals and what role do they play? Who owns the network and what knowledge does it have of the smart card? Who owns the servers and what applications do they run? Finally, what is the unique contribution of the smart card to an open network architecture? The new smart card business model will necessarily be founded on this unique contribution.

A smart card is a personal trust platform. It is a secure, portable, physical token that contains information that links the cardholder to the holder's trust brokers. In the open network architecture this is the smart card's unique contribution. It is where the smart card business model must be founded and where the smart card business battles will be fought.

A key question then in considering the new smart card business model is who owns the card itself; that is, who controls what goes on your personal trust platform? The owner of the smart card is after all the keeper, provider, and guarantor of the trust the card embodies. Today, there is no shortage of companies and organizations wanting to be universal trust brokers. Microsoft, MasterCard, VISA, MCI, JavaSoft, the U.S. Post Office, AT&T, Citibank, Oracle, American Airlines, Blue Cross/Blue Shield, American Express, State Farm, Holiday Inn, and virtually every one of the 50 states would all be happy to own your multiapplication smart card and be your trust broker. Another possibility of course is that you own your own smart card and are your own trust broker.

Since trust and associated dual notions of identity and privacy are going to play such a pivotal role in the new smart card business, we will conclude this chapter with a brief discussion of these concepts and how they relate to the smart card.

Trust

Trust is a necessary component of any commercial transaction. How trust between a buyer and seller is established and what happens when that trust is broken characterizes a commerce scheme.

A wide range of trust instruments is used in modern commerce. Cash, coins, checks, promissory notes, casino chips, debit cards, and credit cards are all trust tokens. Trust is often linked to the object being bought and sold. You trust the U.S. government to stand behind · your money, you trust VISA with your credit line, you trust American Airlines with your AAdvantage points, you trust your doctor with your health records, and you trust the telephone company with your unlisted telephone number. The token used to embody that trust—a dollar bill, a credit card, an ID bracelet, a passport—varies among products and trust providers.

In the digitization tsunami, trust like intellectual property before it is being homogenized and commoditized in the process of being reduced to bits. Stripped from its application-specific token, all trust is fungible. Trust behind money bits is no different than trust behind credit, health record, or passport bits. Anybody can be the trust broker of the trust proposition implicit in bits. All that is lacking is a token that can carry all your trust relationships in a digital form. A smart card is the leading candidate to be this universal digital trust token; a smart card is the Web's trust platform. One reason the battle for the e-commerce standard on the Web is so intense and in a sense so indirect and arcane is that it is the opening battle for universal trust brokerage. Once a trust broker has people using its branded digital trust platform for one trust relationship it is an easy step to add more trust relationships to it.

The most demanded, most compelling, and easiest to understand trust relationship needed on the Web today is small change: pennies, nickels, dimes, quarters, and dollar bills. Coins and bills are perhaps the most ubiquitous and familiar trust tokens. Only about 10 percent of all daily commercial transactions are conducted using a credit or debit card. Almost all the rest use cash. The trust tokens currently used for cash—coins and bills—do not work on the 'Net. The opening trust-platform battle is taking place for this 90 percent on the 'Net. Clearly the banks and bankcard associations would like to expand their 10 percent, but there are new players who would also like to become trust brokers and in the process extract a handling fee for cash transactions.

We conclude this chapter with a brief example-driven discussion of some of the properties of trust platforms, with particular emphasis on smart card trust platforms. While it clearly takes much more than simply providing a trust platform to be a trust broker, such a platform with a number of very practical everyday properties is needed if the trust provided is to be used easily and conveniently in a wide range of commercial settings.

Exchange of Value: The Basic Use of Smart Cards in Web E-Commerce

Whether an e-commerce trust relationship is anonymous (i.e., whether the buyer and seller must reveal their identities to each other to complete the sale) determines many features of the e-commerce system they choose to use. Nonanonymous systems are organized around the creation, transmission, and verification of identity. Anonymous systems are organized around the creation, transmission, and verification of value. As with pre-Internet commerce, nonanonymous systems are preferred when a financial debit or delivery obligation is incurred, typically for large-value transactions. Anonymous systems are favored for small transactions with immediate exchange of goods and payment. Smart cards are used as trust tokens in the establishment of identity in nonanonymous systems and as the repository of value in anonymous systems.

Nonanonymous E-commerce

Four functionalities are needed in a trust platform that supports secure, nonanonymous e-commerce:

1. Privacy—third parties cannot eavesdrop on the negotiations
2. Authentication—each party knows the identity of the other party
3. Authorization—each party knows the other party is able to enter into the transaction
4. Nonrepudiation—neither party can deny committing to the transaction

A smart card can play a useful and convenient role in each of these trust platform functions.

Privacy

Message encryption is the best-known and most widely used method of ensuring privacy of communication on the Internet. It is so fundamental that it is being built into the next generation of Internet transmission protocols.

Since their invention in the 1970s asymmetric or public key encryption schemes have been preferred to symmetric or shared-key encryption schemes. Public key schemes are particularly convenient when the communicating parties are unknown to each other and where there is no out-of-band communication path on which to exchange symmetric keys.

Authentication

Authentication is ensuring that things are as they appear to be; for example, that the people you are dealing with really are who they claim to be and that the order you received is really the order that they sent. Knowing who you are dealing with means that you—whether you are the buyer or the seller—know the identity of the person with whom you are dealing. By identity here we mean a legal identity, something that has assets and can be sued.

Establishing an identity is a two-stage process. First you must obtain a reliable linkage between some unique personal properties and a legal identity. Second, you must verify that the person with whom you are dealing exhibits the personal properties. Having done this, you have a linkage between the person in the packet of bits and the legal identity.

What kinds of personal properties are useful for identity authentication?

1. Something you know (e.g., a password, combination, or your mother's maiden name)
2. Something you have (e.g., a physical token such as a smart card, key, or passport)

3. Something you are (e.g., a portrait, fingerprint, or retinal scan)
4. Something you do (e.g., keys struck during random typing)

Certificate authorities such as VeriSign and GTE Cybertrust are in the business of connecting personal properties to legal entities. This connection is sealed into a tamperproof information packet called a certificate. Inside a certificate one finds a list of personal properties (e.g., public key, fingerprint) together with a list of legal identifiers (e.g., driver's license number, home address, Social Security number, passport number). The entire information packet is signed with the certificate authority's private key and given to the person whose vital statistics it contains. A smart card is a convenient and secure place to store your digital identity certificate.

Authorization

Authorization means determining that you are allowed to do what you want to do after you have proven you are who you say you are. For example, a bank may say "Yes, you are indeed Sally Green but no you cannot spend $4,321.56 because you only have $56.32 in your checking account and $123.19 in your savings account."

A smart card can be an authorization and authentication token. For example, suppose a parent held the PIN necessary to load value onto a smart card but the child was given the PIN necessary spend the value. The parent would load the child's allowance onto the card each week and could be assured that the child could not spend more than this amount in the week. Or suppose that the smart card encrypted each message it sent with an authorization key that said what the bearer of the card was authorized to do. The mere possession of the smart card would grant whatever authorizations it carried.

Nonrepudiation

Nonrepudiation means that you cannot deny having sent a message and the receiver cannot deny having received it exactly as sent. For the purposes of e-commerce the message can either be the offer from the seller to the buyer or the acceptance of the offer from the buyer to the seller.

Nonrepudiation in e-commerce is accomplished using a digital signature. Suppose the buyer has asked the seller to e-mail a nonreputable offer. First the seller computes a unique summary number called a one-way hash of the offer's text. The hash of the offer is encrypted with the seller's private key and appended to the order as its digital signature. By decrypting the digital signature on the order with the buyer's public key and getting the (recomputed) hash of the order's text, the seller obtains nonrefutable evidence that the buyer placed the order (because only the buyer holds the private key associated with the public key that decrypted the hash) and that the order has been received exactly as it was sent (because the hash in the signature is the same as the recomputed hash). A smart card is a secure, reliable place to store private keys and to create digital signatures.

Anonymous E-Commerce

Another kind of e-commerce has nothing to do with the establishment of identities and in fact explicitly works to deny it. This kind of e-commerce, called anonymous e-commerce, tries to be as much like cash as possible.

Because establishing identity in a nonanonymous system entails both time and resource expenses and often third-party fees, anonymous trust relationships are particularly attractive when the value of the transaction is small and overhead costs might exceed the cost of the goods or service being purchased. In addition, there are goods and services that people are more likely to purchase if they do not have to reveal who they are when they purchase them. Since pay-per-click is one of the most compelling and intuitive notions for e-commerce and typically involves small-value transactions, anonymous e-commerce trust relationships are expected to be as important as nonanonymous trust systems on the Web.

Smart cards used for anonymous commerce are called stored-value cards or bearer cards because the mere possession or bearing of the card authorizes one to spend the value contained therein. Stored-value cards are of two types: monetary and token.

The value stored on monetary stored-value cards is money in the sense that it can be spent on any products or services. The bits on the card may represent dollars, francs, yen, or any other currency. The value on a monetary stored-value card is simply a digital representation of the money that was exchanged to purchase or load the card.

The value stored on a token stored-value card is not fungible; it can only be spent for products and services offered by the merchant from whom the card was purchased. Phone cards and loyalty program cards (AAdvantage points) are the most widely used examples of token stored-value cards.

Monetary Stored-Value Cards

David Chaum has done the seminal work in anonymous e-cash, and his DigiCash is the most widely known anonymous Internet e-cash system. While DigiCash makes a number of smart card products, this e-commerce scheme is not currently smart card based. Two smart card–based anonymous trust tokens are used in the United States today for anonymous e-commerce: VISACash and Mondex.

The Mondex system differs from the VISACash system by allowing direct transfer of value from buyer to seller. That is, the seller can turn around and immediately spend the electronic cash he or she receives from the buyer. In the VISACash system, VISA has to turn the electronic cash into legal tender for the seller before the seller can spend it. Monetary stored-value cards are natural candidates for micro or pay-per-click transactions on the Web.

Token Stored-Value Cards

Classic token stored-value cards such as phone cards will find much less application than monetary stored-value cards in e-commerce. First, maintaining a rack of application-specific cards that must be swapped back and forth as one moves among 'Net services is inconvenient. Secondly, the money tied up in these cards will not be earning interest. And finally, to switch services, one either has to get a refund of the unused portion of a card or simply abandon the remaining value.

On one hand, nothing technically prevents nonbank entities from issuing monetary value cards. As long as the cards abide by processing and clearance standards, protocols, and conventions, a VISACash card issued by Nationsbank is identical to a VISACash card issued by Wal-Mart or WebTV. One can easily imagine large retailers using their purchasing and fee payment clout to capture stored-value card float and escheat from their acquiring banks.

A variation on the prepaid stored-value card in a Web setting is the network access card. Rather than paying per click or use, a network access card would entitle the bearer to unlimited access to a data resource, for example, for a fixed period of time—a month, a year, and so forth. Such a card would be sold for a given amount and could be renewed for additional time while in use.

Exchange of Information: The Advanced Use of Smart Cards in Web E-Commerce

It has been observed by Colin Crook of Citibank that "Money is the purest form of information." It is such a special form, however, that we devoted the previous section to showing how smart cards can promote the movement of money on the Web. But just as the Web makes bits out of money so too does it make money out of bits. On the Web, information is the purest form of money.

There is no longer any doubt that information has value. What is in great doubt is who owns this value and how it is converted into common forms of exchange such as cash or stored-value bits. The current debate over the ownership of the numbers generated by a sporting event such as a baseball game, for example, highlights how quickly and easily the Web can convert bits to money. Perhaps it is the speed and ease with which the Web converts between money and information that is at the core of the revolution it is causing in commerce. Conversion to a digital form homogenizes all information and its associated value.

In the exchange of value, the security properties of a smart card are necessary to protect value in the case of anonymous commerce and identity in the case of nonanonymous commerce. In this section on the exchange of information, a smart card is more of a convenience than a necessity.

Bartering Personal Information

Privacy is not secrecy but selective disclosure. A private communication is not silence but a communication to specific people. Thus, data privacy means data control. The hidden but most exciting application of smart cards is not in minting money but rather in putting people directly and explicitly in charge of data about themselves.

Suppose I accumulated on my smart card a record of all the soda I buy. Every time I buy a can in a machine: . . . ka-ching. Every time I buy a 12-pack at the A&P: . . . ka-ching. Every time I buy a 2-liter bottle at the Exxon station: . . . ka-ching. Every time I buy a cup at the movie: . . . ka-ching.

Now clearly, if my dental insurance provider happened to ask me how much soda I drink, I would have no idea, and I certainly would not say "Here, take a look at my smart card." On the other hand, if a soda company came to me and said, "If you will show us your soda records, maybe we can give you a discount," you can bet I would show 'em in a flash. When reviewing my purchase records, the soda company might install a one-year universal discount coupon right on my card, so that for the next year, whenever I buy that particular soda with the card—no matter where or in what form—the discount grant will be applied on the spot. By taking charge of my own personal data, I not only protect my privacy but I become the direct beneficiary of that data's use.

There are a number of inefficiencies and lost opportunities in our current model of personal data accumulation and use. When data are aggregated to protect privacy—average amount of soda consumed per year by a Texan—the value of the data is low because it is difficult to turn it into a marketplace offer. As the degree of aggregation goes down—amount of soda consumed by Scott Guthery in 1996—the value of the data goes up but privacy is sacrificed. The current system mitigates against the accumulation and use of high-value data precisely because the data are not kept and controlled by the person to whom they pertain.

With a smart card a consumer can accumulate in a secure form all sorts of detailed data on himself or herself. Furthermore, the consumer can control the release of these data and realize direct benefit from their use. This is obviously beneficial for the consumer but also to the people to whom the consumer releases data because they can immediately convert the information to a marketplace offer. Not incidentally, they are also avoiding the liability of storing and maintaining detailed data on people.

InfoHits

Currently the going rate for click-throughs—when somebody looking at a Web page on your server clicks on ("clicks through") a URL that goes to my server—is about $5/1,000. In other words, I pay you $5 for every 1,000 people you send my way. Of course, I still have to qualify these visitors to see whether they are potential customers. I may do this by requesting they fill in a form or I may try to deduce something about their interests by watching how they wander around my Web site.

What if a click-through came with some personal demographic information about the person selecting the URL—an infohit. The market for infohits is still in the formative stage but guesstimates are that I would pay 10 times more for infohits—$50/1,000—than I pay for anonymous hits. With an infohit I can immediately start tailoring my presentation to the visitor you have sent me. For some visitors I emphasize features A, B, and C of my goods and services; for others I emphasize features D, E, and F. Some visitors get emotive graphics and some receive technical text.

The personal information accompanying an infohit can come from a smart card inserted in the device the person is using to surf the Web. It might include a selection of the information the person uses to establish identity or an indication of the information the person is using for information bartering. In any case, the information sent with an infohit is controlled and selected by the person to whom the information pertains.

One advantage of using a smart card for this purpose is that if the person decides to buy something, the e-commerce capabilities of the smart card are right at hand. Another advantage is that if the seller decides that the person is a prime candidate for his or her goods and services, the seller can write an electronic coupon back onto the smart card directly from the Web server. This electronic coupon can be redeemed either on the Web or at a local retail store.

Conclusion

The competition of Web e-commerce schemes is only one battle in a much larger war. The war is about being your universal trust broker and about representing yourself in all your trust relationships. This war has been joined because the digitization tsunami has stripped trust from the product- and relationship-specific tokens that previously carried it. Separated from its tokens we can see the commonalities in trust relationships and build platforms that embody these commonalities and thus carry trust of any type.

A successful universal trust platform will blend new ideas from many fields: legal, marketing, distribution, finance, computing, mathematics, and technology. The relationship-specific tokens that people are currently familiar with will be replaced by an all-purpose trust token. A smart card is a leading candidate to be this universal trust token.

In this chapter we have briefly described smart card technology and the smart card industry. We then discussed how smart cards are part of a fundamental change that is taking place in the marketplace, namely the shift away from many product-specific trust relationships toward single-source trust brokerage. Finally, we have illustrated how a smart card can be used as a universal trust token in Web e-commerce.

The trust brokerage industry is still in its formative stage. The initial big players in this industry are still identified with the product-specific industries in which they currently do business— banking, communication, transportation, and health, for example. The opportunities in trust brokerage have also been sensed by players who provide technology and services to today's trust brokers— transaction processors, certificate authorities, computer manufacturers, software developers, and communication companies to name a few. Whether today's trust brokers will be able to generalize themselves out of their current industries or be able to earn their customers' business quickly enough is yet to be seen. What is clear is that reducing anything to bits—intellectual property, value, or trust—fundamentally changes the rules of game.

Bibliography

Abadi, Martin. "Authentication and Delegation with Smart-Cards." Technical report, Digital Systems Research Center, Palo Alto, Calif., 1990.

Allen, Catherine A., and William Barris. *Smart Cards: Seizing Strategic Business Opportunities.* Burr Ridge, Ill.: Irwin Professional Publishing, 1996.

Applications of Computer Card Technology. Washington, D.C.: U.S. Department of Labor, Office of the Inspector General, 1989.

Applications of Computer Card Technology, 1990. Washington, D.C.: U.S. Department of the Treasury, Financial Management Service, 1990.

Arnold, Ken, and James Gosling. *The Java Programming Language.* New York: Addison-Wesley, 1996.

Auriemma, Michael J., and Robert S. Coley. *The Bankcard Business.* Washington, D.C.: American Bankers Association, 1992.

Bank of Canada. *The Electronic Purse: An Overview of Recent Developments and Policy Issues.* Montreal: Bank of Canada, 1996.

Baran, Paul. "On Distributed Communications: IX Security, Secrecy, and Tamper-Free Considerations." Memo RRM-3765-pr, Rand Corp, Santa Monica, Calif., August 1954.

Bright, Roy. *Smart Cards: Principles, Practice, Applications.* New York: Halsted Press, 1988.

Chaum, David. "Design Concepts for Tamper Responding Systems." In *Advances in Cryptology, Proceedings of Crypto 83,* ed. David Chaum, 387–92. New York: Plenum, 1984.

Cordoninnier, V., and J. J. Quisquater. *Proceedings of the First Smart Card Research and Advanced Application Conference.* Lille, France: Université de Lille, 1994.

Devargas, Mario. *Smart Cards and Memory Cards.* Manchester, U.K.: NCC Blackwell, 1992.

Duffy, Francis. *Smart Cards.* Norwalk, Conn.: Business Communications Co., 1991.

EMV '96 Integrated Circuit Card Application Specifications for Payment Systems, Version 3.0, June 30, 1996.

Gobioff, Howard, Sean Smith, and J. D. Tygar. "Smart Cards in Hostile Environments." Technical Report CMU-CS-95–1, School of Computer Science, Carnegie Mellon University, 1995.

Godin, Seth. *Presenting Digital Cash.* Indianapolis: Sams, 1995.

Guthery, Scott. "Java Card: Internet Computing on a Smart Card." *IEEE Internet Computing* (February 1997): 57–59.

Guthery, Scott, and Timothy Jurgensen. *Smart Card Development Kit.* New York: Macmillan, in press.

Hartel, Peter H., Pierre Paradinas, and Jean-Jacques Quisquater (eds.). *Proceedings of Cardis 1996: Smart Card Research and Advanced Applications.* Amsterdam: Stichtin, Mathmatiscly Century, 1996.

ISO International Organization for Standardization. "International Standard ISO/IEC 7816: Integrated Circuit(s) Cards with Contacts, Parts 1–11." Geneva, Switzerland: ISO.

Jeffreys, Denise C. *Smart Cards vs. Magnetic Media in Key Commercial Applications.* Burlington, Mass.: Decision Resources Inc., 1990.

Kaplan, Jack. *Smart Card: The Global Information Passport.* Boston: International Thomson Computer Press, 1996.

McCrindle, J. A. *Smart Cards.* New York: Springer-Verlag, 1990.

McGraw, Gary, and Edward W. Felten. *Java Security.* New York: John Wiley & Sons, 1997.

Oppliger, Rolf. *Authentication Systems for Secure Networks.* Boston: Artech House, 1996.

O'Reilly, Francis J. *The "Smart Card": Projected Markets and Technological Developments.* Stamford, Conn.: Business Communications Co., 1986.

Oton, Jose M. *Smart Cards.* Boston: Artech House, 1994.

Rankl, Wolfgang. *Smart Card Handbook.* New York: John Wiley & Sons, 1997.

Stuber, Gerald J. *The Electronic Purse: An Overview of Recent Developments and Policy Issues.* Montreal: Bank of Canada, 1996.

Svigals, Jerome. *Smart Cards: The Ultimate Personal Computer.* New York: Macmillan, 1985.

————. *Smart Cards: The New Bank Cards.* Rev. ed. New York: Macmillan, 1987.

Wayner, Peter. *Digital Cash: Commerce on the Net.* Boston: AP Professional, 1996.

Yellin, Frank. "Low-Level Security in Java." WWW4 Conference, December 11–14, 1995.

Zoreda, Jose Luis, and Jose Manuel Oton. *Smart Cards.* Boston: Artech House, 1994.

6

Foundations
for Electronic Commerce

Standards and Strategic Alliances

DANIEL SCHUTZER
CITICORP, AND PRESIDENT OF THE FINANCIAL
SERVICES TECHNOLOGY CONSORTIUM

Introduction

Increasingly, businesses are substituting electronic transactions for paper and manual processes in an effort to streamline and provide better, more timely, cost-effective products and services to their customers. With the increasing popularity of the PC and most recently the Internet and on-line services, individuals are spending more time using on-line networks at home and at work. This trend toward getting "wired"—electronically conducting more business, learning, and recreation—is energizing what has been more than a decade-long push to implement electronic banking for home consumers and business users. As more banks develop strategies and implement programs for electronic banking, there has been a parallel growth in the variety of electronic payment systems and the types of electronic money available to consumers.

This chapter first examines the recent surge of interest and development in electronic banking applications and analyzes why this explosive growth is accelerating now. It then relates this growth to the introduction of electronic payments and discusses the various forms it is taking and the need for a common infrastructure to support future development. Within that context, it highlights the roles that alliances and consortia, such as the Financial Services Technology Consortium (FSTC), are playing in facilitating the development of standards for electronic banking.

The Financial Services Technology Consortium and Electronic Commerce

The Financial Services Technology Consortium consists of more than 90 members from the banking, financial services, vendor, government, and academic community who work together to achieve common research goals in a precompetitive environment. (See Appendix B for a list of FSTC's current members and their Web sites.) The FSTC, a not-for-profit organization incorporated in September 1993, is a consortium of banks, financial service providers, technology companies, national laboratories, universities, and government agencies whose original goal was to enhance the competitiveness of the U.S. financial services industry. Since its founding, its interest has expanded to keep pace with international issues in electronic commerce reflecting the global reach of the Internet and the need for solutions that can cross national borders. Today the FSTC includes issues of infrastructure for electronic commerce and precompetitive research goals for the entire international financial services industry within its mission.

FSTC is governed by a board of directors comprising six bank members: Bank of America, Bank of Boston, Chase Manhattan, Citibank, Huntington Bank, and NationsBank. There are three classes of membership: principal, associate, and advisory. Only registered bank holding companies can apply for principal membership, which is the membership class that nominates and elects board members. The board appoints an executive committee that manages the day-to-day business affairs of the FSTC, with the assistance of a professional executive director and staff. More specific information about the FSTC organization, its membership, meetings, and various projects is available at the consortium's Web site at www.fstc.org.

FSTC functions very much as a membership-driven organization and pursues its mission primarily by sponsoring project-oriented collaborative research and development on interbank technical projects affecting the entire financial services industry. Active projects involving development of the Internet and supporting a smooth transition toward integrated global electronic commerce receive particular emphasis. Members subscribe to and fund specific projects according to their interests and willingness to participate. In addition, FSTC holds three to four general meetings each year so that members can learn about some of the latest technology developments that impact the industry and receive updates concerning FSTC's project activity.

Current FSTC projects address electronic payments, with the electronic check project and the bank Internet payment system project; consumer and commercial fraud prevention and detection with the risk management–fraud prevention and control project; and check truncation with the check image exchange project. These projects are aimed at helping banks adapt to the challenges and opportunities presented by the evolving on-line banking and electronic commerce environment. FSTC achieves these goals by cooperating to establish an infrastructure that best supports the needs of its customers and secures a role for the banking community. This chapter will focus on the electronic check and bank Internet payments system projects.

Electronic Commerce Trends

Increasingly our banking customers are demanding services that are faster, cheaper, easier to execute across financial institutions, and with more personal control (see references for some statistics regarding this trend). Advances in technology are making such improved services possible, with or without banks. Individuals and corporations are increasingly turning to on-line services over the Internet to conduct electronic commerce, electronic banking, and electronic collaboration. On-line commerce still represents a rather minor percentage of total commerce but is likely to become a major force in the future. The factors driving this push to automated on-line electronic commerce/banking are convenience, reduced cost of operations, lower risk, more timely information and control over one's processes, and the ability to deliver customization and control on a mass scale.

Electronic commerce, with its greatly reduced cost of production and distribution, makes practical many new knowledge businesses that were previously impractical. For example, a fully realized infrastructure for electronic commerce would make it practical for authors to charge pennies for paragraphs and still make a profit—because they could reach millions of potential buyers (worldwide over the Internet) who might be willing to pay for and download the paragraph at little or no incremental cost to the author. In the absence of a standard infrastructure, however, these types of new business ventures are not possible. As more consumers and businesses connect to the Internet, the demand for payment options and business models that are particularly suited to the on-line environment increases—and so does the importance of establishing standards for validating and securing payments in a global environment.

In addition to the impetus provided by the rapid growth of Internet users, there are other factors driving the interest in electronic commerce payment solutions today. Selling digital objects, or charging for their use, over the Internet offers many advantages over more traditional businesses:

> It provides the customer with more choices and customization options (e.g., choice of font, colors).

> It decreases the time and cost of search and discovery, in terms of both customers finding electronic documents and objects and authors finding customers (e.g., advertising, target marketing).

> It expands the marketplace from local and regional markets to national and international markets with minimal capital outlay and equipment, space, or staff.

> It reduces the time between the outlay of capital and receipt of the digital objects (makes possible a simultaneous exchange).

▷ It permits just-in-time production and payments.

▷ It allows businesses to reduce overhead and inventory through increased automation and reduced processing times.

▷ It decreases the high transportation and labor costs of creating, processing, distributing, storing, and retrieving paper-based information and of identifying and negotiating with potential customers and suppliers. The storage and distribution of digital objects is reduced dramatically.

▷ It enables, through automated information, production of a reliable, easily shared historical database of design, marketing, sales, and payment information.

▷ It facilitates increased customer responsiveness, including on-demand delivery.

Notably absent from this list of drivers is the availability of innovative bank-designed and bank-supported on-line payment applications. Nevertheless, supplying such solutions is becoming a more important priority for the banking industry. Banks need to be where their customers are—if customers work and shop in cyberspace, then banks must be there to handle their customers' transactions.

At a minimum, customers need to be able to access their banks electronically—both on line and via e-mail. They need to be able to provide their banks instructions safely and securely at the same time and place that they are working and shopping, even if that place is on the World Wide Web. These instructions include the full spectrum of services: depositing, withdrawing, paying bills, obtaining loans, making investments, checking on the status of payments, transferring funds, and monitoring account balances, investments, loans, and so on.

Consumers are motivated to go on line because it is more timely, cost-effective, and convenient to do their business electronically. It stands to reason that they will expect and demand the same level of service from their banks. They will expect to be able to bank faster, cheaper, and with more personal control and customization, independently of where they are. This includes being able to access and process all their financial needs and accounts, even if these transactions and accounts cross over among different banks and other financial institutions. For the consumer to get access to integrated payment services and information, the different financial services providers must agree to build their applications around a common standard. One role for FSTC is to provide a model for the secure electronic commerce infrastructure that banks need to meet such demands as quickly and cost-effectively as possible.

From Home Banking to Open Network Standards

Background

In their first foray into electronic banking in the 1980s, banks built bank-specific home banking and treasury workstation software designed to run on the customers' PCs, workstations, and mainframes. This software communicated directly with the banks' processors, usually through dial-up modems over voice networks or dedicated private data networks. These efforts have had only limited success. They never really took off except for a small number of loyal customers (about 1 to 5 percent of the customer base) for a variety of reasons, including

- ▷ Not many people had PCs, and even fewer had modems or other communications capability available at home.
- ▷ The technology and the text interface were too difficult to use.
- ▷ Fees were perceived as too high in relation to the value of the service.
- ▷ Systems were proprietary and of limited utility.
- ▷ Users could not withdraw cash or deposit checks.
- ▷ Systems did not operate across different banks and financial institutions.

In the early 1990s we saw the emergence of a new model. Software intermediaries, such as Quicken for the individual consumer and small business area, and value-added network (VAN) suppliers, such as GEIS and EDS in the corporate world, stepped into a vacuum left by the banks, providing a needed integrator function.

Focusing on the user's total financial needs, assets, and liabilities rather than on a single banking relationship, these packages allow their users to manage their finances in a consolidated fashion, even when they have multiple accounts with more than one bank or financial institution. With the growth of computer networking, this handful of financial software providers (i.e., Intuit, Quicken, Microsoft Money) has begun to transform its popular software packages into a gateway between the customers and their banks and financial institutions.

Customers naturally tend to prefer this model over having to interface with a number of different banking software systems. It provides customers with a common interface and allows them to integrate their various banking accounts, services, and products. These integrated software and network systems have now become the dominant means for banking electronically. They are generally easier to use than the earlier single-bank systems and provide financial planning advice and tools, as well as interfaces to various accounting, charting, and other decision support packages and systems. As a result, they are increasingly replacing the banks' direct lines of communication and interface with their customers.

With the development of secure transactions and financial services on the Web, a new model is emerging, one that further tilts the balance in favor of the customer and one more compatible with the spirit of the Internet—an open, architecturally based solution. This new model permits a user to interface directly with many other users, including merchants, banks, friends, and business partners, through applications that can be built out of software components contributed by many different suppliers.

There are several advantages of this model from the customer perspective:

1. Customers can maintain relationships and deal directly with multiple banks and financial services firms, without the need for and dependence on a single software integrator or network service provider, yet still be able to interact seamlessly on interbank financial transactions.
2. Customers and their banks become less dependent on a single vendor or supplier.

3. Such a model should spur competition, attracting a richer, more competitive array of software components and services, which in turn should lead to better prices and products and a richer diversity of choices for both banks and customers.

4. It enables the banks, financial institutions, and other service providers to maintain a direct interface with their customers and to provide their own unique, distinctive interactive experience.

5. Users can interface directly with all their various financial institutions without requiring different software, network providers, or multiple log-ons and with the same degree of integration of their various accounts and services as with the single software or network intermediary model.

6. Users can continue to selectively upgrade or enhance and personalize their software with little additional cost and effort and at their own individual pace.

7. Once better information and interoperability among banks is achieved, banks will be able to offer their customers many new value-added products and services that can contribute to their revenue base and replace lost revenue as transaction fees continue to drop.

8. It allows banks and other financial services providers to directly interface with each other and their customers and to process high-level interbank customer-to-customer transactions via agents.

9. Open systems have been shown to reduce operating costs because of lower prices resulting from increased competition.

The Internet, and its faster, more secure successors, is seen as a place where these objectives can be achieved because it is becoming ubiquitous, provides access to all products and services without prejudice, is not controlled or managed by anyone, and is completely open. Any and all players can build applications and market their services on the global network, thus promoting competition and attracting even more users. The Internet is serving as a stimulant for the increased use of networked computing and is causing a transformation and convergence of many industries. These characteristics of the Internet promise to both stimulate and transform the nature of on-line banking as it is doing for so many other activities. Its architecturally based model for financial services, including banking, shows evidence of being a superior model that will stand the test of time. One implication of the move from proprietary to open networking systems is that there will be more alternatives for consumers. Another is that a large variety of software and network service providers will continue to compete for the attention and loyalty of these consumers by adding value and enhancements to their products. This combination means that there will be an increased need for standards that will allow all the players to be integrated with each other totally seamlessly.

Fortunately, the Internet's approach to standards differs from the more traditional approach in a way that allows it to become more responsive and quicker than a typical standards committee process. The Internet standards process, coordinated by the Internet Engineering Task Force (IETF), is informal and consensus based. Required standards are identified in response to the evolving needs of the Internet. Parties wishing to propose a standard are required to have a working implementation before submission and to be willing to place it in the public domain and under the control of the IETF. Once proposed a consensus concerning the standard is rapidly reached, and products built around these standards are quickly implemented by multiple parties.

Standards and Requirements: The Next Generation

The majority of Internet standards in the past addressed issues of network operation and interoperability for different types of document and data formats. More recently attention has focused on standards for secure communication, encryption, and authentication of both the sender and receiver of information on the Internet. As more financial and other commercial transactions take place on line, whether via e-mail or Web access, it becomes especially important to have standard means of establishing legal identity and trust among all participants.

In the near future, we should see a broad range of new value-added services on the Internet built around trust and security, including the following:

▷ Authentication over public networks
▷ Certification of information, parties, and transactions
▷ Protection of intellectual property and usage rights
▷ Performance bonding
▷ Electronic escrow
▷ Transaction insurance
▷ Appraisal services
▷ Various electronic broker services
▷ Trusted agents to resolve disputes, claims, and so forth

All of these initiatives must be developed within a common framework or we run the risk of introducing isolated, noninteroperable implementations that will inhibit progress toward truly free, open, and spontaneous electronic commerce. Most of the current solutions being prototyped over the Internet differ in some way in their approach to security and privacy, their ability to handle micropayments, and their applicability to various types of transactions. They also differ in their business models—for example, in their pricing strategies and in their assumptions as to who bears the risk in case of insufficient funds or disputes. Some of these variations are the inevitable result of competitors offering different solutions and are part of the open marketplace that characterizes the Internet. Other differences, however, reflect a more serious lack of standardization that could threaten the acceptance and deployment of secure commerce solutions.

For business and financial organizations, including banks, to develop the next generation of network-based products and services, they must agree to some primary goals and standards. It is especially important to build an infrastructure around the following characteristics: interoperability, flexibility for innovation, increased accessibility, adequate security, adequate search capabilities, and electronic payment options.

Interoperability

Most current implementations depend on proprietary solutions that do not easily interoperate, if they do at all. Internet e-mail and the World Wide Web are notable exceptions. A truly interoperable common infrastructure for applications such as electronic commerce would allow parties to conduct their transactions in private, without paying any fees to intermediaries unless they provide some real added value, such as credit or search services. This infrastructure would make it easier for any and all interested persons to become service providers and consumers.

The infrastructure must be based on a common set of services and standards that ensure interoperability. Preferably, these services and standards can be used as standard building blocks that service providers and application designers can combine, enhance, and customize.

Maximum Flexibility to Permit Innovation

As the Internet and its successors evolve, they will grow and mature significantly—possibly in ways not even imagined today. New services and businesses will emerge. For example, the future electronic marketplace will provide new opportunities for narrow-cast marketing and publishing to very short-lived niche markets. Also, existing services and products will be redefined and modified. The common infrastructure will have to be sufficiently flexible to accommodate all of these changes and be able to address new applications and requirements as they arise.

Increased Accessibility

The consumer cannot usually communicate or transact with vendors in a simple, direct, free-form environment in today's electronic commerce applications. For example, to access most electronic shopping services, a consumer must subscribe to an on-line service (e.g., Prodigy, AOL, or cable TV shopping channels) that then provides proprietary hardware and/or software with which to communicate with the vendors that have also registered with that service. Financial management software may be provided by Quicken or Microsoft, while information about investment options is available from a mutual funds Web site and financial reports on current accounts and assets are delivered as printed statements or accessed via a bank phone system. An individual would benefit from interacting with all these information resources in a single session, using a standard interface.

Adequate Security

The lack of personal contact and the anonymity associated with conducting transactions over a telecommunications network make it difficult to authenticate parties and detect intruders; this in turn makes the system vulnerable to fraud and increases the need for security services. Additionally, the speed with which transactions can be conducted leaves parties with less time to react, check, and respond appropriately—again creating the potential for system fraud and abuse. Lack of sufficient security inhibits the introduction of direct, secure, real-time electronic payment and settlement systems that can support secure exchanges without prearrangements or third parties.

Adequate Search Capabilities

Participants in today's electronic commerce applications must patch together a variety of methods and means of navigating effectively through the sea of rapidly increasing on-line electronic information and services to find trading partners and items of interest. This problem will only increase as more information and businesses go on line.

Electronic Payment Methods

Developing a more robust standard for electronic payments on the Internet is a particular focus of the electronic commerce project area of FSTC. The deployment of safe and convenient ways to pay for things over the Internet and the future information infrastructure is clearly a requirement for the continued growth of electronic commerce. FSTC has identified a number of problems with the current options for Internet payment and designed several projects to create a model for banks to play a significant role in secure, standardized payment models for the future. The emergence of electronic payments and the move to standardization are discussed in the next section.

Growth of Electronic Payments and Electronic Money

The process of transferring money electronically has been with us for a long time and already represents a significant component of the total dollar value that gets exchanged daily. Each day more than $2 trillion is transferred electronically between banks.[1] Collectively, electronic payments constitute 16 percent of the $5.2 trillion payment market. More than 40 percent of consumer paychecks in 1996 were deposited electronically, up from 5 percent in 1995. Of course, this represents a much smaller portion of the actual number of transactions, because until recently only large corporations have been technologically sophisticated enough and have sufficient volume to make electronic payments cost-effective; they make fewer transactions of much larger than average value. But all this is changing as both the price and level of sophistication required for the use of computers and computer networking drop dramatically. Moreover, as the number of people and organizations on line increases, the number of services and products that can be reached over the network increases in proportion, which in turn creates the motivation for more people to work and spend on line in an ever-increasing spiral.

Traditional payment methods, even current electronic payment options, have several deficiencies when applied to public networks, such as the Internet, some of which are the following:

Lack of convenience. One generally needs to leave the Internet and use the telephone or write a letter and enclose a check to make payment.

Lack of security. If one attempts to make a traditional payment over the Internet, it usually involves giving out card or payment account details and other personal information on line. Leaving the Internet and providing the card or payment account details over the telephone or through mail also lacks security and entails some risk.

Coverage. Checks do not work well across borders. Cards work only with signed-up merchants, and do not generally support individual-to-individual or direct business-to-business payment transactions.

Eligibility. Not all potential buyers, or merchants, have suitable credit ratings to allow them access to checking accounts and particularly credit cards.

Cost. Many payments over the Internet are of sufficiently low value that the buyer's cost of a phone call or letter is too high. Some people even talk about micropayments where people would pay very low amounts (e.g., on the order of pennies) for the use of a software program or a page of a document. Similarly, the cost of handling these payment methods is often too high for the seller, making the transaction uneconomical. The transaction overhead cost of credit cards is even higher than debit, check, or funds transfer because it involves the cost and risk of extending credit.

If implemented correctly electronic payment, particularly for the Internet and on-line services, represents a natural progression toward achieving greater convenience, flexibility, timeliness, control, and cost-effectiveness, but it is also a revolutionary departure from the known. In the past people exchanged items with intrinsic value (e.g., precious metals). The change to symbolic currency (e.g., paper money, letters of credit, checks) took many years for full acceptance (to this day a few people still hoard bars of gold) and represented a major departure from the past forms of payment. It offered many advantages—increased convenience and availability to name a couple—but represented a major change. The form of payment exchanged no longer had an intrinsic value even close to the amounts being exchanged. It also introduced new types of risks; based on its dependence on a complex web of loans and credits, the system is more vulnerable to large-scale collapse.

Just as symbolic currency was a major departure from money in the form of precious metal or tangible goods, electronic money is a major departure from paper currency. Electronic money is totally intangible—bits that cannot be seen or felt and are stored in a computer. The digitization of money also brings on a whole new set of risks—vulnerability to remote attacks, ease of duplication, reduced time for risk assessment, the loss of privacy if spending patterns are tracked on line, and the possibility of electronic surveillance if all types of purchases and financial interactions are linked to individual identity.

Nevertheless, as we have seen, there are strong incentives for moving to electronic money, including increased convenience, timeliness, flexibility, and control of payments both on and off the 'Net. When consumers want to purchase items over the Internet, it makes sense for them to also have the option of paying directly over the 'Net. Paying electronically, however, requires some changes in how consumers think about money, and a total shift will not occur overnight.

There is potential value for all parties in a transaction in facilitating a greater percentage of payments electronically at the point of sale in stores and vending machines (e.g., paying by cash and check electronically, as well as credit cards and debit card transactions). It represents increased convenience to the customer by eliminating fumbling for cash and correct change. For the merchant, it reduces the cost and overhead involved in safely handling, storing, and transporting cash and checks, which are the dominant forms of payment today. This is particularly true in convenience-type entities such as gasoline stations, grocery stores, and vending machines. A survey conducted by *USA Today* and the Smart Card Forum found that 53 percent of the customers would like to be able to use smart cards (a form of electronic cash) in gasoline stations and 51 percent in grocery stores.

There is also a strong incentive for banks to move more transactions into electronic form to reduce costs, gain a larger of share of these transactions, and retain their role as the major processor of financial transactions and provider of transaction accounts as commerce increasingly moves on line. Once these new forms of on-line electronic payment become widely accepted and available, they could lead to new services, products, and markets. These new services and products include more real-time cash flow management involving short-term loans and deposits, new services of aggregating information (e.g., point-of-sale data), and the bank playing the roles of information broker, reputation holder, and distribution channel.

However, the concerns over security are particularly strong with respect to payments over the Internet and must be addressed before electronic payments over the Internet can be successfully introduced. For example, the Internet ranks lowest with respect to public confidence in its security, as evidenced by the survey results shown in table 6.1.

Fraud represents a primary concern in the on-line world, where things are less tangible and move more rapidly and where it is possible to conduct fraud remotely. For example, Forrester predicts approximately $1 of fraud per $1,000 of business transactions over the Internet.

Solutions for overcoming these concerns and limitations are beginning to appear. Many predict that these solutions will bring dramatic growth in retail and wholesale sales over the Internet.

TABLE 6.1   **Security Concerns and Electronic Banking Products**

Product/Service	Percentage of PC Users Who Trust It
ATMs	77
Banking by phone	62
Banking by computer	57
Using a credit card/calling card at a public phone	57
Writing a credit card number on a catalog order form	43
Sending a credit card number to a commercial on-line service	34
Giving a credit card number over the phone	31
Sending a credit card number over the Internet	5

Source: USA Today/IntelliQuest Survey

The current and proposed electronic payment systems generally fall into one or more of the following four categories:

1. Adaptation of an existing payment method for satisfactory use over the Internet
2. Dependence on a single, trusted third party
3. Use of Internet cash (electronic cash)
4. Providing a bill-payment service accessible over the Internet

Today there is a rich variety of payment preferences available to meet individual preferences, and we expect at least as rich a variety over the Internet and on-line services as is already indicated by the many solutions appearing and being proposed.

Three of the traditional payment mechanisms, credit cards, debit cards, and funds transfers, are already in the form of electronic payments. Currently they are intended primarily for use over physical point-of-sale (POS) and banking networks and therefore would need to be adapted for secure, trusted operation over public networks such as the Internet.

Credit cards are a popular form of retail payment because customers can buy on credit and are protected by the opportunity to challenge purchases *before* the actual transfer of funds. Merchants like it because they are guaranteed payment the next day, and customers can purchase even if they do not currently have sufficient funds on hand or in their bank accounts. Credit cards are already a well-known and popular form of payment, and their adaptation for secure use over the Internet represents an easy, minimal shift for consumers. But credit card purchases are not well suited to all activities that can take place over the Internet. This payment mechanism only covers transactions among buyers and authorized merchants. It does not address person-to-person (e.g., wiring funds to an individual) or business-to-business payments. It involves an on-line authentication with a trusted third party and limits the size of transactions (transactions cannot be profitably handled if they are too small, and purchases are only good up to the credit limit of the purchaser). These are expensive transactions, since they cost the merchant a percentage of each transaction, but they have been shown to bring more business through the customer's use of credit.

For credit cards to be adapted for secure use on the Internet, one needs to protect customers' account information from capture and fraudulent use, ensure privacy over public networks, and provide the digital equivalent to signing the credit card slip. Both VISA and MasterCard have proposed and are implementing a common solution based on public key cryptography secure electronic transaction (SET).

Debit cards, like credit cards, are intended primarily for POS consumer transactions. Similarly, they do not address person-to-person payments (e.g., wiring funds to an individual) or many business-to-business payments. They also require on-line authentication. Debit cards are linked to an individual's bank account and result in an immediate transfer of funds.

Debit cards have grown slowly relative to credit cards in the United States. By 1985 there were about 12,000 debit card terminals in the United States, but the media had already labeled the technology as a disappointment.[2] Several factors have contributed to the slow growth. Early systems were expensive to operate and there was no common standard. Consumers did not like the product because it provided a shorter float period and did not integrate well with their checkbook routine for keeping records. Consumers cannot question payments made with debit cards as easily as they can those made with credit cards. Credit cards were already widely accepted, and debit cards could not provide significant enough advantage to displace them. The growth of debit cards in Europe has been much stronger—perhaps due in part to the lower penetration of credit cards in that market. Recently, as the processing cost dropped and marketing improved, debit cards have been increasing in usage at point-of-sale terminals. Like credit card transactions, debit card transactions would have to be adapted to be applied securely on line over public networks such as the Internet. The First Bank of the Internet (FBOI) claims to be offering such a solution for secure debit transactions over the Internet, and ultimately we can expect VISA and MasterCard to address this product as an extension of their credit card solution.

Funds and money transfers are electronic payments that are particularly popular for many interbank and corporate-to-corporate payments, bill-payment applications, and direct deposit of salaries. Today these types of payments generally require prearrangement and occur over private banking networks. They would need to be modified to support secure ad hoc (without prior arrangement) payment over public networks such as the Internet. Some third-party intermediaries (e.g., Cybercash and Open Market) and individual banks (e.g., Wells Fargo, First Union, and Security First Network Bank [SFNB]) have begun to provide a software-only solution for payment over the Internet. In these solutions, they act as trusted third parties and require others to authenticate themselves on line. This solution requires both parties of the transaction to be signed up with the same intermediary, limiting interoperability. In addition, although these solutions are similar, they differ enough to each require their own unique software. The FSTC is proposing to develop an open solution addressing this interoperability issue with a standard bank Internet payment system (BIPS) interface and protocol that would allow multiple banks to witness the authentication and authorization for these and debit-type transactions. BIPS is being designed to address any interbank funds-transfer transaction, including debit card transactions and credit card settlement, and other forms of payments, such as bank notes, letters of credit, and bonds.

Standards for the Future: Electronic Cash and Checks

The electronic payments methods discussed do not cover all the possible ways people and organizations are likely to want to pay over the Internet. For one thing they do not address today's two most popular forms of payment. Nearly three-quarters of all consumer financial transactions are still conducted in cash (mostly for small purchases), with checks being the second most popular, as shown in table 6.2.

Issues involving the implementation of electronic cash and checks are reviewed here. However, because these implementations represent a more radical departure from their physical, paper-based cousins, their widespread acceptance is dependent on the establishment of accepted standards and proper positioning and marketing.

TABLE 6.2   **Distribution of U.S. Consumer Financial Transactions**

Type of Transaction	Percentage of All Transactions
Cash	73
Checks	17
Credit Card	5
Electronic Payment	3
Debit Card	2

Source: Bank Technology News

Electronic Cash

The advantages of today's currency in the form of cash are fairly obvious. Cash is generally anonymous (that is, it supports transactions in which the identities of the paying and receiving parties are unknown), can support individual-to-individual transactions, and can increase customer convenience. Cash transactions have the appeal of allowing two people or organizations to make final payment without the direct, on-line involvement of any bank or other intermediary third party; the transaction involves no credit risk and the payment is final. Such transactions therefore represent no direct cost to the transacting parties, although there are indirect costs of storing and handling the cash before and after the transaction.

Cash also has several disadvantages: You need exact change to pay for something. It provides little customer protection—if your cash is lost or stolen you cannot recover it. You lose a float period, because you cannot earn interest on the cash you carry around with you. Paying by cash also makes it more difficult to prove that the party actually received payment. You have no accounting trail and no proof of payment without a receipt.

Electronic cash tends to share in the advantages and disadvantages of physical cash. In addition, the familiar cash we spend now, which involves a tangible physical object, would need to be more drastically redesigned to enable use over the Internet and on-line services since you cannot send paper bills and coins over a network. Electronic cash is the most difficult to protect against counterfeiting because of its relative anonymity—a particularly vexing problem on the Internet. Finally, there is the issue of confidence in who is backing electronic cash. Unlike paper cash, which is backed by the government of the issuing country, electronic cash is generally backed by some private corporation or association.

Several attempts to introduce electronic cash over the Internet already exist, including Mondex, DigiCash, and CyberCash coins. None of these are as compatible or universally accepted as paper cash is in the real world. The two most well-known electronic cash implementations on the Internet—Mondex and DigiCash—are designed to maintain anonymity, whereas other versions of electronic cash such as CyberCash coins and VisaCash—which is currently being developed for use on prepaid cards—are linked to accounts and transactions and are therefore less anonymous.

Generally, electronic cash is implemented by creating a digital token, used to represent monetary value, that can be exchanged, stored, but not copied. It is easy to copy digital information and difficult to distinguish between a digital object and its copy. This makes implementing an electronic cash system that cannot be counterfeited or remotely stolen much more difficult than just using binary digits to represent amounts (such as using the binary digit 10 to represent $2). Solutions require the use of strong cryptography, which is yet another topic of importance. They also require the ability to store and verify electronic money in authenticated, tamperproof hardware (as is the case in Mondex) or risk failing to detect double spending without on-line authentication by the issuing bank, even with the imposition of many restrictions and limitations (as is the case of DigiCash).

Although the various implementations of electronic cash are being designed to mimic the cash transaction, they differ in many important ways:

> ▷ Degree of anonymity provided
> ▷ What gets authenticated, the hardware device, the stored electronic token, whether the use of the device or electronic token is linked to an owner by secrets (e.g., passwords) or biometrics

▷ Where the liability rests (e.g., with the issuing bank or the holder of the electronic money)

▷ How the electronic money is paid for and received (e.g., on line through electronic withdrawal of funds or requiring a physical presence at a branch or ATM)

▷ Whether the electronic money can converted back to real cash

▷ Whether the electronic cash represents actual value or is just a proxy (e.g., an authenticated payment instruction from a bank)

▷ Whether the system is transaction or account based

▷ Whether the electronic cash supports divisibility (an amount can be split into two or more parts)

▷ Whether it can support accounting and auditing

▷ How well it scales

▷ Whether the electronic cash, like traveler's checks, can be recovered if lost or stolen

▷ What kinds of restrictions and limitations it imposes (e.g., can it only be spent at a merchant and then deposited/redeemed by the merchant or can it be exchanged among individuals and organizations indefinitely without the involvement of a bank; is there a finite period during which it is valid; is it backed by real money held in reserve; are there usage restrictions such as a limit to the amount or rate at which electronic money can be spent in a fixed period of time or on what the electronic money can be used for?)

Note that the introduction of usage restrictions can actually be a feature such as when it is used to enforce policies. Examples of such restrictions might be to prevent welfare dollars from being spent on entertainment or gambling. A corporate officer might be allowed to purchase only certain types of business-related goods and services up to a maximum amount. Children under a certain age might be restricted from spending on items rated for sale to adults only.

Electronic Checks

Checks are a very popular payment mechanism that like cash can be used to allow two people or organizations to make final payment without the direct, on-line involvement of any bank or other inter-mediary third party. Unlike cash payments, paying by check is not the final step of a transaction and accepting a check as payment in-volves some credit risk. Unless the check is certified or guaranteed by the bank, there may not be sufficient funds available in the checking account to back the payment. Unlike cash, electronic checks must be linked to a bank account. In fact, the payer and payee both need ac-counts, one to pay from and one to receive payment, although they do not need to be with the same institution.

Secure electronic implementation of checks, like electronic cash, involves the creation of electronic tokens, except in this case the to-kens represent unalterable, verifiable payment instructions drawn off a banking account, so that a fraudulent transaction would be easier to discover and trace. Like electronic cash, hardware devices are recom-mended for storing and validating in order to minimize fraud. Ideally an electronic check standard will provide networked support for all the functions of today's checking applications. In addition, these same standards will be readily extendible to any payment instruction (e.g., credit card receipts). This is one of the goals of the FSTC elec-tronic check project, which is part of the consortium's overall effort to develop the infrastructure for secure banking on the Internet.

FSTC Electronic Commerce Projects

As mentioned earlier, FSTC members work primarily in a project mode by defining a key issue for electronic banking, developing a methodology for creating models, and building a solution. The FSTC strategy for developing an electronic commerce system begins with the creation of a broad architecture to enable all steps in the electronic commerce process to be handled over public networks. This architecture must accommodate the full spectrum of potential users and services including legacy systems and new payment mech-anisms. The next step will be to develop an electronic commerce test bed. The main purpose of this test bed will be to validate the elec-tronic commerce architecture with respect to its technical and im-plementation viability, security, and safety. The test bed will also support an early prototype electronic commerce application. This application will be evaluated as to whether it makes a compelling business case for electronic commerce. Eventually, this prototype could be expanded to demonstrate that the architecture is scaleable and to promote commercialization and widespread acceptance of the electronic commerce system.

Members can elect to participate in one or more projects related to the overall mission of FSTC, depending on their interests. The typical project life cycle includes the following:

1. An initial phase of research and design, in which members analyze the relevant issues, explore alternate scenarios, and agree on recommendations for how to approach creating a prototype, including which standards to adopt, implement, and augment.
2. Prototype construction and testing to detect flaws in the design, usability issues, and other problems that emerge in a broader use environment.
3. Once a prototype has been completed, one or more members implement a limited pilot program to determine what further refinements are required to move the solution into a commercial application.

Among the FSTC projects currently under way are a check image exchange, one supporting risk management, development of the electronic check, and creation of a standard architecture for BIPS. Each project is briefly described in the following sections as an introduction to the detailed discussion of how the electronic check and BIPS projects will help to address some of the most pressing financial services issues and electronic banking challenges.

Check Image Exchange

The FSTC has a vision to build an infrastructure and standards that could support the introduction of a national interbank check imaging system based on interoperable, open systems architectures that provide flexible, economical services for the financial industry and its customers. To successfully implement interbank check imaging, standardized check image representations of acceptable quality levels must be exchanged electronically in a secured fashion among customers and financial institutions and clearly demonstrate check truncation as a viable and cost-effective solution that will benefit the whole industry. That secured electronic exchange is part of the FSTC vision.

Risk Management

Fraud is unfortunately a fact of everyday life and a factor in the cost of doing business in the financial industry. Banking institutions will naturally tolerate a certain level of fraudulent activity so that undue burden is not placed on the bulk of their honest customers. The FSTC is in the process of defining a research agenda to determine whether it can deploy technological solutions that reduce fraudulent transactions and their resultant impact without interfering with the normal course of serving a law-abiding customer base. It will include investigating ways of both controlling fraud, such as the use of biometrics, and detecting fraud, such as real-time anomaly detection. This project is envisioned to include investigating how interbank information sharing can improve fraud detection and prevention, the development of a test bed, associated metrics, and a benchmark database to test, evaluate, and compare various biometric and fraud-detection technologies and methodologies.

Electronic Check Project

The most popular means of payment in the United States, outside of cash, is the paper check. It dominates all other forms of payment, including credit and debit cards. For this reason, the FSTC has targeted the check as one of its first areas of research for safe payment and for making deposits over the Internet and other on-line networks. The FSTC hopes to extend the popularity of checks to the Internet world.

The electronic check project is directed at providing a safe, secure means of paying by electronic check over on-line networks, such as the Internet, that is extensible to other forms of account-based payment, such as debit card and funds or money transfer. It is tied to bank accounts and existing clearing and settlement systems and designed for use at point-of-sale, phone, and other emerging and existing consumer devices, as well as PCs over the Internet. It is based on an electronic analogue to the check but as noted can be extended to other payment types. The electronic check allows two parties to transact direct on-line commerce over public communications (e.g., e-mail, World Wide Web). Like a check, it does not require prior relationship between payer and payee.

The electronic check would normally be sent by the payer to the payee, where it would be deposited by the payee to the payee's bank; the bank would then settle with the payer's bank using standard banking electronic clearing and settling systems. However, with the electronic check other flows can be accommodated, such as the payer sending the electronic check to the payer's bank with payment instructions, including the payee's bank.

The electronic check uses public key cryptography to allow an individual to electronically issue and digitally sign a payment instruction, such as a check. Specifically, the electronic checkbook cryptographically signs an ASCII text block. This signature, along with the electronic check—the payment instructions—can then be safely transmitted over public networks, where it can be verified by the recipient as a legitimate authorization from an authentic account. The process also provides assurance that the check has not been altered. It is based on standards and uses tamper-resistant hardware (e.g., PC cards or smart cards) to add additional security and protection against fraud. To make a fraudulent payment, one must not only know the customer's password but also possess the card. This card also allows for portability. Customers can transact business anywhere. They do not need to own PCs. Customers can transact over any PC or device (e.g., kiosk, telephone) equipped to read their cards. Electronic checks thus support the notion of universal access.

Figure 6.1 illustrates the basic concept behind the electronic check and represents an actual transaction that was prototyped and demonstrated over the Internet last year. In this demonstration a purchase was paid for by electronic check using standard Internet browser and server hardware and software. The customer digitally

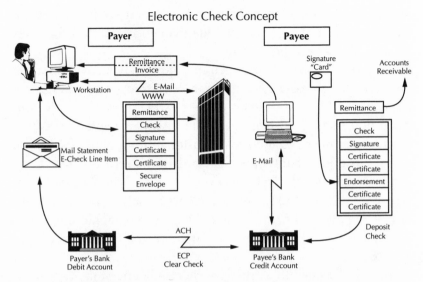

FIGURE 6.1   **Electronic Check Overview**

signed the payment instructions, including remittance information, using a hardware electronic checkbook. The digitally signed electronic check was electronically transmitted to the merchant, where it was verified, electronically endorsed, and electronically delivered to the recipient's bank for collection. The bank then effected the actual transfer of funds between banks and bank accounts through an existing clearing and settlement network, in this case the automated clearinghouse network (ACH). FSTC plans to initiate some pilots with the U.S. Treasury in an effort to further test the security and interoperability of the concept, to refine the design, to test customer acceptance, and to demonstrate the business value of this payment mechanism.

Bank Internet Payment System Project

The bank Internet payment system (BIPS) concept is designed to give banks the opportunity to evolve toward open systems. Banks need to implement secure interbank payments over the Internet in an evolutionary fashion that allows them to interface to the existing payment and settlement systems and to selectively upgrade them over time. BIPS is designed to provide an open architecture for inter-bank payments over the Internet.

BIPS is intended to be an open specification that any vendor can build and sell to banks and that can operate over any number of public networks. FSTC intends to use existing open standards, pro-tocols, and message formats altered to satisfy its requirements that the customer interface and private customer information be known to that customer's bank only. Standards to be incorporated or ac-commodated include SET, electronic check, Open Financial Ex-change (OFX), Joint Electronic Payments Initiative (JEPI) standard for payments selection, and various ANSI cryptographic, digital sig-nature, and financial message standards. A bank's BIPS is shown in figure 6.2.

BIPS is designed to work even when only one of the two banks has a BIPS server because the BIPS bank will have to translate its client's request to something that can be processed within an exist-ing interbank clearing and settlement system. Of course, not all the safeguards and timeliness and payment status information will be

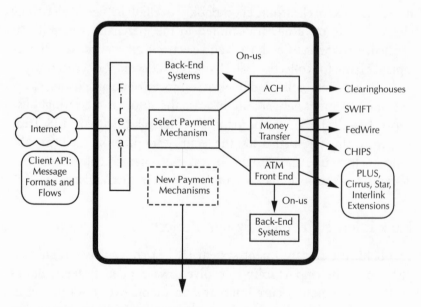

FIGURE 6.2   Overall Model Design

available unless both banks have BIPS servers, as illustrated in figure 6.3.

A complete BIPS interbank system exists when all participating banks have BIPS servers and these servers interface with all the key clearing and settlement systems. A complete BIPS interbank system provides certain advantages.

For banks, BIPS holds the following advantages:

1. Ability to maintain, extend, and further develop their customer relationships
2. Infrastructure on which banks can build new revenue opportunities
3. Reduction of the banks' operating costs in the payments infrastructure
4. Consolidation of banks' preeminent position in the payments world
5. Infrastructure support for banks to implement new products and services

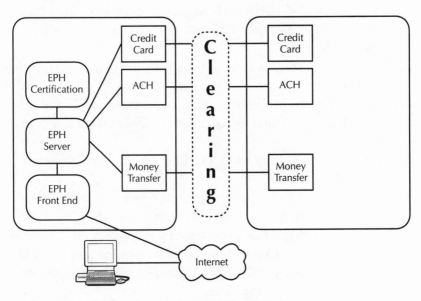

FIGURE 6.3   BIPS Infrastructure for One Bank

6. Minimization of processing errors and reduction of fraud
7. Evolutionary migration path for banks to improve and enhance their existing payment, clearing, and settlement systems and introduction of card-based payment security solutions such as card-secured SET (C-SET) and electronic checks
8. Assistance in meeting the Internet challenge with secure, trusted payment systems developed with minimum risk and cost sharing
9. Increased customer acceptance of Internet banking and payment by providing the critical mass necessary for bringing in new customers and introducing the full banking community

For customers, BIPS offers the following advantages:

1. Increased flexibility of payment options
2. Better management of credit and settlement risk
3. Allowance for a wide variety of devices that could be used to implement payments and settlements, which in turn will facilitate and promote the widespread implementation and utilization of electronic commerce activities
4. Establishment of electronic commerce as an integrated business transaction as opposed to a series of separate business activities
5. Integration of merchants' interfaces with their customers, their own banks, and their customers' banks
6. Faster and more precisely defined payment for goods and services, allowing for quicker completion of commercial transactions
7. Payment over the Internet that is timely, trusted, certain, secure, and reliable
8. Availability of data for better corporate financial information
9. Alignment of banks' payment systems with the emerging corporate business model that provides for on-line shopping, greater dissemination of information goods, widespread implementation of electronic publishing, and more flexible corporate-to-corporate business transactions

Relationship of BIPS to the Electronic Check Project

A fully secure electronic check provides a desirable standardized network payment mechanism. It gives bank customers portability—they can pay anywhere because they carry their profile and authentication with them on a card. They can use it in a business center, on a telephone, on a guest's PC, or anywhere that can read a card. Moreover it represents a more secure solution than most of the current alternatives, because the secrets are kept locked up on a small card or token that the customer possesses and can protect; that card or token will be harder to penetrate because it has only a few specialized functions. Furthermore, payment can occur directly between payer and payee, without the need for an on-line trusted third party. Its use in a retail application is illustrated in figure 6.4, although electronic checking can support many other flows (e.g., from payer to payer's bank to payee's bank) and all manner of transactions (e.g., from individual to individual or corporation to corporation).

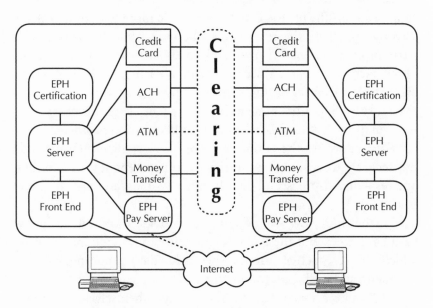

FIGURE 6.4   **BIPS Infrastructure—Complete**

However, electronic checking requires both parties to have cards and the interacting computer devices (e.g., PCs) to have card readers. For electronic checking to be useful, widespread availability of these devices is needed. This will not happen overnight. In the meantime, customers will continue to seek relatively secure software-only solutions.

Providing a secure, software-only solution requires a trusted third party on line who can challenge the user to demonstrate secrets, keys, or biometrics that only the user and the trusted third party know or possess. This is not as secure as the electronic check, which can store these secrets and biometrics on the card that the user possesses, but with the proper design, safeguards, and limitations it should suffice, at least in the interim. This is the type of design currently being introduced (e.g., VISA and MasterCard's secure electronic transaction [SET] specifications). In all cases there is a single trusted third party, either an individual bank or financial institution or an association or clearinghouse. However, for checks and funds transfers, there is no single dominant association or clearinghouse. Therefore BIPS is designed to achieve the same effect by designing an on-line protocol that can include more than one bank, or association, where the trust is distributed among the banks. Each party instructs his or her own bank to either make payment to another party who has an account with a participating bank or to arrange for a transfer of funds from another party with a participating bank. BIPS uses the same technology as the electronic check, digital signatures, but it adds an on-line authentication protocol.

BIPS addresses the entire payment process, including responding securely to customer inquiries as to payment status, handling and resolving disputes, and distributing, revoking, and updating certificates.

Furthermore, BIPS is designed to provide the hooks to allow each bank to extend the BIPS functionality to provide many value-added services, such as warehousing, value dating, netting, bill presentment, and push/pull transactions.

BIPS allows customers to authenticate themselves with their electronic checks even when the other transacting party has no electronic check. When two customers both have electronic checks, the

BIPS design allows them to make payments directly to one another, without the on-line presence of the bank, and accepts the endorsed check electronically, from either the payer or payee.

As such, BIPS represents a generalization of the electronic check server. It supports on-line authentication, extends the number of interfaced interbank clearing and settlement systems, addresses the full required bank payment server functionality (e.g., can handle disputes, queries, and certificate management), and provides banks with the hooks to add their own unique value-added services and branding.

Next Steps in the BIPS and Electronic Check Projects

The BIPS and electronic check specifications are expected to evolve through active use and trial. FSTC will validate the concepts through real-world pilots and expects to put the specification through rigorous tests and certification as to its level of security and safety.

BIPS standards will include evaluation of the suitability of all the evolving open and de facto standards being proposed in the electronic financial arena, including SET and Open Financial Exchange, as well as electronic checking's proposed financial structured markup language (FSML) standard. FSTC plans to propose extensions and modifications it feels are necessary to ensure sufficient security and ease of implementation and use.

Upon completion of these projects, a participating financial institution will be able to develop its interface to the Internet with minimal risk and cost. Each bank will have the advantage of a fully tested and standards-based infrastructure; it will not be out on the Internet alone, and the cost and technical development will be shared by all the members. FSTC hopes to become a voice in shaping, evaluating, and controlling the evolution of financial electronic commerce standards, working closely with the various standards, banking, and financial institution organizations. Because BIPS is a collaborative effort, each bank will be certain that its systems conform to the evolving open standards and are interoperable.

In the case of electronic checking, the FSTC is anxious for the wide adoption of this common standard secure hardware device, such as a smart card. It would like electronic checking to become widely accessible on a variety of end-user devices (e.g., PCs, set-top boxes, and handheld personal devices such as cellular phones and personal information management devices). FSTC envisions that such a device could work over a variety of communications media (e.g., Web, e-mail) over public networks and provide for encryption and digital signatures to occur securely over standard application programming interfaces. It is envisioned that such a card could become sufficiently generic to serve as a user's authentication device for a variety of purposes, including satisfying not only electronic checking and BIPS payments but other initiatives, such as SET and Open Financial Exchange. Ultimately, such a device could evolve to becoming a customer's electronic wallet. This electronic wallet would hopefully become as ubiquitous as real wallets and check registers are today, able to hold a variety of payment instruments and financial documents and applicable for use over a variety of media, across the broadest spectrum of merchants, corporations, and individual users.

Conclusion

This chapter illustrates the growing importance to the financial services industry in general and the banking industry in particular of online distribution of its services and products. It also shows why the open architecture of the Internet is likely to continue to dominate as the preferred means of electronic communication and distribution.

The membership of FSTC is committed to working collaboratively through an industry consortium to help achieve interoperability and sanity against the backdrop of feverish electronic commerce activity, best characterized by an escalating number of uncoordinated activities. Through the efforts of organizations such as the FSTC, we hope to achieve an understanding and consensus as to the best path for the industry and customer to take in this rapidly changing marketplace. In this regard, the FSTC is trying to educate the industry about the importance and relative merits and disadvantages of the various efforts being introduced and proposed, including initiatives of its own when no others are available. As a neutral party,

FSTC hopes to persuade and influence the industry to help shape these efforts so that all can safely and securely interoperate and to achieve a critical mass of acceptance among customers, without hampering the individual innovation and competitive spirit of its members. FSTC is working closely with organizations such as the World Wide Web Consortium and the Open Systems Foundation and has cosponsored an Electronic Payment Forum, along with the Cross Industry Working Team (XIWT) and CommerceNet, to further these goals.

In light of the rapid changes in the industry, FSTC has concluded that the best way to achieve these objectives is to actually build, demonstrate, and pilot these concepts—to act through research and development consortia, influencing by doing rather than by committee, validating a position by demonstration rather than analysis alone. This is a departure from previous standards and industry organizations and more in keeping with the nature of modern standards evolution, such as is occurring on the Internet today. Only time will tell whether FSTC succeeds in its mission.

References

1. David Laster and John Wenninger, "Policy Issues Raised by Electronic Money," paper presented at the Citi Conference on Digital Cash and Electronic Money, New York, 1995.
2. Jay McCormick, "Debit Card Finally May Live up to Its Billing," *USA Today* (June 11, 1986): 4B.

Bibliography

Ernst & Young LLP and the American Bankers Association, "Fourth Annual Special Report on Technology in Banking," *Bank Technology News* (February 1995): 3.

Exploring the World of Cyberpayments: An Introductory Survey: A Colloquium sponsored by Financial Crimes Enforcement Network, U.S. Department of the Treasury, Washington, D.C., September 27, 1995.

Fix, Janet. "Deal Secures First Data's Credit Lead," *USA Today* (September 18, 1995): A1.

Rider, Paul, and Linda Hawkes. *Paying for Purchases Made over the Internet.* Association for Payment Clearing Services, June 20, 1995.

Table comparisons of different electronic commerce systems are available at http://www.fstc.org and under the electronic commerce pages.

Sources for Internet Statistics

Nielsen Study

Some of the key results of a study conducted by Nielsen for Commerce-Net are summarized in the following list. This is the first major survey of Internet use among the general population. The study has found that

1. Adults in the United States and Canada spend as much time surfing the Internet each week as they devote to watching rented videocassettes.
2. An estimated 24 million adults—10.8 percent of the combined population of the two countries age 16 years and older—had used the Internet in the last three months.
3. Based on projections, 2.5 million adults have already purchased goods or services over the Internet's World Wide Web.
4. Internet users tend to be highly educated and affluent.
5. While the Internet remains very much a male preserve, 35 percent of the users were women.
6. About 37 million people, or 16.6 percent of all adults age 16 and older in the United States and Canada, have access to the Internet, either directly or indirectly through a friend, coworker, or commercial on-line service such as America Online.
7. Among the 10.8 percent who said they had direct access, users spent an average of 5 hours 28 minutes a week on line.
8. Among Internet users, 64 percent had spent time on the World Wide Web, the most popular and fastest-growing Internet service.
9. Slightly more than 6 out of 10 adult Internet users said they had access to the Internet from their homes.

10. But the flip side is that 38 percent did not, and their only conduit to the Internet was at the office or at school. Of those who had been on line in the last 24 hours, 66 percent had done so from work.

Those figures suggest that the Internet is approaching mass-market penetration much more quickly than earlier studies had projected. They suggest that into the near future business-to-business Internet services will be at least as important as consumer Internet services. Compared with the adoption rates for other key technologies in the past, the survey indicates that the Internet has entered the mainstream far more quickly than many analysts had projected.

Payments on the Internet: Opportunities in Electronic Commerce—Killen & Associates Study (#392), 1995

This study predicts that

1. Within six years Internet shoppers will purchase $600 billion worth of goods and services—this would represent 8 percent of worldwide purchases.
2. Currently on-line and electronic data interchange (EDI) account for only 4 percent of the credit card market (and Internet represents an insignificant percentage of this).
3. By 2005, Internet-based transactions should increase to $17 billion, approximately 50 percent of the credit card market.

Summary of "Who's Succeeding and How on the Internet?"—ActivMedia Inc., 1995

Growth Statistics

There is tremendous growth of businesses on the Internet. At the end of September 1994 there were 588 commercial World Wide Web sites listed on the Open Market Commercial Sites index, http://www.directory.net. Eight months later more than 6,000 were listed on the same directory.

Sales Statistics

The sales generated between September 1994 and August 1995 were projected to be $118 million, with the sales in August greater than 4,000% of those 11 months earlier. Approximately 21 percent had sales over $10,000 during the prior month. Of these, 2 percent were greater than $100,000 and 1 percent greater than $1 million. This excludes sales by nonprofit organizations and Internet access providers, Web consultants, and so forth. Most of the products sold on line are widely available off line. Most of these on-line sales probably are transferred from another marketing channel.

Cost Savings

Successful marketeers report savings from Internet use over traditional marketing and customer support. "We found manpower to answer 100,000 queries over on-line forums is less than half as expensive as 800 lines."

Handling of Payments

1. Although much has been made of consumer reluctance to provide financial information via electronic media, 35 percent accept credit card information from unsecured sites as opposed to 7 percent from secure sites.
2. Small companies are less likely to report credit card transactions of any type or to bill for purchases.
3. Only 3 percent report accepting some form of electronic payment.
4. Two-thirds accept phone or faxed credit card information.
5. Greater than half accept checks or credit card transactions by mail.
6. Half bill and invoice.

"Battlegrounds in the Payments Industry: Developing Strategies under Uncertainty," presentation by McKinsey, BAI National Payments System Symposium, October 17, 1995.

Payments industry included more than $84 billion in revenue for 1993. Banks have a natural advantage today, but it requires interbank cooperation since most customers have multiple banking accounts.

▷ Outside of cash, payments are still dominated by checks—94 percent of the total 400 billion U.S. payments transactions are paper cash, check, and food stamps, and there is a steady year-on-year growth of checks and cash (3 percent per year).

▷ 90 percent of consumers have at least one checking account, and the average consumer maintains 2.8 bank account relationships.

▷ 89 percent of large corporations use the ACH.
▷ The average business writes 158 checks per month.
▷ Electronic payments are growing at 15 to 25 percent per year, and each share point will shift 4 billion new transactions.

7

First Data Corporation

*Behind-the-Scenes Processing
and Frontline Internet Commerce*

CHUCK WHITE
FIRST DATA CORPORATION

Introduction

The term *electronic commerce* has now become a popular label used to describe the collection of relatively recent efforts to enable the execution of financial transactions over public networking media such as the Internet, cable television, and telephone systems. Of course, in reality, electronic commerce is nothing new. For many years banks and other financial institutions have allowed a subset of their customers to use terminals, PCs, and telephones in the execution of financial transactions ranging from money transfer to bill payment. And certainly the on-line authorization and settlement of bankcard transactions, as supported by the card networks, First Data Corporation (FDC), and other processors, qualify as electronic commerce. The differences between the current definition of this phrase and traditional on-line commercial activity are related to the degree to which the consumer becomes an integral part of the electronic execution of the payment transaction, as well as the context within which these transactions occur.

Current electronic commerce initiatives attempt to place the consumer/buyer, merchant, and potentially the bank together in an on-line environment in which the payment transaction can be initiated and processed without human mediation. Although the initial services being introduced use credit cards as the purchase instrument, the similar use of debit cards, on-line cash, and the digital equivalent of checks is being explored. To give consumers secure electronic access of this sort to both their personal banking accounts and to general merchant storefronts or electronic catalogs via an open network such as the Internet, issues that have no equivalent in traditional electronic commerce must be addressed. And, whenever new issues are raised, new opportunities for business solutions are created.

Historically, electronic creation of financial transactions by customers has been outside of the scope of central payment systems and generally limited to corporate users who access services via closed networks. Although there have been home banking initiatives and explorations of the delivery of financial services to the home, broad focus on the establishment of such access to consumers has been largely nonexistent. This is now changing. Although the forecasts are inexact and vary widely, most credible evaluations forecast that within the next five years from 5 to 20 percent of credit card transactions will be initiated over some alternative medium such as cable, screen phone, or the Internet.

This forecast does not begin to capture the full force of the business impact of moving a significant percentage of financial and banking transactions to the Internet. In fact, such a move will transform the relationships among all participants in the financial services marketplace and provide tremendous opportunities for growth and product development. First Data Corporation, which has established itself over the past several years as a leader in information and transaction processing services for financial institutions and commercial establishments, is now creating and implementing strategies to extend this leadership to commerce on the Internet.

To succeed in this new role, First Data must overcome some of the intrinsic challenges of Internet business models and technology solutions. Because the 'Net is an open, dynamic, and highly competitive environment with almost unlimited opportunities for entry, no one company can know for sure what strategy is going to work, how long a given market will take to develop, or where the next key piece of technology will be found. Even with the most rigorous of planning and analysis processes, there is no reliable method for ensuring that an innovative product or Internet service offering will ever come to fruition much less become a profitable business. Nevertheless, the opportunities for success on the Internet are too large, and the consequences of ignoring this next phase of electronic commerce are too dire, for any company providing financial services to move forward without an Internet commerce strategy.

This chapter describes how First Data Corporation has worked to establish and achieve its strategic goals for commerce on the Internet. One part of this process has been to examine FDC's core competencies and to plan ways to leverage these strengths into Internet-based service offerings. First Data has also created an Internet solution group to coordinate electronic commerce strategies across the company's business units and to identify significant Internet product development and partnership efforts. In addition, First Data's management has evaluated a number of potential Internet commerce initiatives and aims to establish leadership in this new arena. The chapter concludes by discussing how potential Internet initiatives have been analyzed and presenting some of the strategic rationale behind the selection of new electronic commerce initiatives for FDC to pursue.

Overview of First Data

First Data Corporation, with annual sales of almost $5 billion and a market capitalization near $20 billion, is now the second largest independent data services company in the world. FDC aims to be the number one or number two service provider in every market that it serves, including card processing and bill presentment, mutual funds services, information management solutions, and check processing. First Data is currently producing more than 1 billion statements per year for U.S. households, representing 7 percent of the billing market and making FDC the largest statement provider in the country. Over the past several years, First Data has moved to expand its market position by developing new services and by acquiring companies that have already developed market leadership in competitive or adjacent areas of service.

In general, First Data seeks to use its existing business infrastructure, which already supports an intense, high-volume processor model for global electronic commerce, to build the services its commercial clients will need as more financial services, purchasing, and settlement activity take place on the Internet. Because it already offers related services to most of the major markets for Internet commerce, FDC is well positioned to benefit from the increasing demand for secure electronic payment and bill presentment services on the Internet. Among the core competencies and the relevant FDC business units, those that provide First Data with a head start by being most directly relevant to new initiatives in Internet electronic commerce are as follows:

Bill presentment (First Image). First Image is the leading outsource provider of integrated document services in the United States. First Image prints more than 1.1 billion laser-imaged pages, mails more than 200 million envelopes, and scans in excess of 30 million documents each year.

Bill payment (IPS/Western Union). Integrated Payment Systems (IPS) is the leading provider of official checks in the United States. More than 3,500 financial institutions use IPS checks as alternatives to their own products. Western Union provides systems for transferring funds or making payments through 30,000 agent locations in nearly 130 countries and is the worldwide leader in providing these services.

Credit card bill presentment (FDR) and private label home banking (FDR). First Data Resources (FDR) provides a comprehensive line of products and services to bankcard issuers, including processing for credit, debit, commercial, and smart cards; cobranding; fraud and risk management services; and relational database marketing services.

Mutual funds statement presentment (Investor Services Group). First Data Investor Services Group provides integrated and customized mutual fund services to investment organizations and the banking industry. Its clients include more than 100 mutual fund companies that receive daily support for more than $340 billion in assets.

Large biller (merchant) relationships (FDMS). First Data Merchant Services is the world's leading provider of merchant processing services for VISA, MasterCard, and other major credit cards. In 1995 this unit processed more than $144 billion in credit card volume.

Information management (Solutions). First Data Solutions provides information solutions to the financial, retail, collections, and insurance industries.

These and the other FDC business units are working together to develop broader service offerings that will extend current products onto the Internet and develop the innovative Internet processing solutions that will increasingly be in demand. The complete list of business units and core activities is illustrated in figure 7.1 and is available at www.firstdata.com.

As this brief overview shows, First Data Corporation is already a leader in providing electronic processing and financial support services to the market sectors that are affected most directly by the development of Internet commerce, including banks, credit card companies, merchants, investment firms and mutual funds, check and payment clearing firms, and more. The predicted expansion of Internet applications for businesses and consumers will inevitably change the relationships between FDC and its current clients and redefine the services and products these clients will need by the end of the decade. It is also likely that Internet commerce opportunities will attract competitors in areas where First Data is currently an industry leader and will transform the basis of competition. These eventualities are in themselves an incentive for FDC to hone its Internet strategy carefully. In addition, First Data is committed to establishing a leadership strategy that reaches far beyond responding to competitive requirements and takes on the challenge of setting the pace for providing model Internet commerce services to the banking and financial services markets.

FIGURE 7.1   **First Data Corporation Business Units**

Defining the Internet Opportunity

For a company that includes a variety of ways to process large numbers of transactions among its core competencies, the current data and future growth potential of the Internet tell a compelling story. Among the facts that have crystallized the central role of the 'Net in shaping the future of financial services are statistics such as the following:

> ▷ The Tower Group expects North American banks to spend $700 million on Internet sites by 2000.
> ▷ The number of commercial Web sites has increased 26 percent per month since 1994.
> ▷ By the end of 1996, almost 21 percent of 19 million Web users had made on-line purchases.
> ▷ By the year 2000, 55 percent of U.S. households (a total of 103,245,000) are expected to have computers, and of these more than 43 million households are expected to be active on-line users.
> ▷ Estimates of the transaction market size range from tens to hundreds of billions of dollars of sales on the Web by 2001.

▷ The incremental cost of communicating via the Internet with additional business partners and customers is approaching zero.

Strategic Goals and Internet Opportunities

The value of being an early player in Internet commerce markets is high. To understand how the transformation in business models and technology infrastructure is impacting core products and services, it is essential to be engaged with the marketplace and with internal Web applications and development. It is out of this interplay that new business models and the next generation of technology infrastructure for corporations are emerging. Because of the rate of change in this space, a continual, active scanning of the marketplace is required to assess the true value of these emergent markets, business models, and technologies. Because competitors are proliferating and the Internet has lowered barriers to entry in some key financial services sectors, early participation also helps companies to gain mindshare and become identified with the Internet solutions that will become future standards. Early and interactive engagement with the marketplace also helps to reduce the learning curve for future Internet product development and Internet-engendered businesses.

There are numerous points of intersection between First Data's core businesses and competencies and the opportunities that are emerging as a result of the Internet. Figure 7.2 maps some of the most immediate areas of opportunity. These areas include on-line banking services, merchant hosting, retail and commercial bank services, and support for financial services on the Internet offered by card issuers. While not a comprehensive list, it provides a flavor for the breadth of opportunities provided by simply extending some of the services that FDC currently provides on the Internet.

Not all opportunities are equal, however, and an essential step in moving from strategy to execution is determining which of the possible entry points offer the best opportunities for First Data and the greatest value for its clients. From a competitive perspective, it is also

Selected Service Opportunities

Acquiring Banks	Card Issuers	Retail Banks	Commercial Banks
• Basic Services	• Basic Services	• Basic Services	• Basic Services
• Marketing	• Marketing	• Marketing	• Marketing
• Merchant Sign-Up	• Application	• Fulfillment	• Fulfillment
• Merchant Acceptance	Acceptance	• Financial Services	• Financial Services
• Existing Merchants	• Financial Services	• On-Line Home	• Cash Management
• New Merchants	• EU$AVE	and Small Business	• Bill Presentment
• Merchant Hosting	• Transaction Detail	Banking	and Payment
Services	Information	• Balance Inquiry	• Outsourced
• Catalogs, Databases	• Bill Payment	• Funds Transfer	Statement and
• Financial Services	• Bill Presentment	• Statement Detail	Payment
• Delivery of	• Purchasing	• Bill Payment	Processing
Information	Systems	• Bill Presentment	• Purchasing
• On-Line Account		• New Payment	Systems
Acceptance		Instruments	
• New Payment			
Instruments			

FIGURE 7.2   Overview of Opportunities
for Internet Product Development

essential to determine which initiatives will be most likely to establish a leadership position for FDC within a particular service sector. The next section of this chapter reviews some of the strategic issues and the analyses that have shaped FDC's answers to these considerations.

Framework for Evaluation

For FDC, the process of evaluating specific business opportunities is grounded in a clear definition of First Data Corporation's strengths and an analysis of the general opportunities and risks associated with Internet commerce implementation. This understanding provides a framework for a more in-depth evaluation of these investment areas for fit within the overall FDC portfolio of services.

Since First Data is a company that builds its businesses on economies of scale, FDC's entry into the nascent Internet commerce marketplace has not been driven by expectations of direct and immediate financial returns. Rather, the motivation focuses on honing the business knowledge and technical skills that entering these early markets can provide. Such skills are an essential foundation for First Data's future Internet-based business investments and for adapting its more traditional enterprise activities to the 'Net.

FDC's extensive transaction-processing experience and its partnerships with numerous financial institutions across many businesses are assets that underpin a number of potential Internet business opportunities. Also, through the scope of its transaction-processing activities, First Data has developed tangible information assets, including extensive data about aggregate consumer purchase patterns, that increase in value with the growth in electronic transactions. With this asset base and experience as a backdrop, it is possible to summarize the general areas of opportunity for First Data in Internet commerce as follows:

▷ Leveraging existing services and relationships into Internet-based market segments.
▷ Merging information services from different business units in ways that have not been possible with previous technology platforms.
▷ Entering new businesses supporting existing clients on the Internet.
▷ Reducing the network expense and information distribution costs in existing businesses.

Identifying Requirements and Risks

At a very basic level, Web commerce must be based on secure identification of on-line merchants and on-line consumers. The requirement to identify and authenticate participants in networked electronic transactions has created a broad need for services that will certify people, machines, programs, applets, and all of the other players in an open distributed system. Without some means of establishing trust, and some assurance that Internet commerce is supported by the same security infrastructure as other credit card purchases and banking transactions, the potential for Web markets cannot be realized. In the traditional commerce environment, business analogues such as notaries vouch for identity. However, the breadth and scope of these trust requirements for on-line systems, especially the requirement to support commerce among potentially millions of people with whom one has had no previous contact, has created a new class of problems and is calling forth a new class of solutions.

As a large provider of on-line transaction services and an enabler of remote transactions, First Data both requires these services and is well positioned to deliver them to its clients. FDC supports the efforts to implement Internet standards for electronic security and uses the services of Verisign to provide digital certification for merchants on the Web. As the demand for secure identification and certification expands with the growth of electronic commerce, it can be expected that demand for even more secure and more specific trust services will increase. Today's infrastructure, while it serves basic merchant and consumer needs, is not flexible enough to certify the validity of thousands of million-dollar bids submitted during a global on-line auction or to authenticate and then decertify a large number of players in a brief, specific period of time. FDC's infrastructure is well suited to support this anticipated demand for expanded and targeted trust certification on the Internet.

In addition to multiple opportunities, FDC has identified significant risks in entering these new Internet markets. Any time there is a change in the technical infrastructure on which businesses are based, there is a potential downside for the current market leaders. By making it possible for different market participants to exchange information directly, the Internet has the potential to reduce the value of existing, dedicated networks and relationships that First Data has built to deliver products and services. Other companies without market share or capital invested in the existing infrastructure may have the wherewithal to more easily enter the Internet commerce market.

In addition, the Internet is changing the economics of how FDC customers conduct their businesses and how FDC conducts its own business processes. Outsourcing of certain processing functions that have been the mainstay of some FDC business services may be reduced because these can be supported more efficiently, and with less capital intensity, on the Web. Unless FDC maintains a clear focus on evolving its own product set in response to these challenges, the transition from traditional processing models to Internet commerce is likely to reduce the demand for certain FDC products. This in turn would adversely affect the business units that offer products and services geared primarily to current market demand. Realization that such risks are closely associated with the expansion of Internet commerce is another incentive to focus FDC's Internet strategy on areas of high growth potential and to move aggressively to develop a leadership position.

Building on Business Experience

Since it already has a broad base of clients in a wide variety of distinct businesses, the first line of Internet commerce opportunities for First Data includes leveraging existing client relationships and services. As the summary of First Data business units in figure 7.2 demonstrates, FDC products already span a variety of financial and electronic processing realms, and the company's business units number other leading financial institutions among their clients. This network of FDC client relationships provides a basis for aggregation of information and for creating communities of related interest.

Outside of the Internet, for example, First Data has allied with its credit card and banking clients to create a new business opportunity called USAVE. This group, formed in January 1997, is a partnership with credit card–issuing and merchant-acquiring financial institutions. USAVE provides targeted marketing services to merchants who want to deliver special offers to credit card holders. In the current environment of monthly card statements delivered by post, these offers are included in print form with the credit card bills. The advantage of USAVE services for merchants is that their offers can be very precisely targeted to particular combinations of consumer demographics and purchase patterns based on the data available to USAVE from previous transaction-processing activity. This means that a restaurant can send a discount offer only to those consumers who have spent more than $500 on dining out during the past six months, or a specialty store in a particular location can target frequent shoppers at other local stores.

When cardholders wish to take up a USAVE discount offer, they can simply use the appropriate credit card to make a purchase. The value of any discount offered by the merchant is netted against the merchant's credit card receipts in its daily settlement. To merchants, the value of the targeting is related directly to the number of cardholders who can be targeted and the amount of information that is available concerning the consumer purchase patterns. This type of service requires a seamlessly integrated network of issuers, acquirers, and merchants within a business framework that delivers value to all parties. First Data serves as the data integrator, and the USAVE partnership provides the business framework.

In this specific case, the USAVE partners are still developing the discount offers and the business model within the existing printed statement world. Nevertheless, it is easy to see how this model could be extended onto the Internet without requiring significant additional investment. On-line offers could be delivered more frequently and could be exercised directly on the Web for certain categories of goods and services. The types of messages delivered to consumers could be enhanced with graphic and multimedia presentations, demonstrations of products, and other features. Given the projections for future consumer purchases on line and the central position occupied by FDC in processing electronic transactions, working with partners to extend USAVE and similar services to the Internet will provide significant growth opportunities.

Merging the Services of FDC Business Units

The Internet also provides FDC and its clients with an easier way to aggregate services and systems that may have been independently developed or that have different system architectures. The Internet makes it possible to put together diverse systems and, if everything works, convey a single, seamless interface to customers. MSFDC, a joint venture between First Data and Microsoft Corporation, which is discussed in more detail later in this chapter, provides an example of leveraging the core competencies and client networks of different FDC business units. In addition to opening a new avenue for consumer services on the Web, MSFDC creates an infrastructure to meet the requirements of First Image, Investor Services Group, and other FDC clients for on-line statement integration and bill presentment services.

Tracking the Decision Process: Three Cases

To illustrate how this general opportunity and risk framework can inform specific business and strategy decisions, it is helpful to review First Data's decision process in three cases: transaction processing on the Internet, merchant hosting of Web storefronts, and electronic bill payment and presentment. First Data, for example, opted to make an early move into supporting transaction processing on the Internet. As the subsequent merchant Web hosting example will show, despite an initial attractiveness, a careful analysis will sometimes reveal that Internet opportunities do not fit well with First Data's core strengths or will reveal the weaknesses of on-line business models. It is a reality of Internet strategy development, as with strategy development everywhere else, that not every opportunity will become a product. The difference is that business models in more traditional areas have a half-life of more than three months.

Transaction Processing

For First Data, the earliest market to be impacted by the Internet was credit card processing. Early on in the development of the Internet software market, software providers saw that enabling payment was a critical prerequisite for the development of commerce on the Internet. The payment instrument that was seen to be most appropriate, that is, to have the largest market acceptance and the most appropriate risk management infrastructure profile, was the credit card.

Credit cards have been used for years in mail-order businesses; the general business risk of the Internet—consumers purchasing remotely with only the information from their credit cards as identification—corresponds very closely to that market. Also, in the mail-order market, unlike the markets where the buyer and the credit card are both physically present at the time of the transaction, the merchant takes the credit risk. Since merchants have the greatest motivation to sell their products on line, they are the most willing to take the financial risk associated with a new medium.

In 1994 and 1995, the development of a secure payment infrastructure was seen by many market participants as critical to the development of commerce on the Internet. A few credit card transactions had been occurring for some time on the Internet, either by referral to a toll-free number or by passing the credit card information in the clear, but there was a general belief that the mass market of merchants and consumers would not begin to develop until they could be assured that transaction information would be secure. Obviously, many companies saw a role for themselves in the market, as providers of software, standard setters, processors, or merchants. The nature of security on the Internet, with its dependencies on public key cryptography that was, at the time, a relatively arcane discipline, tended to place the software developers in a leadership position.

However, early efforts by software providers to lead the market were notably ineffectual. This was a result of the complexities of the market and the number of market participants who had to work in concert in the delivery of a working solution. Merchants, merchant software providers, merchant acquirers, client software providers, credit card issuers, and credit card associations all had to agree on standards for conducting secure transactions. Overlaying this complexity was the relative fluidity of positions of the various market participants concerning their business models. Who paid whom and for what was constantly shifting as various positions were tested and rejected. The software providers did not have a lot of insight into the complexities of the other market players and their relationships, of the payment systems that were already in place, or of the complexities surrounding transaction risk management. This proved to be a long-term disadvantage that early technical innovations could not overcome.

At First Data, excitement about the market opportunities was tempered with a more realistic assessment of the likely rate of adoption of Internet distribution by merchants. Nonetheless, FDC still believed that entering the Internet market to provide transaction-processing services was a competitive necessity. First, it was clear that merchants would be coming to FDC for support once they decided to venture into the Internet marketplace. If First Data did not prepare an Internet commerce solution, its competitors would. In this regard, it is characteristic of the Internet that competitive concerns at the time were not focused so much on other transaction processors as on emerging digital payment providers that could potentially disintermediate FDC from its key merchant customers. Even though this concern proved unfounded, FDC recognized the clear impact of the Internet on how business would be done and it wanted to gain early experience with the business models and technologies that were emerging.

The Internet transaction-processing market, although on the surface simple, has a number of attributes that make it a useful touchstone for consideration of other markets. The lessons learned during this phase of strategy development provided a useful perspective for subsequent market entry decisions. When everything (business models, technology, and business relationships) is new and the rates of change of all the moving parts are high, it is difficult to construct a coherent strategy. Once the organization has tested its ideas in the market and consolidated partnerships, it can use the experience as a measure for future ventures.

In the excitement that sometimes surrounds the Internet, new entrants can assume that existing business problems can be obviated by technology, only to find that such problems are remarkably persistent. Similarly, market complexities are often dismissed as a simple matter of programming when they manifestly are not. In the transaction-processing case, software providers severely underestimated the extent of development required to support payment processing. This underestimation, along with a resistance from market incumbents, caused a major shift in their business models over a short period of time. Many of the early entrants in Internet transaction processing shifted from expecting to be paid a percentage of each on-line transaction to being pure software providers to completely getting out of the market. Market and technical complexity in this case became an unrecognized barrier to entry.

Initially First Data worked with Netscape to enable transaction processing from its merchant servers. This forced FDC to deal with all of the security issues of doing business on the Internet and required the company to develop the infrastructure to deliver robust and reliable service by working with the relatively immature components available at the time. It also forced FDC business units to modify risk management practices. Typical merchants on the Internet have a different credit profile than average merchants on the street. To develop an acquiring relationship with them, FDC had to change the way it looked at the on-line merchant businesses and how it evaluated the risk of that business. First Data thus developed an understanding of the issues that differentiated Web commerce from other electronic transactions and defined in detail the system requirements of the Internet merchant. This understanding has paved the way for the introduction of new services and products, tailored to the needs of these merchants, that could not have been foreseen without direct experience.

Of course, First Data's investment in this market did not have an immediate return. However, the skills and understanding developed in this area have provided a foundation for its strategies on other services. Also, as a result of this early entry into the market, and despite the entry of many other processors, First Data has emerged with a leading position in Internet payment transaction processing.

Merchant Hosting Services

Business models for merchants on the Internet are changing dramatically. Understanding those changes requires immersion in the market. What do the merchants operating Web sites today really require in terms of services? How significant is the Web channel for their businesses and how quickly will it grow? What are the key services that will accelerate that growth curve and generate demand for expanded services?

To successfully market products and conduct financial transactions with customers in an open on-line environment like the Internet, certain core technical and operational capabilities are required to maintain acceptable levels of service quality. Many, if not most, merchants wishing to participate in this market lack the resources or expertise required to build and maintain the appropriate operational reliability, transaction integrity, access security, and other components of an electronic marketing and distribution channel directly accessed by customers. As the description of its business units illustrates, First Data's fundamental competencies in all of these areas seem well suited to meet this need, capitalizing on the opportunity to add further value to its service and strengthen its client relationships.

One of these capabilities is maintaining the Web site itself. First Data provides services today that mediate electronic transactions between merchants and financial institutions. It would seem only natural to offer a product extension that also provides the services that mediate between the consumer and the merchant. However, on closer examination, there are a number of differences between these transactions. Also, several attributes of the market caused First Data to have second thoughts about entry into merchant Web hosting services.

Supporting the end-to-end purchase transaction cycle requires a number of skills. The development of Web sites does not adapt gracefully to economies of scale since merchants tend to have very individual expectations in both artistic and technical realms. The integration of individual merchant storefronts with a variety of back-end fulfillment and accounting systems also requires more custom software development and system integration, rather than application of the type of capabilities and processing functions that characterize FDC systems. Large merchants require a great deal of customization to support their transaction flow requirements. The development effort required is much greater than First Data typically must expend supporting merchants in other types of transaction processing, and the effort expended is not easily leveraged to serve the needs of other merchants.

At the other end of the spectrum are the many small merchants that have very little customization requirements. While it may be possible to develop a service that fits First Data's strengths supporting these merchant customers, the low-end Web hosting market is also problematic. Many organizations want to offer Web hosting services to these merchants, and most hosting services today are not making attractive economic returns. Also, there are other market complexities. If FDC becomes a major provider of merchant hosting services, it would be more difficult to develop effective channel relationships with other hosting services as distributors for FDC payment services. Since most merchants will be hosted in one form or another, and since this will, in all likelihood, be a fragmented market, the incremental revenue to be gained through hosting does not appear to offset the potential loss to FDC's core payment business.

On balance, therefore, Web hosting turns out to be a market that at first glance appears attractive but that on a more detailed assessment fails to offer a good strategic match to an organization with First Data's skills, business model, and position in the market. On the other hand, the final Internet commerce opportunity analyzed in this chapter, on-line bill presentment and payment, has emerged as a strategic priority for First Data.

Bill Payment and Presentment

At first glance, entry into the emerging market for Internet bill payment and presentment might seem even more problematic than merchant Web hosting services. Although electronic bill-payment capabilities have been available through dedicated, proprietary systems for a number of years, this market has been slow to develop. The number of consumers who make use of electronic payment options today is still relatively small, with estimates at around 2 million. However, the situation is changing. The total number of electronic payments by U.S. consumers has been projected to rise from 361 million in 1997 to 2 billion in 2001.

Bill presentment is seen to be the major factor accelerating this penetration. Consumer research indicates that to attract the widest possible range of consumers the entire process needs to be seamlessly integrated. However, to get support from billers, electronic payments have to become more integrated into back-office processes. Without this integration, and with a relatively tiny percentage of customers opting for electronic payment, the billers cannot realize any economies of scale from on-line payment. Today, the majority of "electronic" payments, because of the lack of necessary account information returning with the payment, actually result in a more manual process for the biller than a traditional check. There is little incentive for merchants to encourage customers to submit payments electronically or to contract with service providers to deliver bills electronically.

Electronic bill presentment fully integrated with the subsequent payment can eliminate this manual process, however, and make the electronic payment cycle much more cost-effective than paper. Recognizing this, estimates of the number of electronic bill presentments project even more dramatic increases than electronic payments, with an expected rise from 12 million bill presentments in 1997 to more than 700 million in 2001.

The Internet makes electronic presentment and payment a viable service offering. The growth of household Internet connections dramatically increases the number of consumers who have easy access to such a service. In addition, using the Internet as a delivery channel also reduces the systems management and network costs associated with this kind of mass electronic consumer service. In fact, electronic bill payment and presentment, especially if they are integrated with home banking and other financial services functions, are likely to become among the first applications on the Internet to appeal to a mass market. Not everyone trades stocks, but everyone pays bills.

Because biller and financial institution relationships are fundamental to success in this market, and because there will be little reason for either financial institutions or billers to establish relationships with multiple service providers, there are clear advantages to being an early player in this market. By the year 2000 the market is likely to be dominated by two or three major players who will be able to deliver the comprehensive, integrated services that offer convenience for the consumer and processing efficiencies for the biller.

The implementation of truly integrated services will require links to processing capabilities that are already a fundamental

strength for First Data. Also, electronic bill payment and presentment provide a logical focal point for increased First Data support
for home banking and related services to retail banks. As a result of
this consideration, First Data decided that entry into this market
would be a major thrust of its Internet commerce strategy.

On considering the capabilities required to create this business,
FDC identified several that constituted success factors:

▷ Ability to develop and manage a large-scale systems infra-
structure.
▷ Close relationships with financial institutions and billers.
▷ Consumer software design skills.
▷ Credibility in the institutional and consumer marketplace.

First Data was well positioned in terms of the first issues, but it
lacked core competency in development of consumer software and
did not have strong recognition or experience in the consumer marketplace. Nevertheless, the evaluation of the bill presentment opportunity indicated that this offering had enough long-term potential to
warrant an extension of FDC business focus into the on-line consumer arena. Rather than develop the required skills from scratch, ex-
ploration of strategic partnerships seemed like the most viable option. As FDC started putting plans together to develop a service for
the electronic billing market, it realized that Microsoft had separately
embarked on a similar project. Upon discussion, both organizations
came to the conclusion that a joint venture could deliver a better service to the market than either organization could offer separately.

As a result, First Data Corporation allied with Microsoft to
announce the formation of MSFDC, a joint venture in electronic
bill presentment and payment. MSFDC provides a fully integrated
Internet-based electronic bill presentment and payment service. It
combines Microsoft's strengths in software development of consumer applications, biller tools, and system design with First Data's
strengths in high-volume transaction processing, database management, information marketing, and bank and merchant relationships.

This new enterprise is based in Denver, Colorado, and will offer
services to banks, to billers, and directly to consumers who want to

receive and pay their bills on line. Figure 7.3 illustrates the major components of the MSFDC system.

Banks are considered the primary delivery channel for MSFDC electronic bills. If a bank already has a Web site with account and transaction information, it can apply its brand to the MSFDC service and offer it through the bank's Web site. Banks are not charged any transaction fee for presenting bills on line, and the service is another means for them to add value to the consumer interface. Billers pay a small charge for each bill presented and paid on line. However, they benefit from the centralization of services and should be able to realize significant cost savings through reductions in direct bill distribution costs as well as efficiencies in processing of on-line payments.

Electronic Bill Presentment and Payment (EBPP) is an Internet-based service that securely and reliably delivers richly formatted bills, statements, invoices, notices, and associated advertising to any online consumer or business, and returns payment, remittance instructions, and related information to the Biller and/or designated payee.

EBPP

What EBPP Is

● EBPP is a new service that Banks can brand and offer to their customers.
● EBPP is a new, more efficient way for Billers to deliver bills to and receive payments from their customers.
● EBPP is an easy, secure way for consumers to receive and pay bills while increasing their control over payment and cash flow.

What EBPP Is Not

● EBPP is not a new form of electronic money. The service uses existing payment vehicles—checking accounts and/or credit cards.
● EBPP is not a Bank or a financial service. EBPP is an online service that any Bank can brand and offer to its customers. It is a great complement to other online Bank offerings.

How Does EBPP Work?

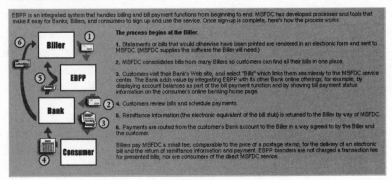

FIGURE 7.3   **MSFDC System Components**

A critical requirement for this and any other consumer-oriented Web product is ease of use and visible value for the end user. The MSFDC product has been designed to take advantage of the lessons FDC has learned in the process of evaluating and implementing a number of Internet commerce services over the past several years. It provides a seamless and integrated front end while assuring security and end-to-end processing of electronic transactions among multiple participants. MSFDC leverages the capabilities of First Data and extends its position into the consumer end of Internet commerce through the Microsoft partnership. Although it is too early to tell whether electronic bill payment and presentment will indeed become high-profile applications for Web commerce, the opportunity it offers is a good match for the next stage of FDC's engagement with the Internet marketplace.

Conclusion

Evaluating the major Internet commerce opportunities in each of First Data's core business areas is more than just a strategic exercise. It has provided valuable insights into the nature and scope of how electronic commerce will shape its business and has improved the company's ability to move decisively into the most promising areas. At the same time, it is clear that every major financial services company has to respond to the competitive challenges raised by the development of Internet technologies. One of the greatest challenges and rewards of working with Internet and electronic commerce strategy development is that today's leaders have no guarantee of staying on top. First Data continues to analyze Internet opportunities to expand its capabilities and to continue its leadership role in the development of Internet commerce.

8

Charles Schwab & Company

Mutual Funds on the Web

MARY J. CRONIN
BOSTON COLLEGE

Introduction

The rationale for putting a Charles Schwab mutual funds site on the Web extends back to the founding mission of the company and forward toward a vision of attracting a growing number of on-line customers with interactive information, products, and services. As the largest discount broker in the United States, with more than $1.4 billion in revenues and more than $200 billion in total assets managed during 1995, Charles Schwab & Company has thrived by serving independent investors and fee-based advisers. In 1996 these investors maintained more than 3.6 million active accounts at Schwab and had driven the mutual funds assets at Schwab over a two-year period from $27.9 billion to $67.8 billion in assets.

Along with this impressive growth, Schwab has developed a reputation for innovative investment instruments and aggressive use of technology. In 1984 Schwab pioneered the Mutual Funds Marketplace, making 140 no-load funds available under one, easy-to-understand umbrella. In 1992 it introduced the Mutual Fund OneSource service, giving investors a way to purchase more than 500 no-load funds through Schwab and track them on a consolidated account statement, with no additional transaction fees. OneSource has become one of Schwab's most popular investment options; assets in this service grew by almost 50 percent in 1995.

The introduction of telephone trading in 1989 and the more recent debuts of StreetSmart investment management software and e.Schwab to support PC-based trading have helped to reduce customer support costs and provide an environment of anytime, anywhere trading and individual account management. Although Schwab also maintains hundreds of customer-access ("high-touch") local branch offices around the United States, the proportion of transactions its customers conduct on line continues to grow, with PC-based services accounting for more than 15 percent of total trading volume in 1996.

It makes perfect sense, therefore, for Schwab to harness the power of the Web at least as an information and marketing channel to technologically advanced customers. But the most significant value of the Web comes from its dual potential to expand investment opportunities and promote growth while reducing Schwab's internal processing costs. And this is the area in which Schwab's use of the Web seeks to distinguish itself by combining core services with innovative options. Founder Charles Schwab notes,

> In many ways, technology is the driver and enabler of all we do, and it's been Schwab's hallmark to enable customers to interact directly with technology themselves. People are anxious to use personal computers to do real, service-based things. The PC is easy to use and Internet trading is even easier to use than StreetSmart.[1]

Internet trading is in fact an attractive convenience for the well-informed and independent investor group that makes up a significant part of Schwab's clientele. As Schwab's customer base grows, however, a less-experienced investor group has joined. One in 10 is a first-time investor, while others look to the convenience of mutual funds as their major investment vehicle. The Web offers another opportunity to reach those investors with introductory and financial planning information.

Charles Schwab & Company opened its first corporate Web site in July 1995 at www.schwab.com. Like many companies debuting on the Web, this first home page focused on information about the company, with extensive descriptions of products and services. Unlike some companies, Schwab's management had already recognized the value of moving the internal communications infrastructure to Internet network standards. During the early 1990s, MIS had developed a corporate-wide networking strategy based on TCP/IP protocols. This infrastructure enabled Schwab to move more quickly from a static public presence to more dynamic interaction with customers and to full trading functions on the Web.

Schwab has also established an electronic brokerage group responsible for developing and managing the infrastructure for secure trading on the Web. This group worked with information technology (IT) to establish a platform for handling secure financial transactions and investor information over the Internet. Once the security issues were resolved, Schwab introduced stock trading via the Web in April 1996. By July 1996 Schwab investors could also check their mutual funds holdings and buy new funds on the Web once they had obtained passwords.

During the balance of 1996, these transaction functions were consolidated on the main SchwabNow corporate Web site, along with mutual funds and investment information. Investors were finding their way to the site in large numbers, and the volume of trading was significant. Nevertheless, Schwab could see the need for a distinctive Web presence dedicated to the mutual funds investor. This site could focus on meeting a variety of customer needs—performance information, analysis tools, portfolio planning, account status, feedback, and, of course, secure, on-line trading.

Within this context, creating a new level of Web service for mutual funds customers raised marketing, positioning, and long-term strategy issues, as well as the immediate logistic matters involved with creating a distinctive home page design, dedicated content development, and site implementation.

This chapter chronicles the process of planning, designing, and implementing the Schwab mutual funds Web site, www.schwab. com/funds.

That process extended over a six-month period, and it highlights the perspective of marketing and customer relationships in addressing some of the critical issues in launching a full-service Web location for mutual funds investors. The chapter concludes with a discussion of the overall impact of the Web model of investment, trading, and support on developing strategies for on-line investing and customer services at Charles Schwab & Company.

Focusing on Mutual Funds

The premise that mutual funds customers had some unique needs and questions that might be more effectively addressed by a distinctive mutual funds home page at Schwab consolidated into a project to design and implement a new Web component in summer 1996. A project team with representation from the mutual funds marketing group, the electronic brokerage group, MIS, and the internal interactive advertising group was established to take responsibility for the project. The mutual funds marketing group was responsible for identifying the on-line needs of a typical Schwab mutual funds investor, analyzing the level of service Schwab wished to provide on the Web, and determining how more on-line functionality might impact Schwab's overall cost structure.

The first challenge for the mutual funds Web project was to figure out what mixture of content and services would best contribute to the on-line relationship with mutual funds investors. The foundation established by the SchwabNow Web site was an advantage, since the mutual funds group did not need to design a dedicated security solution or create all the content from scratch. Therefore, the task of adding substantial new customer value and distinguishing the functions of the mutual funds page became the focus of this project. SchwabNow, the general corporate Web presence for the company, is illustrated in figure 8.1.

As the first stop for on-line visitors to Schwab, this site aims to present integrated, one-stop information and functionality where a

Welcome to online investing the way it should be.

The Schwab Web Difference
Sample our research and investing tools

Web Trading Demo
Online trading has never been easier

Save 20%
When you trade with us on the Web

What's New:

■ Free to Schwab customers—research reports on the
  companies of your choice.

■ Now it's easier than ever to save for college with our College
  Saver Program.

■ Create customized charts in Market Buzz™.

■ More What's New.

Schwab in the News:

Online Investor's Choice. Find out why over half of all online trading is
done with Schwab. Read what Schwab customers have to say

To best view this site, we recommend a frames browser like

Internet Explorer 3.02   or   Netscape Navigator 3.01

Not all securities, products or services described are available in all countries, and nothing here is
an offer or solicitation of these securities, products and services in any jurisdiction where their
offer or sale is not qualified or exempt from regulation.

With over 1,300 mutual
funds to
compare. FREE.

Up-to-the-minute market
highlights. FREE.

e.schwab

Find out about
exclusively electronic
investing for our lowest
commissions.

FIGURE 8.1   **The SchwabNow Home Page**

variety of investing needs can be met. New visitors can click through
a "Tour Schwab" option, access advice on developing an investment
plan, get overviews of Schwab software, or decide to open accounts.
Customers can take advantage of a free Market News section that includes real-time coverage of the financial markets and commentary
on the financial news of the day. If they have technical questions they
can go to a technical support area of the site.

Anyone who has not registered for on-line trading can get a
demonstration of Web trading, including real-time stock quotes,
placing trades, and changing or canceling orders. Registration for
trading requires that a user have a Schwab account and obtain an
initial password over the phone for the first log-on to the trading
section of SchwabNow. The secure trading function, including mu-

tual funds trades, is a critical part of the SchwabNow site. The site also presents the Schwab brand to new visitors and offers education and investment selection tools to customers and prospects alike. In particular, information about investment planning and establishing portfolios is presented in an effective way to attract new customers.

For Schwab's current mutual funds customers who are coming to the Web site with a specific purpose in mind, it was important not to impede the investing process. The mutual funds marketing group worked with other project participants to anticipate the various types of interactions and information required by different types of visitors to the new section. It also laid out the specific steps a customer might take in checking account balances, researching one or more funds, and carrying out a trade. Not only would this type of insight be essential in creating an effective site design, it was also an important factor in determining how well the mutual funds pages could guide investors directly to the information they needed, or answer frequently asked questions, and thus substitute for more labor-intensive customer support services.

How would mutual funds customers differ from the generic visitor to the main Schwab page? Clearly they would want the option of going directly to performance data on specific funds or sorting data based on their own criteria. They may also simply want to execute a trade, which would entail hitting the trade button to move from the mutual funds page onto the secure server, logging on with their passwords, and completing their transactions. Once the steps were outlined in this way, it was easier to ensure that all of them were functioning and clearly accessible from the mutual funds home page.

The goals for adding functions to a new mutual funds page were closely aligned with the presentation of data, particularly account information and performance of different funds groups in ways that would match the needs of individual investors. Since the security arrangements for trading were already up and running in July, the major enhancement goals were consolidating information related to mutual funds and providing options for customized views of existing funds data.

From both a technical and design standpoint, usability was a high priority. The planning group wanted to enhance ease of use from both ends of the investment spectrum. This meant continuing to provide educational materials and guidance for first-time visitors and new investors and also ensuring direct access to the most used functions for regular customers.

The main Schwab page already provided access to large amounts of funds performance data, but when the mutual funds project started the main site offered only a fixed array of information that required a particular path for access and had a fixed option for display. Expanding these options and letting mutual funds customers access and manipulate the data in a way that might make them more valuable were high on the list of desired enhancements.

Site Planning

Framework

Priorities for a dedicated mutual funds page emerged from a series of meetings in early fall 1996. The framework for planning was intrinsically collaborative and included a number of different units internal to Schwab with the following division of responsibility:

Electronic brokerage:	Business and technical perspective
	Continuity of Schwab's overall Web presence
Internal advertising agencies:	Design and creative work
Mutual funds marketing:	Business requirements
	Web site content
	Editorial decisions
IT:	Construction and programming

The networking and programming units also participated at various stages of the planning process to ensure that the Schwab infrastructure could implement and support the functionality called for in the recommendations and to discuss any issues about network requirements. The Schwab project team included representatives from the groups mentioned and consisted of about 10 people at the core and up to a maximum of 14 participants who had some role in the planning process. During the second half of 1996 the core group met on a regular basis, at least weekly and often daily.

In addition to internal discussions, group members analyzed several factors to provide a foundation for their design decisions:

  ▷ What was most interesting to visitors to the SchwabNow site based on traffic and download patterns?
  ▷ What features were offered on the competitors' sites?
  ▷ What were the demographics of the typical on-line mutual funds customer?

The planning group also had to recognize certain limitations in the amount of functionality that could be built into the page. It had a target date of early 1997 for implementation and public launch of the mutual funds page. Meeting this deadline required the group to apply a reality screening to the emerging list of potential and desired enhancements and to agree on a specific list of priority functions that could be delivered by January 1997.

Based on the discussion of customer needs and requests, the ability to manipulate funds data to suit a variety of customer interactions and streamlining access to the most used funds information emerged as the top priorities for the launch of the new page.

Design and Content

Based on the initial decision to organize the mutual funds page around the specific needs and the most frequent activities and questions of funds customers, as well as to distinguish its purpose from the corporate Schwab site, the design team identified four major functions for the page, illustrated in figure 8.2.

Narrowing the page to four major options (View Profiles, Compare Performance, Invest at Schwab, and News Bulletins) provides an immediate orientation for the visitor. Emphasizing the desired actions rather than the depth and complexity of the underlying mutual funds data at the top level makes it easy for users to move quickly to

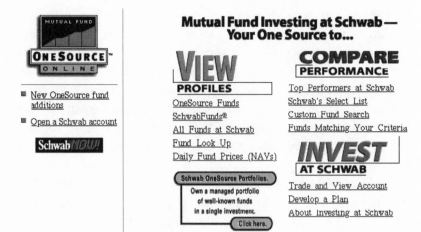

FIGURE 8.2 **Mutual Fund OneSource Online Page**

specific functions. The frame also provides a way to call attention to new or time-sensitive materials.

In reviewing customer feedback on the original SchwabNow site, the planning group also realized that users often had difficulty sorting through long lists of funds to get information about the specific ones they were tracking or investigating. Similarly, funds in the Mutual Fund OneSource service and Schwab's own funds were fairly hard to locate. Highlighting the presence of these funds and allowing users to compare the performance offered important benefits.

Some feedback was available from more technically sophisticated customers who were already using StreetSmart software or the SchwabNow Web site. Popular suggestions or ideas included moving performance information into a spreadsheet and identifying funds based on individual criteria. These suggestions confirmed that the major added value for the mutual funds page would be the ability to customize and interact flexibly with the extensive funds performance data already available.

The new page addresses this demand for customization by building in a number of profiling and search options that offer flexible, personal interaction with the underlying mutual funds data. Users can look up fund families categories or specific funds by name or symbol. They can establish a custom funds list or search for funds that match a set of criteria, such as category and performance, established by the customer. Popular subsets of funds such as the top performers at Schwab and Schwab's Select List are also available as top-level items on the page.

Content and educational information for the new investor or the customer engaged in financial planning or review is a featured part of the "Invest at Schwab" section of the page. Visitors who select the "Develop a Plan" option under this section open up to a five-step investment planning tutorial that starts with setting goals and ends with investing. Along the way, users can complete an investment profile questionnaire, read about what the results indicate in terms of their preferred investment profile (from conservative to moderate to aggressive), see the portfolio breakdown within each plan, and match up their selected plan with specific funds from Schwab's Mutual Funds Select List. The information associated with a moderate plan profile is illustrated in figure 8.3.

Implementation Timetable

Although a good deal of the content for the new mutual funds site had already been developed for the SchwabNow site, there were several time-consuming steps involved in getting from design concept to fully functioning Web resource. One goal of the project was to improve the value of the information by allowing users to access data based on their preferences.

Another issue was ensuring that all information going on the Web page would fully conform to the regulatory requirements that govern descriptions of mutual funds performance and investment options. That existing regulations are designed to fit the world of print brochures, prospectuses, or traditional advertising environments made this process particularly challenging. Rather than following a linear publishing process, the Web implementation involved a

Consider a Moderate Plan

Based on your investing time horizon and feelings about risk, you may want to consider a Moderate Investment Plan. This plan is for longer-term investors who don't need current income and want reasonable but relatively stable investment growth. Some fluctuations are tolerable, but they want less risk than the overall stock market.

Time Horizon: **More than 10 Years**

Average Annual Return (1970-1995): **11.62%***

Best Year: **29.08%**

Worst Year: **-13.51%**

Choosing Investments

To see investments which may be appropriate for this plan,
click on any of the investment categories at the top.

Click on any other plan to see a description.

FIGURE 8.3   **The SchwabNow Moderate Plan Profile**

number of tasks that had to be carried out simultaneously and that were interdependent on the others. In this sense, the project was more similar to product development and release, or to creating software, than it was to producing a traditional mutual funds prospectus.

Each step required the attention of different parts of the planning group and had to overlap with several others for the page to meet its scheduled launch date. In addition to programming, several other major steps took place in the second half of 1996:

July	Set up a planning and implementation group.
August–September	Establish core content for the new page based on internal and external analysis

	of Web sites and investor demographics.
September–November	Solidify business requirements for each piece of functionality identified for the page.
	Resolve all legal and compliance issues.
	Create and test the basic design concept.
	Finalize content and functionality for each section.
November–December	Refine design and content.
	Activate and test functionality.
December	Test for usability with customers.
	Make final adjustments based on feedback from testing groups.

Built-In Security

As more banks, brokers, and investment sites begin to support financial transactions on the Web, providing the appropriate level of transaction security has been a major issue. Unlike some of the Web applications featured in other chapters, the Schwab mutual funds project did not need to spend time dealing with security since the mutual funds site linked to existing functionality within Schwab-Now. The trade option for mutual funds, like other confidential transactions options, links the customer to the secure corporate server, which uses Secure Socket Layer (SSL) technology plus encryption to protect confidential information while it traverses the Internet. Customers who wish to do on-line trading must request authorization from Schwab and obtain a log-on identification and password.

Since this security system resides on a separate Web platform managed by the electronic brokerage group, the specifics of secure trading were not a feature of the mutual funds planning process. The group also took a somewhat different approach to communicating with its customers about the security of the entire site and in particular the trading and account balance functions. The topic of Web security is not in itself given a lot of attention on the mutual funds pages, in contrast to other financial sites that provide more detailed discussion of security and the security process as part of the Web site.

Obviously any break in security would have a negative impact on the credibility of the entire Schwab Web presence, so maintaining the greatest possible level of secure access and trading is of paramount importance to the corporation as a whole. In addition to investing significant time and resources in designing a secure trading capability in the summer of 1996, Schwab has combined internal and external resources to ensure that the company's network security remains state of the art.

The mutual funds planning group, however, decided against highlighting security solutions on the new page. Part of the reasoning was that the general consumer perception of Web security has become more positive now that more transactions are moving onto the Internet. It also seemed likely that the investor who had already done business with Charles Schwab & Company would trust the Schwab brand and feel comfortable trading on the company's Web site. The new functionality in the mutual funds site pertained to mutual funds performance data and therefore did not need to reside in a password-protected portion of the site.

In December 1996, the planning group arranged for extensive usability testing by Schwab customers to determine how successful the new design and functions would be in the hands of real users. This was also an opportunity to determine whether there were any unanticipated problems with the interface.

Listening to the User: Testing and Customer Response

Much of the advance planning for the design and content of the mutual funds pages was based on anticipating customer needs, responding to prior investor requests, and some core market assumptions about the growing demand for Web trading with customized investment information and functionality. Schwab's own competitive research early in the project had indicated that customers wanted an easy and well-integrated way to approach their investment process and that other mutual funds Web sites available at the time did not do a thorough job of meeting the needs of a range of investors.

The usability testing phase provided an opportunity to measure the effectiveness of the new design and also to gauge the readiness of customers to use the expanded functions and information services. Goals for this phase included evaluating the overall amount of functionality and information on the new site from a customer point of view and determining how it compared to competitors' sites. This process also allowed the planning group to observe investors' reactions to the specific descriptions and headers used for each function. It offered an opportunity to fine-tune the design and terminology before introducing the mutual funds site to the general public.

The test program involved a cross section of 15 investors, from active managers of their funds portfolios to those who reviewed their mutual funds less often. The sample also included customers who were already familiar with on-line investment information and those who were fairly new to the Web.

Each usability session focused on a single customer so that individual reactions would not be influenced by group effects. The investors were first asked to look at competitive Web sites and several Schwab prototypes. Each user then evaluated the information and functionality offered on each site. They discussed what type of material they had expected to find, noted anything that was missing, pointed out what sections of the site would be most interesting to them, and highlighted the different ways they would be likely to use the information and functions available.

Participants were also asked to look at the terms used to describe each function and then describe what they thought a particular section would allow them to accomplish. After they had a chance to explore the functions, the same users were asked for ways to describe them more accurately. In cases where the design team had come up with alternate terminology to describe functions, the usability test gave helpful feedback on what made the most intuitive sense to the investor.

The testing included evaluating the deeper layers of mutual funds and investment information that were now linked to the new home page. After looking at all the alternate designs, investors were asked to choose one design scheme based on how well they felt it reflected the richness of the site and the level of information. Finally, participants provided overall comments on the site, describing what they liked most and least and which functions they would expect to use most and least often.

In general, the response from the test group of investors was extremely positive. The usability process confirmed the site design and functionality features, as well as the overall direction of the project in meeting customer needs. Participants understood the general point of the site, used it successfully, and felt that the level of information provided was appropriate and useful. Responses also gave the design team some good ideas about priorities for future enhancements to the home page.

Input from the usability testing and a final evaluation of the site design by the planning group led to a number of small design and terminology changes that preceded the public launch of the mutual funds page in January 1997. Once the public page was up and running, it offered a place for customers to provide feedback directly to Schwab. User comments will be integrated into a continuing planning and enhancement process that will include extensive usability testing with customers before going live with major design and content changes, as well as ongoing comparisons with external Web resources and competitive sites related to mutual funds and investments. The mutual funds group will also keep in sync with the overall SchwabNow site so that any additional functionality designed for the corporate site can be leveraged for mutual funds customers.

Impact: Plans and Outcomes

The planning group had established several objectives for the mutual funds home page: it should provide a positive impression about the information and functionality available to Schwab customers, support growth of investment activity via the Web channel, and enable a long-term reduction of customer support costs. Although it is still too early to document the impact in any detail, initial response to the mutual funds site indicates that these objectives will be met success-fully.

Customer response to date has confirmed that the new page de-sign offers a more straightforward entry point to mutual funds in-formation and investment at Schwab. The functionality and its ease of use are a major improvement over the paper products and that in turn makes it easier for existing customers to help themselves to in-formation and make informed decisions about investments.

For Schwab to sustain its existing growth rates in number of cus-tomers, accounts, and assets under management, it has to attract a steady stream of new investors while encouraging existing customers to expand their holdings. The integration of financial planning, funds performance evaluation tools, and personal account informa-tion provides a one-stop site that is expected to bring more cus-tomers to regard Schwab as their primary financial resource. Not only will the Web site help to drive growth, it will result in a lower customer support cost structure as more trading moves to the Web site.

Schwab saw early that the Web would be a lower-cost channel than the shrink-wrapped versions of trading software such as StreetSmart. Initially, of course, Web trading eliminates the up-front cost of packaging and distributing the software and the maintenance costs of issuing upgrades to individual investors. It also shifts the fo-cus of user support from basic technical issues to more specific ques-tions about personalizing the investment tools on the site and com-paring performance information.

Although Schwab's StreetSmart software lowers costs in compar-ison to in-person transactions at branch offices, it generates techni-cal support calls not related to the software or the investment process per se. It is not uncommon for those support questions to last from 20 minutes to one hour. The initial step of software instal-lation on the local PC also means that many customers who have ob-tained copies of StreetSmart have not followed through and actually used them to initiate trading.

The mutual funds Web site eliminates the steps required for soft-ware installation and maintenance and tends to focus customer sup-port questions on the information about Schwab and its products and services. This in turn greatly reduces the technical support required for purely technical rather than mutual funds–related questions. Issues about basic Web features and navigation, for example, tend to be addressed at the stage of Internet connectivity; by the time users reach the Schwab site they have already become familiar with the underlying technology.

Despite these benefits, Schwab is not ready to eliminate its other trading and customer support channels in the foreseeable future. The plan for the next few years calls for simultaneous support for the proprietary channels like StreetSmart and monitoring the growth of traffic on the Web. Schwab's goal is to provide trading and other services through a variety of channels to meet the diverse needs of customers. Information will likewise still be available in traditional print formats because some users want reports or funds descriptions in hard copy before making investment decisions. The present mutual funds site is aimed at self-directed, independent users who are comfortable making their own investment decisions, and Schwab recognizes that this group is only a part of its overall customer base.

It is still too early to draw many conclusions from the use of the mutual funds site in terms of quantitative measurement. The mutual funds marketing and electronic brokerage groups have identified a number of quantitative evaluation criteria, including the number of hits and the volume of trading, that they will track on a regular basis. They have also established some internal Schwab benchmarks that will be incorporated into regular tracking reports. Another measure of site effectiveness is maintaining a record of how and how often the various functions are used, as reflected in where visitors migrate when they get to the site.

There has already been an impressive stream of traffic to the new pages, accompanied by a major increase in on-line mutual funds trading. Mutual funds trades placed on the Web almost tripled between December 1996 and January 1997, even before the new site had been advertised. A large number of visitors discovered the mutual funds pages through a link on the SchwabNow site, and many customers commented during early 1997 that the funds information was more functional and easier to access. In January there was more than a 50 percent increase in hits to the mutual funds pages.

On-line marketing and advertising are planned for 1997 to stimulate continued growth in Web use and trading statistics. Information about the Web site is now included in Schwab's brochures and mailings. An external marketing campaign will include print and on-line advertising on other high-traffic Web sites. For the project to meet its more long-term goals, the mutual funds site will have to expand beyond encouraging existing Schwab customers to move their interactions onto the Web to attracting new investors in significant numbers.

Mutual Funds on the Web: Added Value and Strategic Issues

Establishing a distinctive Web presence for Schwab mutual funds customers is just the first step in using the Web to add value to investor interactions, stimulate asset and investment growth, and reduce internal support and processing costs. As the Web becomes even more popular among investors and on-line financial and information sites proliferate, the basic Web site functions such as trading and on-line account management will become a competitive necessity. Consumers will expect more immediate response and service as they become familiar with Web functions and comfortable with on-line financial transactions. If a particular Web site does not offer a satisfying combination of content, flexibility, and secure functions, users will be in a position to choose from many other options. Maintaining customer loyalty, to say nothing of attracting new customers, requires a consistently high level of features and functionality. This means that a primary function of the mutual funds site is keeping the Schwab customer base satisfied and retaining loyalty by giving consumers the tools and the services they want.

If the Schwab mutual funds site is to become a vehicle for growth and competitive advantage, however, acceptability is not enough. The company must exceed the present expectations for on-line information delivery and customer service. Figuring out how to develop more high-value functions that take advantage of the growth potential on the Web is a challenge for several reasons. One issue is the amount of regulation that exists in the financial services industry. Any mutual funds product development efforts must be carefully coordinated with the regulatory requirements for financial services. Many of the regulations have not yet been adapted to reflect the realities of life on the Web. Since regulations and a time-consuming approval process add layers of complexity to planning and implementation, substantial effort is needed to roll out new features on the Web.

As a company, Schwab also recognizes the need to make a corporate-wide commitment to supporting and implementing an effective electronic commerce strategy. Once a Schwab Web site is launched, the real work begins. Every aspect of the site needs continual evaluation and updating, as well as regular enhancements with the latest functionality and service options. This is an expensive and time-consuming process, and many organizations underestimate the effort and resources needed to accomplish it. Maintaining momentum over the long term requires an infrastructure to support the entire range of Internet activity from internal communication to public Web servers.

The electronic brokerage group at Schwab addresses this requirement by managing the technical Web implementation and maintenance issues as a centralized service provider with a decentralized partnership model. Since this group does not belong to any one part of the company, it is able to establish partnerships within each of the business units and to implement projects in a timely way. Each unit, like mutual funds, takes responsibility for developing the strategy and business case for additional Web services and functions. As needs and opportunities are identified, the business unit puts together the major points that should be covered, presents them for discussion in a forum or meeting, then works with the electronic brokerage group to make the recommended enhancements and changes. This process helps to keep everyone aware of strategic priorities of putting materials and functions onto the Web and provides an efficient mechanism for implementing improvements that have the greatest corporate value.

This infrastructure worked effectively for the mutual funds Web project and also provides the foundation for Schwab to use the Web as it expands into new areas of business. The lessons learned by Schwab mutual funds group provide a valuable introduction to the potential and the limitations of on-line interactions on the Internet today. Schwab can use this experience to expand its overall strategies for new business development in the United States and internationally.

Conclusion

Moving mutual funds and investment services to the Web involves more than designing an effective user interface for trading. The real potential of a successful business model for mutual funds on the Web also reaches beyond providing value-added information about funds performance and financial planning. The launch of the Schwab mutual funds Web site provides a foundation on which to build a program of long-term growth through on-line marketing, transactions, and product distribution, as well as a more cost-effective model for one-to-one relationships with customers.

Because of the Web channel, brokerage firms must be prepared to compete through their use of technology, products, services, and information. There have already been significant shifts in the competitive landscape for financial services as the Web channel evolves. Charles Schwab & Company's strategies not only take into account the competition from corporations such as Merrill Lynch and Fidelity but also from electronic trading services on the Web, networks such as America Online, and software providers such as Intuit. The range of competition and the scope of competitive services literally change every day.

Schwab has been relatively quick to move forward with innovative technology-based products and services. Today there is even more pressure to innovate aggressively and continuously, because Web functionality and competitive offerings can change overnight. This makes any leadership that is based mainly on technology extremely difficult to defend. In planning enhancements for the mutual funds site on the Web, therefore, the focus is on anticipating customer needs and increasing the personalization and value of on-line interactions and information while reducing costs.

References

1. Carol E. Curtis, "One-Stop Schwab," *Individual Investor* (July 1996): 78–79.

9

Breaking New Ground

WallStreet Electronica

CARLOS OTALVARO, NOAH OTALVARO,
AND FRANCISCO OTALVARO
WALLSTREET ELECTRONICA

Introduction

Even without the explosion of interest in the World Wide Web, Wall-Street Electronica (WallStreetE) might have been an ideal resource for brokers and investors, but it probably would not be a viable business model. It is not just that the Web provides the globally accessible platform and delivery channel that allow WallStreetE to offer secure trading, real-time portfolio analysis, and integrated financial transactions on the Internet. The Web is also attracting, and to a large extent creating, the independent, self-directed, and well-informed investor who has fueled the proliferation of on-line financial resources.

These resources, in turn, have sparked a new form of competition among traditional investment firms and have attracted more and more small brokers and financial advisers to the Internet. It stands to reason that the Web will be the most effective marketing channel to reach those investors and advisers with information about a full-featured trading and financial information site. Not least, the Internet opens a low-cost, high-growth channel to the international investor community, a market that WallStreetE is especially well suited to reach.

The Web's compelling combination of technical capability, global reach, marketing and distribution power, and demographic makeup provide a perfect match for innovative business models. In fact, a vision of redefining the relationships among investors, advisers, and brokers through the Web has informed the mission of Wall-Street Electronica from concept to implementation. Unlike many of the larger investment and banking institutions that have simply appended Web sites to their existing financial services activities, Wall-StreetE defines itself as "a software company with a broker dealer license, not a broker with a Web site." This sweeping redefinition encapsulates a radically different strategy for on-line investment services, a strategy that the founders of WallStreetE believe reflects the business reality of the future.

In March 1997, the WallStreetE Web site received much sought-after recognition of its Web service strategy—a top-10 ranking in "The Best On-Line Brokers" cover story in *Barron's*. The site description noted,

> One upstart that stacked up well is WallStreet Electronica, which provides excellent portfolio analysis tools.... The reports available for account holders include an easily readable list of current holdings, as well as unrealized gains and losses. Separate lists of closed positions and trading results come in handy, and the checks and credit-card activity linked to a Wall-Street Electronica account are easily accessed from the Customer Information page. A box in the upper left-hand corner keeps the major indexes in view at all times. These reports provide more information on your transactions than most other sites have.[1]

This chapter describes how WallStreet Electronica, which had its genesis in years of frustration with the old way of conducting business at major investment firms, has harnessed the Web to change its relationship to the investor community. A combination of advanced technical development, some counterintuitive but Web congruent business strategies, and careful selection of market niches and growth targets distinguishes this firm from some of its counterparts on the Web. If WallStreetE's business analysis is correct, this is indeed the wave of the future. Even if the long-term goals of this on-line brokerage site are not fully achieved, its model of product definition and competitive advantage is well worth watching.

The Long Search for a "Dream Sales Assistant"

Carlos Otalvaro, one of the founders of WallStreetE, spent most of his financial services career working at some of Wall Street's largest investment firms. Even though he was consistently a top producer during those years, he felt that he was laboring with one hand tied behind his back. The lack of up-to-date technology for sales, information access, and customer support meant he had to put more effort into every sale and created a ceiling for the individual producers.

Traditional investment houses spend considerable sums on technology, but that very investment often seems to lock them into complex, proprietary computer systems that are difficult to upgrade so that the technical tools typically lag behind the times. Otalvaro recalls being the head of Latin American operations with a major firm in the 1970s, when even push-button phones were slow to arrive on the sales desks, despite the obvious advantages for convenience and speed. By the 1980s, at Shearson, the issue was introduction of fax machines and once again the sales support services were last in line.

Otalvaro concluded that there is so much emphasis on the bottom line in national and regional sales divisions of the large firms that management would always be reluctant to spend scarce resources on cutting-edge technology or make the commitment to staying current with technical advances. The bulk of the investment that such firms made in technology would continue to be focused on back-end processing and clearing functions rather than on sales and customer support activities. Pointing out that a more effective front end might generate more sales productivity would not change the structural bias and embedded technology mindset.

Rather than putting up with the limitations of technical support at the large firms, Otalvaro decided to develop his own version of a front-end, user-friendly technology. He envisioned an on-line support system that could function as the ideal sales assistant for brokers like himself and put family resources, including the computer skills of his son Noah, to work at designing a sophisticated database that could track customer investments, current financial and stock information, and trading opportunities.

The goal was to create a resource that would improve the efficiency of the sales process and also provide real value-added information for the customers. The major firms at the time were still tied to mainframe-based systems that limited their flexibility to process the constantly changing financial and trading data fast enough to develop in-house sales support systems. Otalvaro saw the need for real-time information to help guide investment decisions and was convinced of the value that information would have for his own productivity and the performance of the funds he was managing. He thought that access to this type of high-level, immediate information and decision support resources would constitute the ideal sales assistant and significantly increase the number of customers he could handle and the way he could interact with them on an individual basis.

To a great extent, this early design effort presaged the development of WallStreet Electronica. The Otalvaros family started to develop the technology for an on-line sales support system within the context of a traditional small brokerage firm in the 1980s. When the Web became a major channel for individual investors, they saw that a whole new platform for investment products and services could open up. More importantly, a Web platform would allow them to offer support for the professional broker community and for the growing cadre of independent investors who wanted the highest quality information to make their own decisions. The combination of sales assistant–quality advice and the ability to trade directly on the Web at low cost would attract both types of markets. By the mid-1990s, they had decided that the best way to put these ideas to the test would be by opening a dedicated trading site on the Web. As Noah Otalvaro, now Chief Information Officer for WallStreetE, observes, "The small companies create the future." Figure 9.1 illustrates the way that future has been implemented on WallStreet Electronica's Web site (www.wallstreete.com).

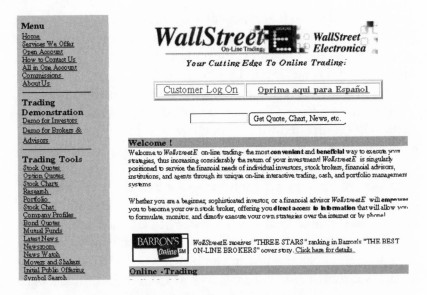

FIGURE 9.1   The WallStreet Electronica Web Site

Creating an On-Line Business Model

It is easy to state that the success of an on-line broker depends on meeting the new information and financial resource expectations of the independent investor. However, it is a completely different story to successfully develop the software, technology, web implementation, and content that make an on-line brokerage site user-friendly and cost-effective while at the same time keeping in place all the safeguards necessary given the nature of the business. While the Web may seem to create overnight success stories, the odds favor business models that incorporate years of experience, planning, and market insights with the most advanced technology.

WallStreet Electronica, which has been 12 years in the making, is rooted in a combination of planning and business strategy. After leaving the environment of major brokerage houses, Carlos Otalvaro became a principal for Winston Rodgers & Otalvaro (WRO) in the early 1990s. There had, of course, been enormous changes in the technology available to support financial services since Carlos Otalvaro first articulated the idea of an on-line sales assistant, the most important of which was the widespread availability of the Web. Instead of creating the on-line sales assistant to function within the brokerage, it had become feasible to deliver a complete package of support services directly to the individual investor.

To create a business that would take advantage of this new platform, WRO contracted with Noah Otalvaro's technology and Internet development firm, Net International. Net International took on the actual Web site development work, as well as fine-tuning the information technology (IT) infrastructure and the real-time interfaces between end-user transactions and trading systems that constitute the backbone of WallStreetE's system. In addition to the design and development work, the content and functionality of the Web site itself took about six months to complete. By 1996 WallStreet Electronica was ready for an official launch as an electronic broker and a fully functional business division of WRO.

Given the dependency of on-line brokerage services on software and technology, a successful electronic broker operating on the Web cannot simply adopt the model of a traditional broker business. The rapid evolution of systems, technology software, and Web implementation techniques makes it imperative for a brokerage firm counting on rapid growth as a provider of on-line services to be as technically advanced in its use of the Web and as flexible in implementing new features as a leading software company. During the design process, it became clear that the following characteristics would be critical for WallStreet Electronica's success:

▷ Ease of use combined with the most advanced technology
▷ In-depth financial information and resources
▷ Real-time, secure transactions and trades
▷ International scope
▷ Scalability of services and content from individual investors to experienced broker agents and firms

Clearly, many of these features are easier to specify than to incorporate in practice. Once WallStreet Electronica had created the infrastructure for on-line brokerage activities, it could also expand its business model to offer other brokers access to these services. Given the speed at which the demand for on-line brokerage services is growing around the world, a firm no longer has 12 years to go through the trials and tribulations of implementing a workable system. Recognizing this fact, WallStreetE has developed a turnkey support technology that allows broker dealers and financial advisers to offer on-line brokerage and other financial services to their customers. Using the WallStreetE Web platform, these independent brokers and advisers can easily offer advanced on-line services to their customers without incurring the cost of buying or developing the sophisticated system of portfolio management, monitoring, and order execution that earned WallStreetE a top rating in *Barron's*.

WallStreetE has designed its business around strategic alliances with forward-looking financial services providers who want to attract more independent, technically inclined investors. The number of independent financial advisers leaving traditional brokers is growing, and the Web allows them to offer their clients the same information, stock quotes, and speed of executions that traditional brokers previously monopolized through their investment in back-end processing systems.

WallStreetE's technological support frees the financial adviser from devoting a good deal of time and resources to routine, unproductive interaction with his or her clients. The individual customer is able to access the rich information resources on the Web, and the adviser interacts with customers at key decision points, when his or her knowledge and expertise can add value to the relationship. In this high-end, independent customer and high-tech adviser relationship, WallStreetE becomes the new channel for information and service delivery, as well as the execution of trades.

Since the Web has no frontiers and the number of Internet connections outside the United States continues to grow rapidly, providing services to the international investment community becomes a natural business opportunity. Because of the close ties between the company's founders and the Latin American, Spanish-speaking countries, developing business in these areas has been a particular priority. As in the United States, the business plan for international growth combines access for the individual, sophisticated investor with a focus on serving the information and customer support needs of the independent broker and financial adviser. By providing instantaneous flow of information in all directions, the Internet allows all those connected to WallStreetE's International Network to receive and disseminate information from any part of the world. Figure 9.2 illustrates the Spanish language version that is already a feature of WallStreetE's Web site.

In summary, the business strategy developed by WallStreet Electronica's founders includes several key components:

▷ Derive revenues from a combination of transaction fees and value-added services
▷ Build volume of transactions through strategic partnerships with independent brokers and financial advisers who will use the Web site to support their own customers
▷ Market to the self-reliant, independent investor who is already familiar with the Web
▷ Make international growth and partnerships a top priority and provide appropriate support services

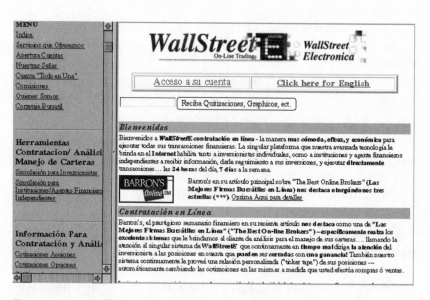

FIGURE 9.2   **WallStreetE's Resources in Spanish**

To measure the success of this strategy in practice, WallStreetE also identified its short- and long-term business objectives as follows:

Short-Term Goals

 ▷ Extend an international reach in Latin America, Spain, and the Philippines
 ▷ Become the on-line support system of choice for domestic and international financial advisers and institutions
 ▷ Attract high-end individual investors (those who can invest $5,000 or more)
 ▷ Provide the highest quality investment resources and customer service for WallStreetE clients

Long-Term Goals

 ▷ Extend an international reach to other countries, including Germany, France, Japan, and others in Asia
 ▷ Develop strategic alliances with broker dealers and financial services providers, both domestically and internationally, to comarket products and services

Market and Competitive Analysis

The on-line brokerage business is rapidly gaining a significant foothold in what was once considered the exclusive domain of traditional brokerage firms. There are numerous studies showing that the number of individual and home PC users is growing rapidly.[2] This in turn will enable more and more users to go on line to the Internet. Worldwide Internet commerce is also expected to grow at a rapid rate. In the next several years, there will be a huge explosion in the growth of on-line trading accounts. According to Forrester Research, in the United States alone the number of these accounts will grow from 1.5 million in 1996 to an estimated 10 million in the year 2000.

It is harder to find specific market studies that focus on how the availability of on-line brokerage will impact the number of independent brokers and financial advisers in the United States and internationally. Certified financial advisers are one of WallStreet Electronica's primary market targets because they will influence the behavior of a large number of investors and find high value in the features of the Web site. There are approximately 35,000 financial advisers in the United States according to 1996 data, but these numbers do not reflect the rapid growth of financial services on the Web during the past year.

While some analysts predict that investors will move away from direct Web trading and fuel the demand for adjunct services, quantitative estimates are scarce. WallStreetE's market model is premised on rapid growth in the number of independent brokers and advisers who will use the Web to compete effectively with the large brokerage firms. At the same time, individual investors will continue to come directly to the Web for some services and trading functions but will also prefer the services of brokers and advisers who are able to offer the latest technology.

For the next several years, especially, new Web users will require technical advisers to get the most out of the technology and resources available. Once individual users master the technical side of on-line brokerage, many investors will take responsibility for their own financial decisions while others seek financial advice and then carry out the recommendations on their own. In fact, the Web seems likely to create a larger number of fee-only financial advisers who leave the execution up to the individual investor. Since there are no strings or commissions attached to such services they will be more cost-effective for the investor. But for the advisers to reach enough customers to operate profitably, they will need the support of a WallStreetE-type infrastructure.

Even investors who want to continue to engage the advice of financial experts and are willing to pay fees based on trades and transactions handled by their brokers will expect to be able to track performance and receive updates about activities on a real-time basis. All of these types of customers are potential market targets for WallStreetE.

The competition is going to be intense. WallStreetE recognizes that there will be many competitors with bigger budgets and more resources. The technology is widely available and implementation is a matter of staff competency. Therefore, one must expect to encounter an increasing number of direct competitors on the Web including the following:

▷ Traditional brokerage firms
▷ Discount brokers with large customer bases
▷ Virtual Web-only trading and financial advice options
▷ Banks
▷ Service providers from outside banking and finance

Separating WallStreetE from the others are its marketing and product differentiation strategies:

▷ Building its brand—the focused marketing of its brand to prospects on a global scale
▷ Personalized, one-stop, in-depth information, services, and support it can offer to financial advisers, brokers, and individual investors
▷ International orientation and value-added information

In the present and immediate future, the most important objective for a firm that wants to be relevant in this market is to position itself by establishing brand recognition and creating customer dependency on the quality and breadth of its services. Accomplishing this requires a period of intense work to be able to benefit in the future. Since price is one of the main reasons independent investors are attracted to on-line brokers, profitability can only be a function of developing high transactional volume. This high volume in turn will make possible considerable savings in executions of transactions because of the automatic execution inherent in the WallStreet Electronica systems.

The current experience with on-line brokerage accounts that are trading with WallStreetE makes it clear that a substantial number of clients will not be exclusively self-service customers but investors who will use and pay for personalized service and support provided by the company's team of technical consultants. WallStreetE technical support staff must provide a high level of personalized service that pure discount brokers cannot match at a price that full-service brokers cannot touch.

A typical customer service representative at WallStreetE has a series 7 license and is trained to provide customer support. He or she will explain and guide investors on use of the various on-line trading tools but will not make any investment recommendations or give financial advice. The ability of the firm to aggressively and effectively compete and survive in the rapidly changing Internet rests on its flexibility. This flexibility is attainable because of WallStreetE's relatively low fixed-cost structure made possible by its advanced technology.

The Front End: How WallStreetE Empowers the User

The welcome screen on the WallStreetE Web site encapsulates the market focus and the target audience in one sentence:

> Whether you are a beginner, sophisticated investor, or financial advisor WallStreetE will empower you to become your own stock broker, offering you direct access to information that will allow you to formulate, monitor, and directly execute your own strategies over the Internet or by phone.

The long list of products and services available on the site backs up this claim:

▷ On-line trading of stocks, bonds, options, and mutual funds
▷ On-line credit card and banking services
▷ Clearing services for on-line brokers
▷ Clearing services for investment advisers and institutions
▷ Financial counseling
▷ Investment banking

▷ Private banking
▷ Fixed income securities
▷ Corporate, trust, and retirement accounts
▷ Market and economic research

Not leaving anything to the imagination of the prospective customer, the Web site also offers separate demonstrations of the online trading and account management features available to account holders. The broker and financial adviser demonstration highlights how participation in WallStreetE assists brokers in tracking the activity for all of their customers individually and on the whole. They can view detailed account statements and position analyses, including account value, balance, cash available, buying power, margin calls, and money market fund activity. The broker/adviser service also provides a history of all account activity, interest earned, and other client transactions as well as tracking a broker/adviser's own order and portfolio management activity. A sample client report is illustrated in figure 9.3. All Web users are welcome to take advantage of the free information resources on the site and to sample some of the other fee-based services.

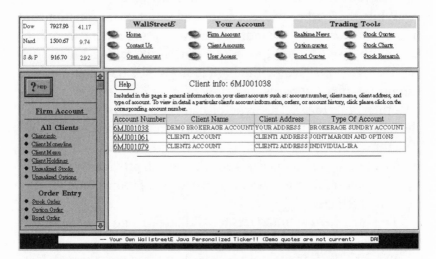

FIGURE 9.3   **Sample Report for Brokers Using WallStreetE Services**

The Back End: Client/Network
Replaces Client/Server

The financial services industry has always invested large amounts of money in information systems. A typical traditional broker has a complex network of mainframes, minicomputers, client/server systems, and desktop PCs all communicating with each other with various levels of network protocols and software. These traditional brokers in turn have dedicated links and connections to other financial institutions, exchanges, and data sources. The traditional brokerage business, because of its need for speed and security and the huge volume of transactions it generates, has been one of the best customers and main engines for development of software and hardware.

Before the Web, the considerable investment large brokers made in software and hardware served them well, since it was the key to maintaining control over investors and over the brokers' sales forces. Investors were literally held hostage by the brokerage firms, since with the exception of very large institutional investors, they did not have any access to convenient, inexpensive information or systems that would allow them to act independently to manage funds, monitor their portfolios, and execute their transactions.

While the Web provided a front-end point of information and transaction access for the individual investor and independent broker, it also created a need for a completely different technical back end that would overcome the limitations of the traditional model, run on Internet standards, and provide a scalable turnkey solution for other brokerages. This type of back end requires a shift from client/server computing to a fully functional client/network infrastructure. Developing this infrastructure and interfacing it with the front end of full functionality through the Web provides WallStreetE with another significant advantage in bringing products and services to the marketplace.

The key back-end interfaces for WallStreetE and how the system handles them are illustrated in figure 9.4.

WallStreetE clears its stock and trade transactions through Herzog, Heine, & Geduld, a large traditional clearing firm whose systems

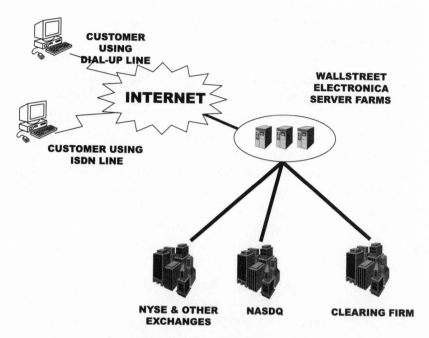

FIGURE 9.4   WallStreetE System Diagram

are mainly comprised of the setup illustrated here. One of the main hurdles to successfully implementing WallStreetE's vision has been setting up the communications between the legacy mainframe systems of its clearing firm and server farms. Two important integration steps are needed when communicating with a clearing firm. The first is an end-of-the-day batch download, and the second is a real-time data link to the clearing firm that will execute all the trades placed by WallStreetE's customers. The end-of-day downloads are automatically performed by servers at the end of each business day to update all customer records—account balances, stock positions, credit interest rates, credit card and checkbook transactions, and so forth. This download is achieved using special communications boards that convert EBCIDIC files (mainframe format) to ASCII files (PC format). Once the downloads are converted to the ASCII format, various servers perform the tasks of updating the different tables in Wall-StreetE's databases.

The real-time data link is based on a dedicated frame relay point-to-point connection. Essentially what this means is that the live connection to WallStreetE's clearing firm is a private link as opposed to a public link (the Internet) whereby the connection is always on. Using LU 6.2 protocol (a standard communications protocol for mainframes), CGI and PERL scripts were created to execute a trade from a customer on the Internet to WallStreetE's clearing firm; this order in turn is routed to the exchanges. This combination of complex network integration from the mainframes to the servers makes it possible for the client to view his or her account and place trades through a simple and easy-to-use front-end application such as the browser.

This process is the true definition of *client/network,* the term that will define Internet applications. As opposed to client/server technology whereby several desktop computers in a corporation communicate with the corporation's main servers within a physical area, client/network computing is browser–Internet computing. The end user's experience is that of the Internet being one huge computer, where the front end, which in this case is the browser, sends commands over the Internet and travels throughout a complex network of computers, each command going to its appropriate place on the network. In Wall-StreetE's case, some commands go to the mainframes of the clearing firm, some to mainframes of the exchanges, and some to the servers.

Profiling the WallStreetE Customer

Although all types of investors and institutions are clearly welcome and encouraged to do business at the WallStreetE Web site, it is useful to focus on the profiles of a select target group of ideal customers for long-term growth and competitiveness. One such target customer is the well-established independent financial adviser. The following profile is based on a real WallStreetE customer and helps to illustrate how the company positions itself to add value to such users, who will in turn promote growth and revenues for WallStreet Electronica.

A specific adviser has been in the financial services business for more than 20 years and prides himself on offering the highest quality of service and the best possible return to his clients. He works out of his home through an ISDN line that previously was needed to bring in individual, proprietary financial information resources and services. Now that he has transferred his accounts to the WallStreetE service, this is the only interface he needs. He has well-established relationships with his clients and does all their trading for them. Typically these clients do not care who the adviser uses to handle clearance and transaction issues. They trust his advice and are happy to leave the details to him.

Using WallStreetE as his primary interface makes it possible for the adviser to carry on his business in a much more convenient and cost-effective way and to dedicate the majority of his time to activities that directly benefit his clients. Among the major advantages are the following:

> ▷ He saves on the commissions that he previously paid for transactions, a reduction from around 20 to 25 cents per share to only 2 cents per share with WallStreetE.
> ▷ He charges a fee for managing the account and now has the management tools to do so without inputting the information by hand; this in turn has allowed him to reduce staffing costs.
> ▷ Previously he had a staff of three people just to help him input information and download stock market and financial data but even with this expense it was impossible to keep up with the speed of the market.
>   Now he has only one assistant and has all the information at his own PC, in client portfolios' screens and each individual screen. The WallStreetE master screen displays his clients' total number of shares so that he can determine which account has what holding and automatically place orders based on the latest information.
> ▷ He is able to budget his own time much more effectively; the basic concept is that the computer can now do the routine, linear functions quickly and correctly and provide the

support for the adviser to do the creative part of adding value to the relationship with the client.

▷ WallStreetE provides Web activity tracking software that can determine whether the adviser's clients are coming directly into their accounts or doing other searching on the site and can offer advice to make conversations with individual clients more helpful.

▷ He has flexibility about whether to give individual clients access to the WallStreetE data depending on what he feels is appropriate.

▷ The most expensive part of business had been the back-office information gathering and staffing; now this is taken care of and the adviser has all that information available to him 7 days a week, 24 hours a day.

▷ He can do an asset allocation account for all of his accounts in one simple transaction, monitor banking without any other contacts, and be much more efficient at giving consolidated and high-value advice to his clients

In fact, the value of WallStreetE has been so compelling for the adviser that he wants to become a subregional director for the company and recruit other financial advisers. Not every customer is expected to be quite so involved, but it is clear that this service gives individual or small brokers tremendous value and convenience in conducting their investment management activities. Upon request, the company can also track click streams to let customers know how they are using the information on the site and what they might be missing.

Strategic International Role

One of WallStreetE's objectives is to attract the established broker dealers in other countries because they can add content that will make the site even more valuable. For example, a dealer in Colombia who has a seat on the exchange in Bogota will know more about the local situation in Colombia than a central information service is likely to provide. When international brokers become WallStreetE customers, they receive free spaces on the server to set up a site for their personal customers. This promotes cobranding and helps to increase recognition of the company's global reach. It is also a major advantage for the local broker because WallStreetE will register the brokerage domain name and directory structure through Net International and feed in the capability of the WallStreetE site directly to this customized home page in the local country.

In turn, these international brokers provide the local information that can be integrated with the WallStreetE site and also post a page about the local stocks that they are trading; that content will then be accessible through either the region of WallStreetE restricted to members or to the public Web site. Through this type of network flexibility, the local adviser can edit all the information to suit his or her own customer base, which may vary by country. WallStreetE receives revenues from the volume of transactions handled through the site, but there is no charge for the Web site, local information option, or domain names.

Just as in the United States, the brokers and agents who have worked for the traditional firms in Latin America and Canada now see the possibility of doing international business through the Web. With a local Internet connection they can have access to quotes and execute transactions that were previously only possible though expensive dedicated lines. The real business challenge is to develop and grow technology to support the volume of trading that can be anticipated from these international initiatives. The company has already established a beta connection with Argentina, Peru, Chile, Colombia, Brazil, and Spain. WallStreetE has a program and broker in each country and sees rapid growth of interest in marketing efforts targeted to the international community.

Conclusion

Innovative software applications and solutions have been changing all facets of our lives. Now the Web is making it possible for investors to benefit from and keep updated on the evolution of software not in the traditional calendar time but in Internet time. The unique investment audience that has been attracted to the Web in the American do-it-yourself tradition is taking its investment destiny in its own hands. This expanding investment audience is made up of independent-minded, outspoken, self-directed investors who have found in the Web a very convenient, inexpensive, and efficient means to receive information; analyze, manage, and monitor their portfolios; and execute their transactions without being subject to input from a broker.

On-line brokerage firms that successfully meet the challenge of providing financial services to the growing number of such investors and the adviser and independent broker community that is forming to serve them will be a retail success story as we approach the year 2000, much in the manner that Wal-Mart was the retail success story of the 1980s. Wal-Mart gained a considerable edge over its competition by implementing the most advanced technology for inventory control and distribution, which allowed it to give customers what they wanted, when they wanted it, where they wanted it, at a price they liked.

For on-line brokers to be the success story of years to come, they must meet the expectations of Web-enabled investors by giving them the convenience, efficiency, information, and cost structure that match the highest expectations. This is the ultimate goal of Wall-Street Electronica. Only on-line brokers who accept this challenge will reap the rewards from the opportunity to do business on the Web.

References

1. Theresa W. Carey, "Surf's Up," *Barron's* (March 17, 1997): 33–43.
2. Forrester Research, On-Line Brokers, 1996.

10

International Banking
and the Internet

ANDREAS CREDE
UNIVERSITY OF SUSSEX

Introduction

As the Internet continues to attract users and commercial applications around the globe, its relevance for the international activities of major commercial banks and the international investment banking community is on the rise. This chapter examines the expansion in international banking and securities markets in the past 50 years and the implications that the Internet has for the further development of these markets. The chapter focuses on the international activities of major commercial banks and the investment banking sector. The first three sections provide some general background on the growth of the international banking industry since 1945 and the specific technological requirements that have arisen over this period. This will include a general discussion of existing international payment systems and an overview of how major commercial and investment banks have started to respond to both the challenges and threats posed by the Internet. After examining the impact of the Internet on major banking institutions in more general terms, five specific key issues are addressed by the chapter.

Firstly, the chapter considers the role of the Internet in providing new access channels for customers to commercial banks. Historically, banks have emphasized personal direct contact with customers, particularly for larger banking transactions. Large branch networks have been established together with complex hierarchical organizational structures that function to deliver the personal level of contact traditionally required by customers. Because the costs of these more traditional delivery channels have risen, banks are increasingly considering other technologically mediated solutions. The Internet is viewed as one of several important alternatives in this respect.

Secondly, the Internet's effect on the way in which large commercial banks communicate internally is considered. In view of the existing nature of branch networks, international banks have far-reaching needs for facilitating intraorganizational communication. This section examines whether there is any evidence that the Internet is being used to facilitate internal communication and whether existing proprietary networks will continue to dominate.

Thirdly, the chapter considers the role of the Internet in changing the market for debt and equity securities. The securities markets are expanding rapidly internationally but continue to be dominated by a small group of institutions that have enjoyed rapid expansion over the past 10 years. The Internet offers a potentially powerful platform to deliver information to prospective investors directly rather than in a mediated form. A number of initiatives are taking place in the investment banking sector where incumbent players and new entrants are seeking to gain advantage from the Internet as a radically new distribution channel.

Fourthly, the impact the Internet is having on existing international payment systems is examined. This section of the chapter describes existing methods for cross-border settlement but then focuses on how the Internet is establishing a requirement for, as well as enabling new methods of, settling small-value cross-border payments. Most transactions continue to be predominately settled using cash as the means of payment. Electronic smart card technology is seen as a potential bridge between the two, offering an alternative to small-value cash transactions while also providing a technological solution for secure payment transactions over the Internet.

The fifth and final area is the extent to which the Internet is stimulating the growth of new virtual international banks similar to the start-ups being established in domestic retail banking markets. This covers initiatives in the areas of commercial, payments, and investment banking. This section discusses some of these initiatives and examines the regulatory and socioeconomic issues raised in this respect.

Expanding International Financial Markets

A wide range of economic indicators points to growing global economic interdependence since World War II. The principal OECD economies are increasingly intertwined in terms of trading and cross-border investment relationships in a way that qualitatively distinguishes the postwar period from previous times. This ever-greater global interdependence has brought with it an increasing globalization of the commercial and investment banking industries. At the same time, the rapid internationalization of key financial markets has in turn acted as both a cause and effect of this phenomenon. These features become mutually reinforcing as global banks increasingly seek to expand in locations where financial markets are more open and where banking markets are more competitive.

International banking has been dominated by very large banking institutions for more than 150 years. Up until the nineteenth century, international banking was largely the preserve of specialized finance houses providing trade finance and raising debt in the form of securities. Progressively, the major commercial banks founded in the second half of the nineteenth century have taken over, and established finance houses such as Rothschilds, Barings, and Hambros have lost their preeminence or have themselves been absorbed by larger banking groups. The most rapid period of expansion has been in the last 50 years. During this period, commercial banks have shown themselves adept at managing technological change. As new information and communication technologies emerged, banks were often among the first commercial bodies to modify their existing organizational routines to take advantage of the resulting efficiencies.

In particular, commercial banks were at the forefront of using new digital computer technologies that became available in the 1960s to automate highly labor-intensive clerical procedures for payments and bank accounting systems. Similarly, because banking has become a global activity, extensive telecommunication networks were established throughout the 1970s and 1980s to manage the associated data flows.

Three waves of internationalization of banking have occurred in the postwar period. In the 1960s, U.S. banks rapidly expanded the number of branches they operated overseas. This was in part a function of the expansion in overseas investment and the increases in international trade. There was a second wave of international expansion in the 1970s by European and Japanese banks that has been followed by a further period of expansion in the 1980s by banks located in Asia and Latin America. The three periods of expansion have seen the emergence of major banking centers, principally London, New York, Tokyo, Singapore, and Hong Kong. However, the pace of expansion when measured in terms of international branches and representative offices accelerated markedly in the 1970s and 1980s. For example, the number of overseas branches and subsidiaries of U.S. banks increased from 131 to 899 between 1960 and 1986. In the case of Japanese banks, the percentage increase was even greater, with overseas offices increasing from 37 to 380.

A major factor in the expansion of international banking has been the expansion of the world economy and the associated increase in trade. It is estimated that the growth of merchandise trade since 1945 at a rate of around 7+ percent per year has led to a similar or greater expansion in offshore banking assets. In the 1960s, the expansion experienced by international banks accelerated. Between 1964 and 1985, international banking, as measured by net international bank credit, grew at a compound rate of 26 percent per year while international trade grew at 12.5 percent per year and national output at an average of 10.5 percent per year.

However, despite the increasing importance of telecommunication networks, international expansion of commercial banking services has been almost exclusively through an expanding network of branches that in most cases are registered in the home country of the bank. Thus major U.S., U.K., French, Japanese, and German banks have followed their corporate customers to where they invest and trade. New branch locations or wholly owned subsidiaries were established rather than sharing the production process with local banking firms, creating joint ventures or other forms of interbank networks. Despite the availability of already existing networks of correspondent banks, which could have been used to provide the necessary institutional conduits, international expansion has predominantly come through the creation of local offices. For example, Citicorp, which has activities in more than 58 countries, operates through more than 3,500 individual offices worldwide. Similarly, other major commercial banks continue to add to the geographical spread of locations while already operating out of 50 or more individual countries.

A significant element in the globalization of international financial markets has been the eurocurrency markets that emerged after World War II. The euromarkets have grown significantly in size and stature and now account for a large proportion of bank lending to international companies as well as securities underwriting worldwide. They have contributed to a concentration of international banking activities and are still predominantly based in London, which has become the world center for international lending, eurobond securities underwriting, and eurobond trading. London remains the preeminent global international banking and financial center. There are more than 540 banks represented compared to 450 nondomestic banks in New York and 220 nondomestic banks in Tokyo. At the end of 1994, the United Kingdom accounted for 17 percent of international bank lending, a higher proportion than any other country. London is also the largest global foreign exchange market, its average daily turnover of $464 billion in 1995 being more than that of the next largest centers (New York and Tokyo) combined.

The term *euro* is slightly misleading since these markets now operate on a fully global basis. Eurolending and securities markets are defined in terms of the nature of the associated liabilities. They all involve the acceptance of deposits and the extension of credits in currencies other than those of the country of location. The eurocurrency markets have grown substantially over the past 20 years but remain concentrated in a small number of major global financial centers. Although subject to the specific banking and financial regulations of their particular host countries, the eurocurrency markets have generally been less constrained by regulation than the respective domestic capital markets. They represent a response to a requirement for globally based financial services in a rapidly growing international economy.

The Role of the Internet to Date

To consider the impact of the Internet on international banking, it is necessary to take a brief look at the technological trajectory banks have followed in the use of information and communications technologies (ICTs). Despite moving progressively to distributed computing networks, banks remain much more dependent on mainframe-based computing to process large transaction volumes on a batch basis than their counterparts in the manufacturing sector. This investment in large-scale processing power is complemented by a major infrastructure that exists largely to facilitate communication, particularly within their branch networks, often serving to repersonalize communication that is separated by either geographical or temporal space. For more than 100 years banks have relied on their extensive branch networks to facilitate the requirement for personal communication. Branch networks remain an integral element for most of the major commercial banks. In many cases existing extensive international branch networks continue to expand, requiring an increasingly complex communications infrastructure.

With a cultural tradition that has emphasized the dissemination and sharing of information and knowledge, the Internet has until quite recently been viewed with mistrust and suspicion by the global banking community. The Internet, with its emphasis on facilitating open communication, is essentially at variance with banking culture, which emphasizes the importance of safeguarding information in its privileged form and minimizing its perceived misuse. This cultural contrast led to an understandable initial reluctance by major banks to embrace the new opportunities that the Internet had to offer. However, from an initial position of hostility and mistrust, interest in the Internet has grown significantly over a very short period of time as banks have come to acknowledge its critical role in providing the platform for global electronic commerce. Increasingly there is a recognition that banks have to embrace this new opportunity and view it as a replacement rather than simply an alternative to some of their existing proprietary networks.

The driving forces for change appear to be twofold. On the one hand banks recognize the need to meet the new requirements being generated by commercial activities taking place on the Internet. The resulting forms of electronic commerce are putting much stronger pressures on traditional methods of making payments and in particular forcing a comprehensive review of the still relatively labor-intensive, unautomated methods presently available for making smaller-value international payments. On the other hand, the Internet is starting to offer alternative solutions to problems that banks continue to face in managing their very large communication and information management requirements. The Internet is being actively explored as another way in which banks can reach out to new and existing customers by providing an alternate distribution channel. Furthermore, equally important have been the opportunity to facilitate further communication channels for internal communication and especially the integration of externally generated data with intraorganizational information.

In the past 18 months, there has been a significant change of perspective regarding the Internet on the part of the commercial and investment banking industry. In early 1995, there were only a handful of banks running World Wide Web sites and the majority of institutions had no presence whatsoever. However, during the course of 1995, initial concerns and reluctance to embrace a network that was seen to be vulnerable and that had no discernible owners or means of control gave way to a more balanced view of the commercial potential. By the end of 1995, more than 200 banks had Web presence, including 80 European banks, 100 U.S. and Canadian institutions, and the balance spread across Asia and Latin America. A recent survey by Booz Allen Hamilton found that more than 600 banks in the world have Internet sites. These numbers are confirmed by other sources. FiTech, which provides details for many of the bank Web sites worldwide, lists more than 650 banks in the United States and 180 spread across Europe, Asia, and South America. Similarly, the Monetary Institute at Göttingen University lists around 200 international bank Web sites located outside the United States. These figures suggest that at the end of 1996 there were already more than 850 banks with direct Internet presence, of which more than 650 were located in the United States. The pace of growth is clearly accelerating. Currently, the number of banks with Internet presence is already more than 1,000, including more than 400 banks outside America. At this rate of expansion, banks without Internet presence are likely to become an increasing rarity in the near future.

The evidence therefore suggests that the Internet is regarded as an increasingly important commercial tool by a growing number of banks. In the past 12 months, most of the world's top-50 commercial banks have created some form of Web presence. Initially, Web sites represented little more than electronic brochures. As a result of initiatives currently led largely by U.S. banks such as Wells Fargo and Bank of America, Web sites are being expanded to offer full banking services. In its survey, Booz Allen found that around 1 to 2 percent of banks were offering full banking services, with another 80 percent of respondents confirming that they have plans to upgrade their Internet sites to permit financial transactions within three years. Given the large numbers of banks that already have Web sites, a distinction is increasingly being made between true Internet banks that already offer some form of direct transactional services over the Internet and the rest that do not. NetBanker provides a growing list of such institutions that currently number around 80. These include a number of world-class commercial banks (Deutsche Bank in Germany, Royal Bank of Scotland in the United Kingdom, and Bank of Montreal in Canada), as well as a handful of smaller start-up operations based in offshore banking centers such as Antigua.

Innovative approaches are no longer the sole preserve of U.S. banks. A number of European institutions are moving to second-generation Web sites that permit access to existing bank networks. Barclays Bank in the United Kingdom was one of the first non-U.S. banks to establish a virtual shopping mall called Barclaysquare. A number of U.K. retailers were located in the virtual mall when it opened for business in May 1995; it provides an environment for making security enhancement payments using credit cards. The site received more than 500,000 visits in the first eight months and has since expanded to include most of the major U.K. names in retailing. Bank of Montreal based in Canada is developing an interactive lending decision system for mortgages, credit cards, and student loans on the World Wide Web. Similarly, Deutsche Bank, the largest bank in Europe, has rapidly expanded its Web site to provide enhanced facilities for its existing telephone banking service called Bank24. In April 1997, the Royal Bank of Scotland launched the United Kingdom's first major fully fledged on-line banking service over the Internet. Customers are able to access their account details, authorize bill payments, instruct payment transfers, and view transactions with a search-and-sort facility. The services available match those of its existing telephone-based banking service and in addition provide an interface with Microsoft Money '97. The rate of change is perhaps best illustrated by the fact that there are now already more than five banks in Russia that have comprehensive Web sites, something that would probably have been inconceivable as little as five years ago.

The greater willingness to embrace the Internet opportunity has in part been a competitively based response. Nonbanks are showing increasing willingness to ignore traditional boundaries between banking and nonbanking services. This phenomenon has already been apparent for some time in the United States but is recently becoming the norm in Europe and Asia. In the United Kingdom, one of the largest supermarket chains, Sainsbury's, recently announced plans to establish a new banking joint venture with the Bank of Scotland while another retail chain, Marks & Spencer, has progressively introduced new investment-based financial services that compete with similar offerings from the major U.K. commercial banks. Similarly, also in the United Kingdom, Virgin Group has achieved a notable success in selling financial investment plans called personal equity plans (PEPs) to investors using direct telephone-based selling techniques rather than more traditional forms of financial intermediary.

International bankers are responding to a perceived need for what is sometimes irreverently referred to as "Martini" banking (banking that occurs anytime, anyplace, anywhere). This is driving a desire to supplement the more traditional delivery channels, which focus on the bank branch, with other electronic forms of access. In this respect, the benefits of the Internet are seen to arise from significantly lower overall transaction costs. Commercial banks are increasingly coming to terms with the fact that the more traditional proprietary networks on which they have relied in the past are unable to deliver small-value transactions at a sufficiently reduced level of cost because of the lack of flexibility and the requirement for non-standard computer equipment and software.

The scale of future opportunities can be put into context by considering the case of automated teller machines (ATMs), which have become synonymous with bank automation. In most of the major industrialized countries, ATMs account for more than 50 percent of transactions involving cash acquisition from the banking system (i.e., cash withdrawals from individual bank accounts). ATMs have earned increasing customer acceptance and trust. In the United Kingdom, for example, the volume of cash withdrawals from ATMs increased by 400 times between 1976 and 1995, a time that saw a corresponding increase in the size of the ATM network from 676 to 21,000 units. Although ATMs started out as proprietary networks, there is increasing interconnectivity through a web of reciprocal links that permit cardholders to use ATMs belonging to other commercial banks. With the creation of worldwide ATM interchange arrangements orchestrated by VISA and MasterCard through the Cirrus and Plus networks, ATM cardholders are able to withdraw cash from the majority of the 500,000 ATMs in operation around the globe.

However, despite having become ubiquitous and representing a significant achievement in its own right, ATM technology networks remain costly, with single transaction costs typically in the order of $0.50 to $1.00 depending on the type of network switching required. Furthermore, it has taken more than 20 years for the technology to become fully accepted by customers, and a significant number continue to depend on bank branches for all their banking transactions. The relatively high cost of ATMs reflects specific technological priorities concerned with guaranteeing the necessary level of confidence and trust on the part of customers while ensuring high levels of security in networks. At the same time, ATMs illustrate the competitive threat and opportunities presented by the Internet, which has the potential to deliver commercial transactions at a cost measured in a few cents once similar issues associated with trust and customer confidence can be successfully addressed. In other words, the emphasis on creating proprietary, directly controlled networks has been influential in establishing the current levels of consumer acceptance but at the same time has created a cost structure that is now vulnerable to the vast network externalities the Internet has to offer. This has led to growing initiatives for creating electronic purse–based payment systems that can be used over the Internet and that permit low-value payments to be transacted securely. These initiatives, particularly the creation of Mondex International, in which MasterCard has recently acquired a 51 percent controlling interest, will be discussed in further detail in the next section.

The Internet and Bank Communication with Customers

Commercial banks have historically made major investments in their branch networks. In many instances, the total book value of buildings and associated fixtures exceeds ICT investments by a factor of three times or more. This is a reflection of a traditional need to locate banking personnel in the geographical vicinity of the customer base. The expansion of international bank branch networks that began in the 1960s is continuing. International banks are opening offices in what 10 years ago would have been considered remote international locations. However, despite this traditional emphasis, banks are increasingly embracing the opportunities to obtain a wider reach using new electronic delivery channels like the Internet. Increasingly, there has been a progression to more sophisticated interactive access points that permit new and existing customers to transact real banking business. In July 1996, Wells Fargo offered its customers the opportunity to pay bills and give account instructions using the bank's Internet site. New customers were invited to sign up directly for the Wells Fargo bill-payment service, using the bank's

Internet home page. Bank of America likewise offers Internet-based mortgage advice and most recently the ability for customers to build their own banks, whereby individuals can customize access to a wide selection of pages available from the bank's Web site.

Where U.S.-based banks have often set the pace for change, European and increasingly Asian institutions are following. The previous section highlighted the fact that these initiatives are rapidly being emulated internationally, with banks in Canada, China, Finland, Germany, Paraguay, and Scotland more recently launching similar services. According to Ernst & Young, 6 out of 10 major U.K. banking institutions are already conducting Internet banking experiments, while Netscape is reportedly working with 16 European banks to launch interactive Web sites to support transaction in 1997. The market research firm Ovum predicts that more than 300 banks will be offering full banking services over the Internet within less than 10 years. In some cases, similar electronic banking services are still being offered on existing proprietary networks. For example, HSBC, based in Hong Kong and the owner of Midland Bank in the United Kingdom, is launching a PC-based version of its Hexagon cash management service previously made available only to corporate customers. HSBC is quoted as arguing that using proprietary networks will ensure a higher level of customer service since control will permit greater security and an avoidance of Internet overusage problems. However, this approach is increasingly in the minority because other banks such as the Royal Bank of Scotland are already accepting the need to offer customers full Internet services without imposing the constraints associated with a limiting proprietary network.

Progress is taking place at a rapid pace. At the beginning of 1995, banks with Web sites on the Internet remained a novelty, whereas only 12 months later most major institutions have now established some limited presence.

This process of differentiation appears to be a global phenomenon, with individual institutions like Banco Bradesco in Brazil, Advance Bank in Australia, Nedbank in South Africa, and OKOBank in Finland maintaining pace with the leaders in North America and Europe; their less-adventuresome peers continue to provide Web sites that offer little more than electronic brochures. The rapidly expanding sphere of Internet-based banking has seen a growing differentiation between banks that have historically responded more quickly to technological opportunities compared to many of their peers whose rate of advancement has been much more muted. In many cases, responding proactively to the opportunities available on the Internet is part of a longer technological trajectory and a reflection of a strong grounding in communication- and information-based technologies. Brazil's Banco Bradesco recently expanded its Web site to 800 pages of financial information and access to a home banking network that allows customers to transfer funds, make bill payments, and check account statements. Similarly, OKOBank and Merita Bank in Finland are some of the first banks in the world to offer electronic funds transfer directly from the client to customer over the Internet. The innovative approach of these banks to the Internet reflects a growing confidence in establishing themselves as technological leaders in bank technology systems. Bradesco was the first bank in Brazil to install computers in 1962 and the first to go live on the Web in 1995. Similarly, Merita Bank has been at the forefront of electronic banking initiatives in Finland for some time and is in turn responding to a high level of consumer awareness that is reflected by one of the highest Internet user densities of any country in the world.

There are strong indications that banks around the world are taking much more innovative approaches to establishing new delivery channels for their customers. Telephone banking, which was still a restricted and novel service in the late 1980s, has expanded dramatically, particularly in Europe. In the United Kingdom, First Direct has emerged as a major banking operation, with more than half a million customers, without operating a single branch. Although First Direct is owned by one of the major U.K. commercial banks (Midland Bank), it has nevertheless achieved an independent existence, with separate management controls and a head office based outside the main banking center in London. Similarly, Deutsche Bank is achieving success with its telephone banking operation in Germany, Bank24, which has now been in operation for more than three years. Increasingly the emphasis is on creating a variety of ways to reach the customer, with the Internet providing a key platform. Bank24, for example, has a separate Web presence that permits both new and existing customers to access some of its services. It has permitted Deutsche Bank to launch a compatible and complementary banking service that extends the reach of the existing telephone-based commercial banking and investment-related services.

The overall picture suggests that the Internet is rapidly establishing itself as an important complementary distribution channel for a growing number of alternatives to the traditional branch-based model. A select number of international banks is showing increasing willingness to experiment with the opportunities available. The global dimension in these developments is particularly significant. Individual banks in countries like Brazil, Finland, Russia, Thailand, and Malaysia are maintaining an aggressive pace in pushing forward these developments, while technological leadership continues to rest with a handful of major banks based primarily in the United States but to a lesser extent in Europe. While existing regulatory obstacles stand in the way of an immediate breakthrough to new virtual banking forms, developments are taking place at an increasing pace and the picture is changing quickly.

The Internet and Intrabank Communication

Large international commercial banks have a major requirement for internal intraorganizational communication. Large sums of money are spent on maintaining networks of leased lines that permit secure voice and data transmission. As awareness and confidence in the Internet grow, many commercial banks are giving serious consideration to using intranets as part of a wider internal communication network. Intranets offer significant cost advantages to other methods of disseminating corporate information and are beginning to impinge on the role traditionally reserved for groupware products such as Lotus Notes. Intranets are particularly useful when several different types of network technology (e.g., Macintosh, PC, and DEC) are being used within different parts of the organization, as is frequently the case for major global banks. In this situation, intranets can provide users with the capability to access the same level of information that is then hardware independent. In addition, intranets permit the combination of external and internal information in ways that limit expensive new programming.

The existing and future Web tools being developed by major suppliers such as Microsoft, Netscape, and others offer cost-effective solutions for problems that have preoccupied bank ICT departments for some time. For example, banks obtain large quantities of economic and pricing data from commercial suppliers such as Reuters, Bloomberg, and Telerate. In the past this information was often delivered to dedicated terminals, with suppliers resisting until very recently the broader trend toward the integration of data sources. The emergence of the Internet and the creation of corporate intranets offers a completely new solution by permitting external data from both proprietary and public sources to be combined and given a common access point. The developments are being accelerated by the increasing volumes of financial information being made accessible. Data feeds from the London Stock Exchange, NYSE, and NASDAQ, among others, are already provided from several Web sites on a quasi-real-time basis, often with no more than a few minutes delay. Similarly, current information on commodity prices is available from the Chicago Mercantile Exchange directly using a specially created Internet Web site. The need to integrate data with other corporate sources, as well as the inherent fragmentation of existing bank information systems, makes the Internet an increasingly attractive solution.

A similar pattern of technological diffusion is being witnessed with respect to the bank-customer interface. Once again, North American banks are providing the new organizational templates as they rapidly introduce intranets to form another layer in an intricate web of internal communication facilities. European, Asian, and Latin American banks although initially more reticent to embrace the new opportunities are starting to emulate these examples. While there remain a number of residual concerns associated with security and a general desire to maintain the integrity of existing networks as the basis of customer confidentiality, intranets are offering overwhelming advantages to non-U.S.-based commercial banks that often have more extensive international branch networks and therefore greater needs to improve on existing proprietary systems. A similar process of global differentiation can be found occurring in respect to other Internet-related banking developments. For example, Banco Bradesco in Brazil plans to be the first institution in the country to establish a bank-wide intranet as an alternative to the current internal e-mail system, which has 23,000 users and handles 24 million transactions per month. Similarly, Merita Bank in Finland, already at the forefront of developing secure payment transfer systems, is also instituting a company-wide intranet that became fully operational in early 1997.

The process of catching up is highlighted by comparing Wells Fargo bank, based in California, and the HSBC Group. Wells Fargo has been one of the more enthusiastic pioneers of exploiting the opportunities presented by the Internet. Intranets linking the various branch offices have been in operation for more than 18 months and barriers separating *inter* and *intra* Internet components are being broken down. Customers are given direct access to Wells Fargo's internal banking systems to get information, transfer funds, and pay bills on line. The bank's Web pages encourage new customers to sign up immediately for the Wells Fargo bill-payment service, using the bank's Internet home page.

HSBC is one of the world's largest global banks, with major operations in Asia (HongkongBank), Europe (Midland Bank), the Middle East (British Bank of the Middle East), and North America (Marine Midland). In contrast to Wells Fargo, HSBC still maintains a much greater dependence on proprietary and closed networks. In October 1996, HSBC announced that it was updating its 13-year-old X.25 packet switch network with frame-relay technology. Initially the bank will upgrade its 400 Hong Kong branches, but eventually the project will be expanded to its entire global data network, which connects more than 3,000 individual offices operating out of 72 countries. HSBC's IT group specifically considered TCP/IP as an alternative to frame relay but chose what they considered to be the more robust technology, capable of handling voice as well as the data generated by the bank's large transaction volumes. For example, HSBC has 17 million individual accounts in Hong Kong alone. Frame-relay technology will increase capacity by more than 100 times and has been chosen to permit thin-route multiplexing. The bank's IT group believes that it will be sufficiently versatile to meet future requirements, ultimately incorporating a multimedia branch terminal application.

The contrast presented by Wells Fargo and HSBC highlights a number of issues. In practice, commercial bank intranets are likely to vary in importance depending on the particular technological trajectory adopted. Banks like Wells Fargo and Bank of America have already operated at the forefront of technological developments for some time. Together with a number of other leading North American institutions, they view the significant network externalities available on the Internet as creating a series of technological imperatives that will determine the software and hardware options available in the future. The emergence of the latest version of Lotus Notes as another Web-friendly software package appears to confirm that choosing proprietary and closed-network solutions will increasingly be the higher-cost solution. However, existing dominant international financial institutions such as HSBC are likely to experience growing competitive pressures in the individual local markets in which they operate if they do not respond more quickly to the communication opportunities of the Internet. Pressure will come from local banks that, although much smaller in terms of asset size, are able to offer an increasing subset of the international banking services that were previously dependent on having a very large global branch network. Based on recent announcements, HSBC's proprietary frame-relay network will require a global rollout of at least five years and an economic life of 10+ years in order to generate an appropriate return. In an environment where significant technological changes are taking place in 12- to 18-month intervals, such time horizons may rapidly prove impractical.

However, in many respects, the creation of intranets represents a rather tame and unexciting application of Internet technologies. While the potential exists to develop radically new business models based on electronic commerce, intranets seek much more modest objectives. Their benefits derive largely from saving on the substantial costs currently expended in keeping employees fully informed and encouraging better group working with colleagues. The reluctance of many commercial banks to more fully embrace the benefits of establishing intranets is therefore in itself a reflection of a growing divergence between institutions that are positioning themselves to create seamless electronic trading networks for their customers and banks unwilling to break free from existing closed-network infrastructures. These new commercial networks will depend in part on the adoption of systems that overcome the limitations of payment architectures that date back to the Europe of the medieval period. The key issues involved form the main element of the next section dealing with electronic payments and the Internet.

Smart Card Technology and Electronic Payments over the Internet

International payment transfers have to be considered in terms of a contrasting mismatch between volume and value. This is also the case for domestic payments. While in value terms, more than 95 percent of all domestic and international payments are made electronically, in transaction volume terms, the figure is less than 10 percent, even when taking into account all forms of electronic transfer including payment by credit card. When considered in terms of transaction volumes, payment systems continue to be dominated by paper-based systems, with transactions involving $10 or less almost exclusively transacted using cash. This is in part a function of cultural factors. Paper money is a relatively recent innovation that has required more than two centuries to be fully trusted as a secure repository of value. However, the selection of payment method is also determined by the underlying economics of the alternatives. For example, credit card usage offers one of the most cost-effective means of settling transactions electronically, particularly for smaller-value cross-border transactions. However, fees payable by the merchant make transactions that amount to less than $10 unviable since the cost of processing the payment will absorb more than 25 percent, which is frequently more than the retail margin. This makes credit cards unattractive and often unacceptable for the large majority of low-value payment transactions. In the United States, where credit card usage is most developed, there are approximately 360 million individual payment transactions each day, of which 94 percent are settled by checks or cash (with 300 million transactions estimated to consist of cash payments amounting to $1.00 or less).

The economics of operating ATM networks were discussed in an earlier section and point to significant barriers to introducing cost-effective electronic payment systems using existing architectures. At the same time, cash as a payment medium is increasingly coming under critical scrutiny given its high cost, the increasing risk of forgery, and the difficulties it poses for controlling illegitimate activities such as drug dealing. A recent study in the United Kingdom by the Boston Consulting Group estimated the overall costs of handling cash to banks, retailers, and customers at more than $7.4 billion, a figure roughly equivalent to twice the total cost of all other forms of money transmission (including paper and electronic transfers). Central Banks are increasingly becoming concerned at the growing volume of forged banknotes entering circulation. In many jurisdictions, retailers refuse to accept high denominations on the grounds that they may be exposed to nonpayment if the banknote proves to be a forgery. In Germany, detected forgeries of banknotes increased more than 10-fold between 1990 and 1993, and in the United Kingdom, the Bank of England estimates that on the basis of random sampling, as much as one banknote in a thousand in circulation could be a forgery. Similarly, estimates for the amount of illegal money laundering vary from one to tens of billions of dollars.

To date, issues concerned with commercial transactions over the Internet have largely focused on establishing the necessary levels of security so that existing payment methods, primarily involving the use of credit cards, could be conducted securely. Increasingly there is recognition that new solutions will need to be found, particularly if the opportunities for selling information-based services are to be realized. The Internet is potentially a very powerful tool for distributing digital data in its various forms at extremely low cost. It could radically transform diverse areas including the music, publishing, and investment advisory industries. However, to offer an attractive alternative, these new services will need to be delivered without incurring the levels of transaction costs associated with the existing payment system. In particular, there is a requirement to accommodate purchases denominated in fractions of a dollar rather than tens of dollars so that customers are able to purchase individual pages of information, sound tracks, and investment tips.

To date attempts to create new payment methods have focused on establishing secure procedures that permit the transfer of sensitive data associated with credit card details or payment-transfer instructions. Both Netscape and Microsoft are progressively incorporating further refinements to their Web browser software that reduce the risk of unauthorized disclosure of such data. Various initiatives are being undertaken to ensure that the necessary levels of security can be achieved. MasterCard, together with computer companies, including IBM, is developing the secure electronic transactions (SET) protocol that will permit secure card payments over the Internet. In March 1997, Microsoft announced the launch of a new technology, code-named Marble, which is expected to be formally released in the fall of 1997. Marble operates on the Windows NT computing platform and is based on the Open Financial Exchange (OFX) technical standard that has also been adopted by Intuit and CheckFree Corp. It is designed to facilitate the creation of transactional bank Internet sites. OFX provides standard instruction sets that permit bank and customer computers to communicate financial data securely.

However, transferring payment instructions securely over the Internet does not guarantee a low transaction cost. Payment instructions still have to be processed using existing systems and routines designed at a time when electronic transfers were seen as the preserve of large-value payments. One solution is to create new forms of money that assume a purer electronic form. Some initiatives have also revolved around the creation of digital cash, whereby payment is made in the form of electronic coupons that can subsequently be redeemed with a limited number of financial institutions. While some progress has been made in developing these forms of payment, the actual volume of transactions remains modest.

With the dominance of small, cash-based payment transaction amounts and the lack of an effective and secure means of settling payments over the Internet, a number of major financial institutions are looking at smart card technology as the means to bridge the gap between the two. Several major commercial banks, together with

AT&T and MasterCard, have chosen to adopt innovative smart card technology that was first developed by National Westminster Bank in the United Kingdom under the name of Mondex. Mondex has been in development for more than six years and now consists of a separate organization that is owned and controlled by MasterCard and 17 founder banks. While VISA is developing its own branding of smart card technology, Mondex appears, with the recent formation of Mondex USA, to be achieving a greater degree of the critical mass required to successfully launch a global smart card that can be used for small-value Internet payments. Mondex USA includes Master-Card, Chase Manhattan, Wells Fargo, AT&T, Dean Witter Discover, First Chicago, and Michigan National Bank and recently received approval from the Office of the Comptroller of the Currency for each organization to invest in the venture.

Mondex will permit the storage of electronic cash on a smart card. With the help of special card readers that can be linked to either a PC or a public terminal, individuals will be able to make payment transfers across the Internet at a very low transaction cost and without any of the payment security issues currently impeding greater electronic trade. Mondex permits users to load their cards with cash from their own homes via telephone lines and PCs, as well as in public locations using cashless ATMs. Mondex is the only smart card technology developed to date that permits direct transfers of electronic cash from one Mondex card to another. Wells Fargo and the other members of the consortium are convinced that smart card payment technology will be able to offer a single global solution for making small-value payments without the need for cash or expensive payment transfer. MasterCard's controlling 51 percent stake in the overall consortium signifies its level of commitment as an organization having relationships with more than 13,000 financial institutions worldwide. With this level of support, Mondex smart card technology may emerge as a viable solution to achieving two related aims, a dramatic reduction in transaction costs over the Internet and a progressive substitution for cash as the predominant method for making low-value payments.

Europe has been at the forefront of smart card technology, with the number of cards in circulation estimated at around 50 million, accounting at present for more than 95 percent of the global total. This figure is expected to grow to 100 million by year-end, as several new initiatives presently underway take hold. Smart cards have already been used extensively in France, where they provide superior authentication when used for traditional credit and debit card payments. Mondex and the more established Danmont card in Denmark represent two of several initiatives to institute smart card technology as a solution to very low cost, low-value payment transactions. They represent relatively unique applications of smart card technology in offering a stored-value solution only. Other smart card initiatives include the introduction of a Eurocard smart card (Geldkarte) by German banks and the Proton card system. These smart card initiatives differ by offering a combination stored-value/debit card. Both Geldkarte and Proton keep track of the remaining value on the card by maintaining shadow accounts on the relevant bank accounting system. This approach is potentially more costly but has the advantage of fuller auditing control and permits banks to reimburse customers if they lose cards before all the stored monetary value has been spent. Overall, smart card technologies offer the promise of providing secure payments at a sufficiently low cost competitive with cash obtained from an ATM. While the use of the associated technologies has been largely limited to Europe, MasterCard's Mondex and other related ventures by VISA International, if proved successful, have the potential to radically transform existing global payment systems.

The Internet and Investment Banking

Like their commercial banking counterparts, investment banks are rapidly embracing some of the opportunities of the Internet. In the United States, at least 70 separate brokerage firms have established Web pages on the Internet. A few of these companies are moving beyond an electronic billboard-type presence to offering interactive on-line services. Increasingly, investment banks are considering the use of their Web sites to market securities directly to the end investor. For example, in April 1996, Salomon Brothers, which was the lead underwriter for a public offering of Berkshire Hathaway's new

Class B stock (an investment company with major holdings in Coca-Cola, Boeing, and other blue-chip shares), created an Internet site devoted to the upcoming public offering. Another pointer is the launch of related specialist publications that are often associated with the emergence of new industry sectors. It is therefore interesting to note that in November 1996, a new publication, "Securities Interactive," was launched specifically to respond to the needs of "Internet and technology analysis for investment professionals."

Retail investors, particularly in the United States but also in the United Kingdom, have benefited from the emergence of a number of on-line stock brokerage firms. There are currently an estimated 15 brokerage firms on the Internet that together already service 120,000 investors who are trading stocks, bonds, and in certain cases mutual funds at commissions up to 80 percent below those charged by more traditional discount brokerage firms. Companies like Charles Schwab, which have traditionally been major players in the private investor brokerage world, have responded vigorously by offering expanding brokerage services on the Internet to complement their telephone-based business. Schwab estimates that out of the 100,000 daily trades instructed by its 3.5 million customers, already 20 percent are conducted on line using the Internet.

An increasing number of Web sites provides research services to investors; one example is Researchmag, operated by *Research* magazine, which gives individuals access to a powerful stock screening facility that can sort 9,000 individual stocks by a number of different criteria such as earnings growth and share price volatility. Similarly, major exchanges like NASDAQ provide sophisticated Web sites that permit current trading data to be displayed. There is an increasing level of added value to information obtained from these sites. Stock movements can be examined historically using graphs and compared in relative terms to other shares trading on the exchange. Web companies like Quote.com permit portfolios of shares to be reviewed and will arrange to deliver relevant articles carried by the major news services (e.g., Reuters, Businesswire) directly by e-mail to an individual account.

The Securities and Exchange Commission (SEC) has also recognized the benefits of the Internet in making information on publicly listed companies more readily available. Since June 1996, all SEC filings by U.S. companies are made electronically and are available on the SEC's EDGAR database. In addition to providing historical data often going back more than two years, EDGAR offers the major advantage of making newly published financial information almost instantly available. Users of the service are able to download complete documents including annual reports, proxy statements, and virtually any other document without charge. Private investors are effectively given the same level of access as major financial institutions.

Other areas of investment banking, particularly the sale of securities in new ventures, are subject to greater constraints because of the regulatory issues involved. Nevertheless, new start-up ventures are increasingly viewing the initial public offering market as potentially being serviced by the Internet. For example, a new start-up firm, Ben Ezra Weinstein & Co., expects three of its clients to post public share offerings on the Internet in the next 12 months. Existing established players are also giving the opportunity serious consideration. Deutsche Morgan Grenfell, the investment banking arm of Deutsche Bank, is currently funding the development of an elaborate World Wide Web site that will be used to trade international stock indices. Similarly, Yamaichi Securities, one of the larger Japanese investment houses, is using the Internet to post mergers and acquisitions opportunities, including companies looking to buy, sell, or restructure. Even the more traditional world of trust private banking is exploring new methods of delivery using the Internet. US Trust, which has more than $53 billion under management in seven states in the United States, is using a Web site to introduce itself to new clients. Likewise, Northern Trust, which provides personal and institutional money management services, has won a steady stream of new clients by offering free economic reports at its Internet site.

At present major investment banks continue to dominate the issuance of new debt and equity instruments. In the United States, in the first nine months of 1996, underwriting volume was $691 billion, which in turn represented a 33 percent increase over the same period in 1995. Despite the amounts of capital involved, only three institutions, namely Merrill Lynch (16.4 percent), Lehman Brothers (11.1 percent), and Salomon Brothers (10.7 percent), accounted for more than one-third of the total. In other words, around $300 billion in new funds was raised by just three major investment banks. Similarly, in the market for initial public offerings of equity securities (IPOs), which has grown dramatically over the past two years, one investment bank (Morgan Stanley) had a dominant share of 16 percent on $5.7 billion in volume. Internationally, with the growth of the euromarkets in particular, large investment banking firms are becoming dominant, with a handful of U.S., European, and Japanese institutions vying for position as one of the top 5 to 10 firms that are expected to dominate large-scale wholesale investment banking into the millennium.

The limitations and opportunities of Internet-based investment banking are well demonstrated by E*Trade Securities, a start-up company that also now enjoys a public listing on the NASDAQ exchange. E*Trade established its operations by offering Internet on-line discount brokerage services. As of the middle of 1996 it had a customer base of approximately 80,000 accounts, which were growing at around 10 percent per month. E*Trade recently established E*Trade Securities, headed up by David Traversi (a former managing director at Montgomery Securities), which became operational in early 1997. Its aim is to offer comanagement using the Internet. This involves traditional underwriting of securities, but E*Trade can only make information available using the Internet rather than using the more traditional approach of personal investor presentations. E*Trade focuses on companies in the technology and emerging growth markets that have capital requirements of at least $5 million. Unlike the traditional campaign, E*Trade's marketing is based entirely on the Internet and aims to take advantage of rapidly expanding multimedia capabilities including videos of production demonstrations or management presentations.

The Securities and Exchange Commission is reportedly looking favorably on the emergence of E*Trade Securities and similar companies, such as IPOnet, that will be restricted to presenting exactly the same message to each individual investor, whereas traditional marketing provided greater opportunities to deviate from the information contained in the prospectus. However, E*Trade is restricted to working with other larger investment banking firms as a comanager. It will therefore continue to form part of a larger, more traditional securities business that in the short term appears destined to be dominated by the larger players.

E*Trade and similar emerging Internet-based investment banking firms face a highly regulated market environment in most industrialized countries that has evolved to protect potential investors from various abuses practiced in the past. This may mean that investors have to prequalify to have access to new investment opportunities. In the United States, venture capital opportunities involving unlisted securities cannot be marketed directly to investors. Instead, only accredited investors are able to access such new stock offerings. Such regulations severely constrain the opportunity for marketing new investments over the Internet since there has to be some system for prequalifying investors electronically. Companies like IPOnet and E*Trade are developing systems in which investors are screened through an electronic questionnaire that then releases the potential investor to browse through potential opportunities. In the case of large new stock offerings, the Internet infrastructure is still too undeveloped to compete with existing delivery networks, particularly in view of the constraints on using the Internet to effect direct electronic settlement.

In summary, while the wholesale investment banking markets are responding more slowly, there are already strong indications that the Internet is starting to significantly affect the economics of offering investment services at the retail investor level. A significant number of Internet-based brokerage firms have already emerged and are achieving growth in subscriber numbers as much as 10 percent per month. Firms like E*Trade, which have already established successful electronic brokerage businesses, are increasingly looking at other elements of investment banking business, in particular the flotation of companies and the sale of new securities directly to end investors.

While a number of regulatory obstacles remain, it is clear that some of the traditional functions that investment banks perform are likely to be challenged by the economics of competitively priced alternatives on the Internet. These trends are being accelerated by the move in both the United States and Europe toward giving individuals greater opportunity and responsibility for managing their own savings, particularly pensions. In the postwar period, the emergence of major pension funds and life insurance companies has been reflected in an increasing institutional ownership of shares. However, as a result of regulatory changes and the need to reduce state-based pension provisions, individual households are becoming more active investors, placing more emphasis on direct choices rather than purchasing packaged investment products. The ability to purchase the associated financial services from Internet service providers (e.g., brokerage, investment research) at increasingly competitive prices is in itself reinforcing these trends.

International Payment Systems

The expansion of international goods and services and the growth in investment has been accompanied by an exponential increase in the volume of cross-border payments. However, the emergence of major international markets in foreign exchange and debt and equity securities has resulted in a hierarchy of payment systems dominated in value terms by the electronic systems used for settling large payments such as Clearing House International Payment System (CHIPS for U.S. dollars), Clearing House Automated Payment System (CHAPS for Sterling), and SWIFT (Society for Worldwide Interbank Financial Telecommunication) in respect to large cross-border, interbank payments. In the majority of cases these payments are only indirectly related to concrete trading transactions involving the actual exchange of goods and services. They represent the results of the many thousands of daily financial trading transactions that take place in the major financial centers around the world. For example, the foreign exchange market alone involves the daily settlement of $1.230 trillion in payments, while total daily average payment flows including all the different categories of securities transactions amount to $3 to $4 trillion. These figures can be compared with the volume of annual merchandise trade between Europe and North America that amounts to less than $1 billion per day.

The requirements for settling transactions generated by the world's international financial markets have increasingly absorbed the attention of central bankers in view of the potential dangers associated with the related systemic risks; that is, the danger of bank failure triggering a wave of defaults throughout the payment system. To minimize these dangers, large-value electronic payment systems are progressively moving toward single-day settlement. In April 1996, the Bank of England introduced a system of real-time gross settlement for large-value payments being handled by the CHAPS. This involves each sterling payment being settled individually in real time, across accounts held by the Bank of England. Previously, all payments were netted out at the end of each business day, creating potentially large single-day exposures among individual institutions. The design constraints and associated costs with such sophisticated systems, however, make them unsuited for anything other than very large payments since the individual cost per transfer can exceed the total value of the underlying transaction. Typical costs of using the CHAPS system for same-day settlement are on the order of $20 per transaction to an individual end user. Similarly, the cost of same-day U.S. dollar payment routed through CHIPS is $10 to $15. Future developments are expected to further maintain and accentuate this divergence. The European Commission and EU member states are presently grappling with the issues associated with the planned introduction of a single European currency in 1999. A planned system for settling intra-European very large–value payments (Target) will cost an estimated $7 to $10 per settlement transaction, even though it will be able to use the latest networking and computer processing technology.

SWIFT remains the preeminent electronic payment system for large-value cross-border payments. Based in Brussels, SWIFT was set up in 1977 and provides electronic payment services to around 5,200 financial institutions worldwide in 137 different countries. Although the SWIFT system enjoys worldwide acceptance it is dependent on the same heritage that forms the basis for the majority of all non-electronic cross-border payment transfers. Payment messages follow the routing determined by the respective correspondent network. Interbank payments remain the principal activity, although other forms of messaging, specifically those related to securities transactions, have seen more rapid expansion. SWIFT operates on a proprietary network centering on two major mainframe systems, one based in Leiden in the Netherlands and one located in the United States near Washington, D.C. In 1995 603 million SWIFT messages were sent, of which 71 million originated in the United Kingdom. Given the importance of London as a financial center, it is not surprising that the United Kingdom remains the second largest sender after the United States of SWIFT messages throughout the world.

Although operating as an electronic messaging network, SWIFT follows the historical precedent for cross-border payments that operates on the principle that a bank initiating a payment should be able to select its routing. For example, a U.K. bank will maintain a U.S. dollar account in the United States (nostro) while the U.S. bank will have a corresponding sterling account with the U.K. bank (vostro). This system facilitates currency transfers by allowing the crediting or debiting of the respective nostro and vostro accounts, essentially a series of accounting entries rather than actual payment transfers. Thus a U.K. bank can arrange for its customer to transfer funds to U.S dollars by simply instructing its U.S. correspondent bank to debit its U.S. dollar nostro account. Correspondent banking arrangements have survived and continue to be the principal means of effecting cross-border transfers throughout the world. The underlying concepts of correspondent banking date back to the merchant-based trading systems established at the time of the twelfth-century trade fairs in Europe. The system was originally devised to eliminate the need for medieval merchants to settle transactions in gold currency, given the risks involved in transporting valuables in medieval Europe. SWIFT automates what was previously a series of manual entries, but the underlying principles remain the same.

Despite the growth of SWIFT, costs associated with making low-value cross-border payments remain high. In practice, the cheapest option for making such payments is to use an internationally recognized credit card. This is reflected in the payment statistics, which show that in 1995, U.K. banks cleared only 513,000 cross-border payments with an aggregate value of £9.6 billion. This compares with the 58 million cross-border credit card payments valued at £3.93 billion in the same period. The inability to establish cost-effective cross-border payment systems has become a major political issue in the European Commission (EC), which estimates that every year individuals and small businesses make more than 200 billion cross-border payments within the European Community. A recent study commissioned by the EC has revealed that costs and service levels are very poor. The EC has established a directive that will require EU banks to reduce costs and improve service levels.

Significantly, SWIFT does not at present have a Web site or immediate plans to establish one. The Internet itself is not viewed as a viable alternative and is therefore not considered an immediate threat to SWIFT in the short term. SWIFT believes that the Internet can only become a viable alternate network when certain key issues are addressed, including identifiable ownership. It argues that since no one owns the Internet there is therefore no liability, no support, no effective audit trail, and consequently no reliable security. In contrast the SWIFT network operates on an independent web of leased data lines that connect individual nodes to the principal processing centers in Belgium and the United States. The network uses the older X.25 standard rather than TCP/IP. SWIFT operates the total network, which means that it can ensure that issues of control and throughput are addressed. However, SWIFT is able to carefully monitor messaging volumes and to bring on new capacity as required. This is seen to be in contrast to the Internet, where capacity constraints appear quite randomly.

All SWIFT messages are subject to seven separate levels of security and are archived at various stages so that there is always a clear audit trail for every individual payment. Each day SWIFT processes more than 3 million payment messages. These are predominately interbank cross-border payment messages, which account for 70 percent of the total. However, a growing percentage is associated with securities trading (15 percent) and foreign exchange settlement (15 percent). One unique feature of SWIFT is that once a message enters a local country node, SWIFT takes on associated financial liabilities associated with the message being misused in any way. SWIFT ensures that if the receiving institution does not properly confirm that it has received the message, an acknowledgment confirming nondelivery is sent back to the sender. SWIFT is considering the Internet as a possible means of disseminating user support materials and other relevant information. However, there are some potential difficulties given the organization's broad global reach, covering institutions in more than 150 countries.

While the volume of SWIFT messages continues to grow, the system of correspondent banking-based payments on which it is based is now increasingly cumbersome and costly. In a location where a bank has no correspondent banking relationship, payments have to be routed via a third bank that acts as correspondent to both the remitting bank and the bank in the country of receipt. This means that up to four different banks can be involved in making one payment. The correspondent banking-based cross-border payment system is built on the requirements of client confidentiality, trust, and secrecy. Payments are routed through friendly correspondent network banks that are trusted not to leak any of the information resulting from payment instructions. Its stands in contrast with an electronically networked solution, which would permit fewer intermediaries and therefore more efficient instruction transfer.

With the emergence of very low-transaction-cost-payment solutions on the Internet, international payment systems are experiencing a further divergence. On the one hand, increasing investments are being made within restricted, expensive, and highly secure, real-time payment systems that are used to handle very large payments, averaging $1 million or more. These payments account for more than 90 percent of the volume of international transfers in value terms. However, the vast majority of these payments have no underlying merchandise transaction. They represent purely financial transactions, typically foreign exchange trades where major banks buy and sell currencies in amounts of $10 million or more at a time. The particular requirements of large-value settlement systems mean that new alternatives are required to satisfy a growing volume of low-value cross-border transactions whose volume growth is being accelerated by the expansion in international trade and commercial opportunities on the Internet. Existing providers like SWIFT appear as yet uninterested in meeting this need, while some of the more technologically proactive banking institutions appear more focused on considering alternatives such as smart card technology. Overall, there is clearly a divergence between the systems that will be used to settle nonmerchandise-related international financial transactions and the settlement systems required to spur the growth of internationally based electronic commerce.

The Internet and New Models in International Banking

While initially reluctant, commercial and investment banks alike have proved increasingly willing to embrace some of the opportunities available through greater use of the Internet. At the same time, new start-up ventures such as Security First Network Bank in the United States and BankDirect in the United Kingdom in commercial banking and Wit Capital and E*Trade Securities in the investment banking sector have emerged as new virtual banking operations. It is too early to establish what impact these smaller start-ups will have on the existing market incumbents. However, major banks enjoy special advantages in respect to new start-up ventures because they are able to exploit existing relationships of trust and overall name awareness among existing and future potential customers. Furthermore, regulatory constraints have an important impact on new initiatives as reflected by the requirement on the part of Mondex US members to receive OCC approval before confirming their interest in the venture. To date, initiatives involving banking and the Internet have remained the preserve of existing established industry players. A similar pattern has been followed with early initiatives involving primarily U.S.-based institutions being rapidly emulated by a wide range of large- and medium-sized internationally based banking organizations.

Commercial banking in its present form dates back almost 150 years. A variety of technological developments have helped to mold banking institutions but have not dramatically changed the nature of banking in substance. The Internet presents yet another challenge for banking institutions to adapt these new technologies successfully in the same way in which they became some of the most successful early adopters of computer mainframes and proprietary digital data networks. There appears to be strong evidence that after

some initial delays a similar process of technological adoption is occurring. Up until 18 months ago, international commercial banks
were relatively skeptical of what the Internet could offer that was
not already achieved on existing proprietary networks. However,
the explosion of bank Web sites, which have grown from 200 to
more than 1,000 in less than 12 months, signifies a major change of
perspective.

The Internet is changing banking in a number of ways. New opportunities for low-value payment systems are emerging that could
help to replace the overriding dependence on cash as a payment
medium and that makes electronic payment transfer for very low-
value payment prohibitive in terms of costs. Initially in the United
States but increasingly worldwide, banks are adopting the Internet
as an effective means for intraorganizational communication, using
a combination of e-mail, Web server, and groupware technologies.
Similarly, commercial banks worldwide are beginning to embrace
the possibilities for greater direct customer contact, with a number
of banks moving to second-generation sites that provide true transactional capabilities and represent a significant extension of functionality compared to the electronic brochures that initially pre-
dominated.

There are increasing signs that creation of Internet-based
banking may ultimately have a very dramatic effect on commercial
banks as traditional savings intermediaries. Individual households
are being offered highly cost-effective tools that can be used to
manage savings and to effect payments. At the same time there is
an increasingly global dimension to the changes, as a variety of
geographically dispersed institutions are established, creating a
vanguard of change. The nature of future developments is still un-
certain, particularly given the key role banks have in creating an
environment of trust and therefore authentication of information
for the financial system as a whole. However, there are clear indications that the pace of change is accelerating and that the Internet's
wide-ranging network externalities will start to create major competitive pressures first in domestic and then in international banking markets.

Bibliography

Allsopp, P. "Settlement Risk in Foreign Exchange Transactions: The G-10 Central Banks' Report." *Payment Systems Worldwide* 7(2) (1996): 3–11.

Alper, A. "Hong Kong Bank Trading in Packets for Frame-Relay Net." *Computerworld* (October 1996): 5–6.

"Banking on the Internet." *Banking Automation Bulletin for Europe* 141 (1995): 1–5.

Banking Technology. "The Cost of Contact." *Banking Technology* (May 1996): 32–34.

"Banks Gain Net Interest." *Computer Weekly* (October 1996): 46.

The Ernst & Young/American Bankers Association Fifth Annual Special Report on Technology in Banking. New York: Ernst & Young/American Bankers Association, 1996.

Fox, R. G., ed. *Electronic Data Interchange: Strategies for Success.* Lake Forest, Ill.: F.I.A. Financial Publishing, 1996.

Gandy, D. A., and D. C. Chapman. *The Electronic Bank: Banking and IT in Partnership.* London: Chartered Institute of Bankers, 1996.

Gandy, T., and G. Geenty. "Systems Go Back to the Future." *The Banker* 146 (848) (1996): 106–8.

Graham, G. "New Euro Clearing System Could Ease Target Tensions." *Financial Times* (December 14–15, 1996): 2.

"The Growing Impact of the Internet." *Electronic Payments International* (March 1996): 10.

Hitachi Research Institute. *Payment Systems: Strategic Choices for the Future.* Lake Forest, Ill.: F.I.A. Financial Publishing, 1993.

"The Intranet—Beyond e-mail." *Management Review* (November 1996).

Kim, T. *International Money and Banking.* London: Routledge, 1993.

Metais, J. *International Strategies of the French Banks: Banking in France*, ed. D. Boisseau. London: Routledge, 1990.

Moshella, D. "Why Intranets Are a Missed Opportunity." *Computerworld* 30 (33) (1996): 37.

Porter, R. D., and R. A. Judson. "The Location Of U.S. Currency: How Much Is Abroad." *Federal Reserve Bulletin* 82 (10) (1996): 883–903.

"Pulling the Plug on TV Banking." *Electronic Payments International* (October 1995): 7.

"Stockbrokers on the Web." *Securities Interactive* 1 (1) (1996): 4.

"Tunnel Vision—Virtual Private Networks." *Client Server Computing* (December 1996): 530.

Wagner, M. "Lines Blur between Internal, External Nets." *Computerworld* 38 (1996): 6.

World Telecommunications Development Report. Geneva: International Telecommunications Union, 1996.

APPENDIX A

Banking and Financial Services Resources on the Web: Directory of Directories

Banks

AAADirectory WorldBanks

http://www.aaadir.com/index.htm

This site contains a very comprehensive list of domestic and international banks and credit unions. Many of the listings have links and e-mail address connections; others have information only. The site also contains cyber and Internet banking sites worldwide and selected links on banking organizations, finance, financial and news publications, data sources, reference books, and business law.

Banking.Com

http://www.banking.com/

Links to two Internet banks as well as site sponsors. Limited value outside of this role with paying sites and a directory of banking and financial conferences and magazines on the net.

Bank.net

http://www.Bank.net/

Created by Virtual Office, Inc.

This site contains a collection of sources for securities and finance industries. There is a full description of each Web site so that the surfer knows what is there before visiting. The sources range among investment firms, internationals, and academics in the field. This site also contains a good area to jump into several directories on the Web.

Bank Web.com

http://www.bankweb.com/
Sponsored by RJE Internet Services. The site contains bank listings (domestic and international banks) on the Web. The listings are divided by state and continent. There are also links to travel, government, weather, financial, technology, and commercial banking.

CNNfn—the Financial Network

http://www.cnnfn.com/markets/
Created by CNN. This site has a plethora of information on finance and investing. Lots of up-to-the-minute information. Updated daily.

Commercial Finance ONLINE! sm

http://www.cfonline.com/cgi-win/cfonline.exe/
A very comprehensive list of financial institutions and related topic sites. Users must register to retrieve data from the site.

CorpFiNet

http://www.corpfinet.com/
Sponsored by Duncan Resource Group.
An e-zine focused on comprehensively covering issues that executives and decision makers in the financial industry need to compete in a wired world.

The Finance Area

http://www.tsi.it/finanza/
Sponsored by Top Services International and includes a long list of banks (domestic and international); links to all sorts of financial analysis tools; market information links for stocks, bonds, futures, options, mutual funds, and currencies; "green" fund links; directories; offshore banking links; and various other financial sources.

Finance Hub

http://www.financehub.com
Sponsored by Intersoft Solutions, Inc.
More than 97 links to North American banks, seven of which are in Canada. More than 50 European, Asian, South American, and African banks. Fifteen credit unions. Fifteen quote servers, 12 exchanges, 13 brokers, and other financial service companies. Twenty-three futures sites, 23 newsletter links, software, economic information, legal information, and other sources.

IBanker Index

http://www.ddsi.com/banking/
Sponsored by Comerica
The value of this site is in its concise summaries of each link contained within the service. This site includes a list of domestic and international mortgage banks, each with interesting summaries and e-mail connectors. The list of banks is broad in terms of number. There is a collection of banking and Internet technology companies and a list of investor-service-related Web sites. It also includes the *ibanker newsletter,* an Internet electronic banking magazine (www.ddsi.com/ibanker).

IfBG Gottingen

http://www.gwdg.de/~ifbg/bank_2.html
Created by the Institute of Finance and Banking at the University of Göttingen. This site provides lists of U.S. banks and a comprehensive bank list from more than 50 different countries. Also includes offshore banking directory, investment banking directory, and cyberbank sites.

Killen & Associates

http://www.killen.com/
This research and report-oriented site contains many studies on electronic and Internet banking, as well as some general Internet studies.

Mark Bernkopf's Central Banking Resource Center

http://adams.patriot.net/~bernkopf/banks-1.html
There are links for central banks in most of the countries, but the depth of information varies from excellent to minimal (address and phone number).

The Money Page, Inc.

http://www.moneypage.com/banks/index.htm
This site has links to hundreds of banks in the United States, foreign banks, investment banks, and much investment information and links.

MyBank-US Directory

http://www.mybank.com/
Sponsored by FiTech Inc.
A listing of links to more than 700 U.S. banks subdivided by state, alphabetically. Also includes a list of international banks divided by continent.

NETBanker

http://www.netbanker.com
This site includes a listing of Internet banks, the 100 largest financial institutions with statistics and the appropriate link for each, and a comprehensive list of financial Web site resources. There are also technology links and the *Online Banker Report*, a magazine for home banking decision makers. This site has a search tool for finding information within the site.

Online Banking and Finance

http://www.orcc.com/banking.htm
Sponsored by Online Resources & Communications.
There is a list of domestic and foreign banks with links. Short listing of other sites related to money. More than 20 different financial service sites. Short list of breaking news stories in the financial- and Internet-related areas.

Qualisteam Worldwide Banking Guide

http://www.qualisteam.com/aconf.html
This site contains a list of banks in the United States and many international banks. Its total directory of listings includes financial sites from more than 55 countries. French and English versions.

Street Eye

http://www.efrontier.com/efindex/toplevel/bankstop.html

A financial services resource center. This site contains a relatively long list of banks in the United States and the world, an outstanding list of investment banks and brokerage houses, and a large selection of financial- and banking-related resources on the Web.

www Virtual Library: Finance and Investments
http://www.cob.ohio-state.edu/~fin/overview.htm
Created by Ohio State Finance Department
This site has a wealth of information on finance. Information ranges from banks, to quote servers, to financial and investment sources, to company information, to a myriad of Web resources and links. Very detailed, the site has different areas for students, researchers, investors, executives, investment bankers, and educators.

Electronic Currency

BanNet Electronic Banking Service
http://mkn.co.uk/bank
This site is an access point for companies seeking to engage in transactions over the Internet.

Banxquote
http://www.banx.com/
The site has a listing of Internet banks with a chart of fees and services. Marketable treasury services, FAQs, and hundreds of other tidbits of information vary from credit card rates to income and business tax information.

CyberCash
http://www.cybercash.com/cybercash/news/directory.html
An alphabetical listing of many banks on the Web. The site includes links to domestic and international banks involved in electronic commerce.

Digicash
http://www.digicash.com

The site tells browsers about DigiCash and e-cash and how to use them. It also includes links to Internet companies.

MasterCard

http://www.mastercard.com
This site details the products and services available to MasterCard cardholders and merchants.

VISA

http://visa.com
The site provides information on all of VISA's products and services, for both merchants and potential customers.

Credit Unions

Credit Union Land

http://www.culand.com/links.html
A very thorough list of credit unions in the United States and world-wide, with links to each one.

Credit Unions Online Organizational Link

http://www.creditunions.com/
This site has a directory of credit unions, domestic and international, a newsletter, employment opportunities, and a trends and technology section.

Ultra Data Credit Union Web Services

http://www.udweb.com/other.htm
Sponsored by UltraData Web (Credit Union Web services). A full listing of domestic and international credit unions, along with leagues and organizations.

Initial Public Offerings

Alert IPO

http://www.ostman.com/alert-ipo/

Offers subscribers a weekly e-mail update of all IPOs listed on the Securities and Exchange Commission's EDGAR database for companies filing for initial public offerings. The e-mail is a report containing detailed information about the companies that have filed during the week.

Capital Markets Financial Center

http://www.capmarkets.com/index.html
The Capital Markets Financial Center contains a number of financial services providers' links on the Web. Its goal is to provide visitors with cutting-edge financial information to inform and facilitate commerce in the initial public offering industry and continuation as emerging public companies. It includes information on the latest IPOs, a digest of emerging IPO companies, IPOs presently being filed, and the IPO Insider (a report on IPO companies).

The IPO Center

http://nestegg.iddis.com/ipo
Provides a comprehensive list of mortgage brokers by categories: purchase or refinance loans, home-equity loans, manufactured housing and mobile-home loans, imperfect credit loans, and commercial loans. The site also includes a number of other resources including a reference desk, mortgage forum, interest rate trends, tools for measurement of rates and pay tables, and a directory of related services.

IPO Central

http://www.ipocentral.com/
A service of Hoover and Edgar's Online services. The service includes an IPO directory of all filings since May 1996, with links to the companies' IPO-related SEC filings, as well as recent filings, and a directory of IPOs by state and by metro area.

Investment Brokers

FinWeb

http://www.finweb.com/

Sponsored by FIA Financial Economics www server.
Contains a list of Internet resources providing substantive information concerning economics- and finance-related topics. Many Web links included, as well as journals and working papers in the field.

Invest$Link

http://www.Investlink.com
Sponsored by the IMF Corporation.
The site offers a compendium of resources from updates on stock and fund prices to opportunities to trade over the 'Net.

Investment Brokers Guide

http://www.cs.cmu.edu/afs/cs.cmu.edu/user/jdg/www/invest_brokers/index.html
This site provides detailed information on finding a broker, addresses, FAQs regarding brokers, a collection of associations, and an outstanding collection of domestic and international brokerage firms with links.

Personal Finance Web sites compiled by Ira Krakow

http://www.tiac.net/users/ikrakow
This site is evolving into a general Web resource. Its finance categories provide a variety of links.

A Trader's Financial Resource Guide

http://www.cob.ohio-state.edu/~fin/overview.htm
Self-proclaimed a "filtered guide to the Internet," this site highlights almost 100 financial resources for investment strategies.

Wall Street Directory

http://www.wsdinc.com/
This site claims to have more than 7,500 pages of information for electronic traders and brokers. It includes stock quotes, and a searchable subject index directory.

Mutual Funds

Bank CD Rate Scanner

http://bankcd.com/
The site searches more than 2,200 banks for the nation's top CD rates. Also includes FAQs on CDs and links to various financial institutions and government agencies in the industry.

Investor Guide to Mutual Funds

http://www.investorguide.com
This site covers mutual funds and stocks with more than 4,000 links to related sites. There is information and a detailed instructional component for stocks, mutual funds, bonds, and futures, IPOs, personal finances, loans, and venture capital. The site includes a comprehensive guide on each subject (i.e., mutual fund investing along with a list of mutual funds with links to the sites).

Mutual Fund Company Directory

http://www.cs.cmu.edu/~jdg/funds.html
Almost 1,000 domestic and international mutual funds are listed, with typically just the toll-free number. A majority of the sites do not have links.

Mutual Fund Investing on the Internet

http://www.indexfund.com/links.html
A very comprehensive site with links to virtually all mutual funds–related sites. Written by the author of the book *Mutual Fund Investing on the Internet*, Peter Crane, the site walks through each chapter of the book, with hyperlinks to all sites included in the book, as well as related updates.

Mutual Fund Investors Center

http://www.mfea.com/
Sponsored by the Mutual Fund Education Alliance.
There is a list of hundreds of mutual funds, with a complete summary on the actual site (many have links). The site has a planning area where it makes investment recommendations based on different investment scenarios. There are also a number of articles on the process of investing and maintaining mutual funds.

Mutual Funds Interactive

http://www.brill.com/
Sponsored by Brill Interactive Services.
Analysis of mutual funds from top funds investors, as well as links to mutual funds companies through Fundlink—a frames-based link engine—and a link to CNN Financial Network for fund quotes. The site also includes a reference center with articles, indexes, and so forth.

Mutual Fund World

http://www.MutualFundWorld.com
Sponsored by 1800 Mutuals Inc.
The site selects from more than 8,000 mutual funds and provides data as well as links on selected mutual funds. There are many investor tools that allow you to apply them to the mutual funds that you select. The site is well designed to lure investors into trading through the firm.

Nestegg: Tradeline Mutual Fund Center

http://nestegg.iddis.com
Sponsored by IDD Enterprises.
This site reviews 524 mutual funds groups and more than 8,010 actual mutual funds. It also includes a top mutual funds reference and weekly updates on information in the mutual funds area. This site has four components, including IPOs, mutual funds, stocks, and planning and financial tools. It includes an e-zine entitled *Nest Egg Magazine.*

Networth

http://networth.galt.com
Created by GALT Technologies.
This Web site includes a directory of mutual funds and background information on funds and equities. The site has several search engines that allow you to search by stock, fund, or ticker.

Quicken Financial Network

http://www.qfn.com
Created by GALT Technologies.
This site catalogs mutual funds and offers information and analysis to investors. The site also contains information on banking institutions for on-line transactions.

E-Zines

The ABA Banking Journal Online

http://www.banking.com/aba/
A journal source from the American Banking Association, with updated information on banking and technology.

Crestar's On-Finances

http://www.crestar.com/
Another e-zine detailing different finance-related suggestions from experts.

Internet Banker

http://www.ddsi.com/ibanker/
An online newsletter covering data, new technologies, and implementation of on-line banking services.

iworld's Guide to Electronic Commerce

http://e-comm.iworld.com/
The site details information on electronic commerce, including reviews and benchmarks of products available on the server, as well as new products being marketed.

NestEgg Magazine

http://nestegg.iddis.com/nestegg/
Interesting and informative articles on financial issues (e.g., retirement, rainy day funds, real estate, insurance, college funds, tax information, and investment strategies). The site is associated with four other very strong financial references (see Tradeline Mutual Center).

NetBanker's Online Banking Report

http://www.netbanker.com
This publication includes reports on on-line marketing, trends, products, and industry news.

APPENDIX B

Financial Services Technology Consortium Membership

Advanced Technology Group	//www.iitri.com/iitri/atg
Agorics	//www.agorics.com
AT&T	//www.att.com
American Bankers Association	//www.aba.com
American Express	//www.americanexpress.com
BancTec	//www.banctec.com
Bank Administration Institute	//www.bai.org
Bank of America	//www.bankamerica.com
Bank of Boston	//www.bkb.com
Bank of Montreal	//www.bomcc.com
Barnett Bank	//www.barnett.com
Battelle	//www.battelle.org
BBN (Bolt, Beranek & Newman)	//www.bbn.com
BBN (Bolt, Beranek & Newman)	//www.bbnplanet.com
Bellcore	//www.bellcore.com
Beneficial Corp	//www.bnlcorp.com
BottomLine Technologies	//www.bottomline.com
Broadway & Seymour	//www.bsis.com
Canadian Imperial Bank of Commerce	//www.cibc.com

Certicom	//www.certicom.ca
Chase Manhattan Bank	//www.chase.com
CheckFree	//www.checkfree.com
Citibank	//www.citibank.com
Columbia University	//www.columbia.edu
CommerceNet	//www.commerce.net
Copyright Clearance Center	//www.copyright.com
Corestates	//www.corestates.com/
CU Cooperative Systems Inc.	//www.primenet .com/~co-op/
Credit Union National Association	//www.cuna.org
Cybercash	//www.cybercash.com
Deluxe	//www.deluxe.com
Digital Equipment Corporation	//www.digital.com
DOE/Sandia Natural Laboratories	//www.sandia.gov
Export-Import Bank of the United States	//www.exim.gov
Federal Reserve Bank	//www.ffiec.gov/nic/
First Union Bank	//www.firstunion.com
First Virtual	//www.fv.com
Ford Motor Credit	//www.fordcredit.com
Global Concepts	//www.global-concepts.com
GTE	//www.cybertrust.gte.com
Hewlett-Packard	//www.hp.com
Huntington Bank	//www.huntington.com
IBM	//www.pc.ibm .comwww.poly.edu
Information Systems & Technology	//www.insyte.com
Infostructure Services & Technology	//www.infostructure.com
Interval Systems	//www.interval.net
IRE Inc.	
Kinza	
Lifecycle Technology	//www.lctech.com
MasterCard	//www.mastercard.com
Mellon Bank	//www.mellon.com
Mentis Corporation	
Mitre Corporation	//www.mitre.org

Motorola	//www.mot.com
National Automated Clearinghouse	//www.nach.com
National Security Agency	//www.nsa.gov:8080
National Semiconductor	//www.national.com
Nations Bank	//www.nationsbank.com/
NCR	//www.ncr.com
NEC	//www.nec.com
New York Clearinghouse Association	//www.nych.org
Northeastern Parallel Architecture Center	//www.npac.syr.edu
Novell	//www.novell.com
NTT	//www.nttca.com
OKIData	//www.okidata.com
Open Market	//www.openmarket.com
Open Software Foundation	//www.osf.org
Oracle	//www.oracle.com
Polytechnic University	//www.poly.edu
Premenos	//www.premenos.com
Raptor	//www.raptor.com
RDM Corporation	//www.rdmcorp.com
Royal Bank of Canada	//www.royalbank.com
Royal Bank of Canada	//www.royalbankci.com/
Spanning Tree Technologies	info@spanning.com
SSDS	//www.ssds.com
Sun Microsystems	//www.javasoft.com
Superhighway	//www.shol.com
SWIFT	//www.towergroup.com/ noncust/notes/v3/high/ v3_014.htm
Tandem	//www.tandem.com
Telequip	//www.telequip.com
The Tower Group	//www.towergroup.com
Toronto Dominion Bank	//www.tdbank.ca
Unisys	//www.unisys.com
U.S. Postal Service	//www.usps.gov
U.S. Department of Treasury	//www.streas.gov
Verifone	//www.verifone.com

Verisign	//www.verisign.com
VISA	//www.visa.com
Wells Fargo Bank	//www.wellsfargo.com/
World Wide Web Consortium	//www.w3.org
YCS, Inc.	

CONTRIBUTORS

Andreas Crede is currently a visiting research fellow at the Science Policy Research Institute at the University of Sussex, England. His research focus is technological change and innovation in the commercial banking sector. He has more than 17 years of experience in the financial sector and also works as a consultant. He holds a masters degree from the School of Advanced International Studies at Johns Hopkins University.

Mary J. Cronin is Professor of Management at Boston College, with a research focus on electronic commerce and Internet business strategies. Among her books are *Doing Business on the Internet: How the Electronic Highway Is Transforming American Companies* (Van Nostrand Reinhold, 1994, 2nd ed, 1996); *Global Advantage on the Internet* (Van Nostrand Reinhold, 1996); and *The Internet Strategy Handbook: Lessons from the New Frontier of Business* (Harvard Business School Press, 1996). Dr. Cronin is a contributing writer for *Fortune*, with a regular column on Internet business, and has published numerous articles on electronic commerce. She holds a Ph.D. from Brown University.

Frances X. Frei is Xerox Assistant Professor of Operations Management at the University of Rochester. Her current research focuses on the financial services industry. Areas of particular interest include examining drivers of performance and efficiency, process analysis, electronic payment systems, on-line financial services, and supply chain management. Before moving to the University of Rochester, she taught at the University of Pennsylvania, where she also received her Ph.D. in operations management.

Scott B. Guthery is a scientific adviser in Schlumberger's senior technical community, currently working on advanced smart card development at Schlumberger Electronic Transactions in Austin, Texas. He has spent 16 years in various roles at Schlumberger. Previously, he worked at Bell Labs. Guthery holds a Ph.D. in probability and statistics from Michigan State University and has published numerous articles on programming and Internet applications. He is coauthor of *The Smart Card Developer's Kit* (Macmillan, 1997).

Kim Humphreys is Director of Public Relations with Security First *Network* Bank and Security First Technologies, Inc. Previously, she served as a magazine editor, and as a marketing/public relations account executive with a small marketing firm catering to the golf/resort industry. A graduate of the University of Alabama with a bachelor of science degree in communications, she also serves on the board of directors of the Magazine Association of Georgia and is editor of the association's newletter.

Iang Jeon is vice president of electronic commerce at Liberty Financial and leads Liberty's corporate strategic initiative to expand e-commerce. Jeon came to Liberty Financial from Forrester Research, where he served as senior analyst in the Money and Technology Strategies Group. Prior to joining Forrester, he served as director of electronic marketing at Fidelity Investments. Iang's marketing background also includes senior positions with Hewlett-Packard, Apollo Computer, and Norsk Data in Oslo, Norway. He has more than 14 years experience in the financial services and computer industries.

Ravi Kalakota is Xerox Assistant Professor of Information Systems at the University of Rochester. He is lead author of *The Frontiers of Electronic Commerce* (Addison-Wesley, 1996) and *Electronic Commerce: A Manager's Guide* (Addison-Wesley, 1996). He taught at the University of Texas in Austin from 1991 to 1993, where he also received his Ph.D. in information systems. His current research focuses on electronic commerce, with an emphasis on strategy and new business models, new product development for on-line retail banking, on-line markets, and electronic brokerages.

Carlos Otalvaro Coronado founded WallStreet Electronica after a successful career in investment services, including experience as president for Latin American investments at two major brokerages. He is a graduate of the Columbia Graduate School of Business.

Francisco Otalvaro is a graduate of Villanova and provides support services to financial advisers using WallStreet Electronica.

Noah Otalvaro is a graduate of Boston College and the Chief Information Officer of WallStreet Electronica. He has 15 years of experience in computer programming and has designed and implemented a number of hardware and software projects ranging from legacy mainframes to UNIX systems to client server and the Web.

William Rice is Director of Corporate Marketing at Liberty Financial Companies. Before joining Liberty Financial in 1992, he managed media and investor relations at Colonial Mutual Funds and The Boston Five Bancorp. He began his career at Fidelity Investments. Mr. Rice is a graduate of Northeastern University, with a degree in business communications. He also holds a graduate certificate in business management from Harvard University and is a NASD-licensed Limited Principal and a Registered Investment Advisor.

Daniel Schutzer is Vice President and Director of Advanced Technology at Citibank, with responsibility for company-wide research, and president of the Financial Services Technology Consortium. He also teaches part time at Iona College and George Washington University. Schutzer has authored more than 65 publications and 6 books, including titles on parallel and distributed processing and emerging technologies in business. He received his Ph.D. and MSEE from Syracuse University.

Chuck White is President of Electronic Commerce Payment Services at First Data Corporation. His responsibilities include developing electronic commerce businesses. Previously, he was a Senior Vice President at VISA International, where he was responsible for the development of technology strategies and the engineering of VISA's global network and systems. Mr. White holds an M.B.A. from the University of California at Berkeley and a B.S. in computer science from the University of Florida.

Index